# PUPPETRY IN EDUCATION AND THERAPY

## Unlocking Doors to the Mind and Heart

**Edited by**
Matthew Bernier and Judith O'Hare

**Foreword by**
Susan Linn

authorHOUSE™

1663 LIBERTY DRIVE, SUITE 200
BLOOMINGTON, INDIANA 47403
(800) 839-8640
WWW.AUTHORHOUSE.COM

First published by AuthorHouse 12/22/05

ISBN: 1-4208-8460-3 (sc)

Printed in the United States of America
Bloomington, Indiana

This book is printed on acid-free paper.

All royalties from this book will be donated to the Puppeteers of America, Inc.
www.puppeteers.org
to support puppetry in education and therapy initiatives and projects.

Front cover photo of 6th Grade Students Performing Tales of Greek Mythology by Judith O'Hare.

The authors of this book welcome your comments and questions. They can be contacted through the editors:

Matthew Bernier
Graduate Art Therapy Program
Eastern Virginia Medical School
P.O. Box 1980
Norfolk, VA 23501-1980
757-446-5895
berniemg@evms.edu

Judith O'Hare
You and Me Puppets
74 Hillcrest Rd.
Reading, MA 01867-3311
781-944-0965
jaohare@gis.net
www.youandmepuppets.com

## DEDICATION

We dedicate this book to those children, teachers, students, parents, therapists, patients, and puppet enthusiasts who have been nurtured by the experience of working and playing with puppets.

# FOREWORD

## Susan Linn

In the hands of an artist, the power of puppetry to entertain is breathtaking. As seen in this thoughtful collection of essays, when that artist is also a teacher or a clinician, the power of puppetry to educate and to heal is boundless.

One theme repeated throughout this book is the astonishing capacity of puppets to affect people who are hard to reach through more traditional means. The answer to why this is so lies in the nature of the medium. Puppetry is evocative because it is a three dimensional symbolic art form with the capacity for movement and speech. Static puppets, like dolls, or stuffed animals, exist as symbols for the creatures they represent. Yet puppets can be made with no distinguishing features at all; mittens, paper bags, scissors, hands, and lobster claws can all be brought to life by puppeteers. Once they begin to speak, regardless of their physical characteristics, they become people. After all, the ability to translate thought into speech is a uniquely human characteristic.

As "nearly humans," puppets elicit identification from audiences. We see ourselves in them, or parts of ourselves. Once that occurs, we see them as being "like us" and in doing so invest them with our own thoughts and feelings. These processes can happen almost instantaneously. The puppets become simultaneously, "me" and "not me," and therein lies their power. For an audience, this paradox means that through watching puppets perform we can learn some things about ourselves—including new ways of being and relating to the world—without feeling defensive or threatened. In this way, puppets can serve as models for behaviors and values.

Speaking through puppets also provides a "me/not-me" experience that allows us to say things we might not be able or willing to say directly. The "me" part means that talking through a puppet elicits honest expression. That the puppet is clearly "not-me," makes talking through them feel safe. I was once making puppets with a group of emotionally disturbed children. One boy worked feverishly on his puppet, and when he was finished, he put it on his hand and began using it to say terribly mean things to everyone in the room. "Peter!" his exasperated teacher called to him. "Stop it!" Peter's eyes got very big. "It's not me," he announced pointing at his puppet. "It's him."

How we, as educators and therapists, harness the power of puppetry depends on our experience, inclinations, and training. There is no "right way" to do it and one finds enormous variety, ingenuity, and creativity in the types of puppets described in this book, and in the ways they are used. Educators such as Judith O'Hare, Bruce Chessé, Marlene Joyce, and Sharon Peck describe working with children in schools—to promote literacy, to preserve cultural heritage, to teach music, or explore multiculturalism. As an important complement, Carol Sterling contributes an important piece designed to help puppeteers learn how to describe their work with children as it contributes to Core Curriculum Standards.

In addition to transmitting knowledge, puppets also transmit the self, making them invaluable tools for therapy. Therapists like Matthew Bernier and Mickey Aronoff begin to delineate the theoretical underpinnings of puppet therapy, and describe a range of ways of facilitating growth and development by using puppets as a safe vehicle for bringing forth, examining, and working with our unique, inner experience of the world.

Those of us who use puppets for education or for therapy are a quirky, creative bunch. Driven by our commitment to the medium and to the people we serve, most of us have found our own way, learning from each other and taking what we can from other disciplines. *Puppetry in Education and Therapy: Unlocking Doors to the Mind and Heart* does a great service in bringing together a wealth of expertise in one volume. If you're already using puppets it will inspire you to understand your work differently and to explore new possibilities. If you're a teacher or a therapist and you've never used puppets before, it will open a whole world of possibilities and new ways of communicating.

Susan Linn
Boston, 2004

# ACKNOWLEDGMENTS

There are many people we would like to acknowledge who have helped to make this book a reality. We would like to thank the members of the Puppeteers of America Puppetry in Education and Therapy Committee for their input and support of the project. Thanks to the participants of the many presentations and workshops previously led by many of the authors. Your comments and responses to the ideas and techniques represented in this book have greatly influenced their success. Thanks to all the educators and therapists across the country and all over the world who are dedicating their talents and energy to making puppetry a part of the lives of children and adults in a way only possible through personal contact, teaching, and sharing of talents. Thanks to the faculty of the Graduate Art Therapy Program at Eastern Virginia Medical School for your support. Thanks to Kiera Dorsey for your technical assistance. And finally, we would like to acknowledge the many students, clients, and patients who have inspired this work.

# CONTENTS

# INTRODUCTION

## Judith O'Hare and Matthew Bernier

In 1989, the Puppeteers of America held its National Puppet Festival in Cambridge, Massachusetts. One of the unique features of this festival was an education overlay called "Puppets: Education Magic" that ran concurrent with the Festival. It was exclusively for local educators and therapists from many different settings: teachers from preschool through grade 12, religious educators, after-school educators, special educators, hospital personnel, etc. Thus began a unique conference for educators and therapists that continued to be offered each summer in the New England area.

The concept of Puppets: Education Magic, workshops targeted for educators and therapists, was then added to many Puppeteers of America Regional Festivals in the Mid-Atlantic and Northeast Regions, with graduate credits offered for participants. Along with this opportunity for puppeteers, educators, and therapists to join together to offer workshops, performances, exhibits, discussions, and sharing of ideas and expertise, came Education and Therapy Symposiums at Regional and National Festivals.

Puppeteers in other parts of the country and Canada also offered regional conferences for educators and therapists with workshops that taught skills in puppetry and how to apply these skills in educational and therapeutic settings. These sessions brought together puppeteers, educators, and therapists to talk about the unique aspects of working with puppets in educational and therapeutic settings of all kinds. People from across the country and Canada began to articulate what they meant by "puppetry in education" and "puppet therapy" and how it is the same or different from "puppet theatre." As new books were published, the authors came to Puppets: Education Magic and offered book signings and their books were reviewed and discussed.

Simultaneous to the Puppets: Education Magic events, several therapists who use puppetry in therapy, and puppeteers who do therapeutic puppetry, began to dialogue about the theory and practice of therapeutic puppetry. Various workshops were presented at puppetry festivals and arts therapies conferences. Several practitioners of therapeutic puppetry independently began teaching workshops and making presentations promoting therapeutic puppetry.

Articles about therapeutic puppetry have been published since the1930s, but interest in the topic increased with the publication of several books in the 1980s and 1990s. Clearly, many divergent concepts and approaches to therapeutic puppetry were being explored.

It became apparent to us and others that there is a need for more study, research, and reflective writing about the power of puppets in education and therapy from the point of view of the puppeteers, therapists, and educators who use puppets in their work. There is a need for thoughtful discussion about the unique characteristics of puppetry in education and therapy, the skills it takes to be successful in these areas, and the skills that are passed on to the children and adults who use puppets for personal expression.

There are many fine books that discuss using puppets in the classroom, in religious education, and/or for therapeutic situations, and ways to construct and manipulate puppets, but few books focus on the theory of puppetry in education and therapy. Why use puppets? What and how do children, teens, and adults learn when they use puppets? What are some processes to assess the impact of puppets on learning or behavior change? How are the multiple intelligences concepts relevant to puppetry? How does puppetry affect literacy? What is a rationale for engaging in the process that people go through when they become immersed in puppetry activities? How is the process different from the product when working in puppetry arts? How can puppets benefit participants in a therapeutic setting? How does involvement with puppetry affect the puppeteer/teacher? How have lives been altered or changed by involvement in puppet art and drama? These questions and more are addressed in the following chapters.

Puppets do have power and what better gift for a child or adult than the opportunity to play with puppets. Puppetry changed our lives and we have seen puppets work their magic on countless children, adolescents, and adults and we know their lives were changed too. It is our hope that this book will illustrate that puppetry arts can affect learning and behavior and that puppets indeed have the power to unlock doors to the mind and heart.

# PART ONE:

# PUPPETRY IN EDUCATION

# CHAPTER 1

## INTRODUCTION TO PUPPETRY IN EDUCATION
## Judith O'Hare

Judy performing her toy theatre version of The Three Bears.

The book, *Champions for change: The impact of the arts on learning (Fiske, 2000),* commissioned by the President's Council on the Arts and Humanities, is a collection of research projects on the positive impact of the arts on education. The studies found that "involvement in the arts provides unparalleled opportunities for learning, enabling young people to reach for and attain higher levels of achievement" (p. viii). The researchers found that "the arts can help 'level the playing field' for youngsters from disadvantaged circumstances" (p. viii), and they found that group learning, as exemplified in putting on a play, deepens the learning process. The findings also illustrated that "learning in the arts has significant effects on learning in other domains." These studies are very important because they provide educators with research to support taking time to provide active stimulating arts experiences in classrooms, libraries, after school enrichment programs, clubs, and other learning environments.

One of the crucial issues in education today is testing, evaluating student learning. There is a pressing need by everyone from the president of the United States, to state governors, to school boards, to school administrators, to teachers, parents, and taxpayers to have an educated populace. With the pressure of mandated evaluations in mind, teachers and administrators often say, "There is no time for puppetry. We would love to do more arts, but the children have so much to learn to pass the tests." A well-planned puppetry program taps into all of the multiple intelligences, the many ways people learn, and puppet play exemplifies the levels of literacy as described in Bloom's Taxonomy (1956). Recreating characters and stories with puppets helps children to absorb and remember what they have learned and internalize information so that they can retell the stories from the mind and the heart. Puppets make an emotional as well as cognitive connection to ideas, information, stories, characters, literature, and historical and life situations. It is one of our goals to illustrate that the time spent on a well developed puppetry program is indeed *time well spent.*

In 2003, in an urban multi-ethnic elementary school, a group of fourth grade children were preparing a Toy Theater production of "The Lion and the Mouse," one of several of Aesop's Fables the class was working on for a literature project. The day the children were going to share their work, one of the children came to me and said that the boy who was playing the hunter was not in school that day. He looked disappointed, but then said that he could play that boy's part, and his own as well. I said, "Fine, give it a try," and I sat back to watch. The boy got the other students in his group organized and told them that he was going to play both parts. He then outlined how the story would go and who would move where and who came in next and so forth. His classroom teacher was also watching, and as the story progressed and the puppets moved and spoke, she looked at me and said, "I have that boy listed as retarded. I can't believe what he is doing!"

The boy knew the story and all of the parts and could direct all of the other students. The play was not ready for an Emmy, but it worked. He indeed had processed the story, had an organizational plan, had administrative skills, and he "pulled it off." The next day, we selected a few of the many puppet plays for the Massachusetts Cultural Council representatives to view. The boy's play was one of them. His teacher was amazed and while she had been reluctant to take time away from preparing for the MA state mandated MCAS tests with her fourth grade students, she realized there is more than one way for children to learn. The teacher had labeled the boy retarded. Perhaps he could not express himself well in spoken or written words for a variety of reasons, but he illustrated that he had more complex thinking processes that were apparent as he worked cooperatively with his group, and planned and presented a puppet drama. This is an isolated example of how children can be assessed through their puppet play and how one child illustrated what he knew, grew in his sense of self-worth and changed in the eyes of his teacher. The process illustrated that there are many ways to teach children and how a totally linguistic approach had led to inaccurate conclusions about a child's ability.

The following articles describe a variety of puppet programs and projects with children and training programs with educators. It is evident from reading these articles, that those children and teachers have gained success, understanding, pride, and a sense of accomplishment from their involvement in puppet construction and puppet drama. Even the youngest children can be included, and children from isolated cultures in places like Alaska can be touched by the power of the puppets. Technology can be used to connect people across continents and to share expertise and information about puppetry. Puppets can stimulate learning by involving the multiple intelligences and promote active learners in literacy, social studies, and history programs. Puppets have a magic and a power when we think of puppets as metaphors, and through the symbolic nature of puppets children can begin to grapple with sensitive issues such as bullying and conflict resolution. Not all puppets are for little children; middle school and high school students can find ways to communicate through an inanimate object, and some of the tedium of education can be eased through an artistic and expressive use of puppets.

The articles in this section are written by puppeteers and educators who know about the art of puppetry and the art of teaching.

## References

Bloom, B. (Ed.) (1956). *Taxonomy of educational objectives: The classification of educational goals.* Boston: Addison Wesley.

Fiske, E. (Ed.) (2000). *Champions for change: The impact of the arts on learning.* Washington, D. C.: The Arts Education Partnership/ The President's Committee on the Arts and the Humanities.

# CHAPTER 2

## THE PUPPET AS A METAPHOR

### Tova Ackerman

Their world is a poem, not a short story.
They are, by their very nature, images coming to life.
When the puppet bridges the gap between his seeming
limitations and his coming to life,
He has made a moving comment on the human condition
And even the puppet's death can be moving,
As having given us the gift of his breath,
He then takes it back.
And yet, in the next moment, he lives again - immortal,
A dream or memory in the actor's hand.
The actor can play this role too,
But the puppet is this.
He is naturally tragic-comic
Naturally abstract - a detail.
In the human world, he is a visitor
And we must see ourselves through his eyes.
(Bass, 1992)

Tova Ackerman

Puppet drama, while a form of creative expression, differs from other performing arts in that the world designed by the puppeteers consists of animated objects, a theatre performance whose actors are not human. The performance may parallel human reality, but the "actors" have much greater freedom. A puppet can be an inanimate object, a distortion or exaggeration of reality, or a being that can move in ways impossible for a human actor.

The actual puppet creation process may be quite simple. A few pieces of fabric, a bit of glue and glitter or a folded paper plate may be all that are needed. The interaction between person and character, however, is complex. The character that is created comes from some aspect of its creator that may not even be consciously expressed in everyday life.

The puppet, then, is put into the role of actor, mirror, and critic. It has lines to speak, and its oral environment takes place within the context of other "actors" in a particular place and time set by the puppet producer. In much the same way that ordinary discourse takes place, the interaction between players on a puppet stage is always more than the words expressed. The puppets not only mouth words, but transmit a message through body language and visual aspect. In contrast to human interaction, that of the puppet is an exaggeration, often a comic one, of some aspect of the character portrayed. It may be an abstract shape, an object, or a realistic figure, but it is always symbolic. A puppet is created with the audience in mind. Its body language is purposeful with no movement un-intentioned. The mind of the puppeteer interacts with the audience with the freedom of anonymity and the urge to portray that which may normally not be portrayed. At the same time, the stimulation of the medium affects both the puppeteer and the audience.

## Imagination and the Puppet

The word, imagination, is usually defined as a power of the mind to form a mental image or concept of something that is not real or present. In Hebrew, the word, imagination, is dimyon, which means to be similar to. If the two definitions are combined, in terms of puppet creation, the question then arises as to the origin of an "imaginary" puppet character. The answer, then, lies in the basic nature of the puppet as a metaphor. Puppets become visual metaphors for ideas, characters, or emotions that may not have been consciously thought of as connected by the puppeteer until the puppet is made.

Once made, the puppet has an external look and an inner "anima" that is the gift of its builder. When Rudolf Arnheim (1974) wrote about artistic imagination, he described it as the,

> capacity to invent a striking pattern, especially when applied to such familiar shapes as a head or a hand... (p.142). Imagination is by no means (primarily) the invention of new subject matter, and not even the production of just any kind of new shape. Artistic imagination can be more nearly described as a finding of new form for old content, or - if the handy dichotomy of form and content is eschewed - as a fresh conception of an old subject. (p.142)

Arnheim (1974) wrote further about the relationship between the artist and the object being portrayed. He described the object as being able to dictate a bare minimum of structural features and therefore calling on the imagination of the artist in the literal sense of the word. It is the imagination of the artist that must turn the object into an image. In the case of puppetry, in which the object itself is the active voice, what does the artist/puppeteer do to embody it with spirit?

In an interview with Joseph Krofta, conducted by Hannah Kodicek (1992) for a BBC documentary of Czech puppetry, Krofta spoke of the animation of an object:

> We need to remind ourselves often that the words "to animate" does not mean "to make move," but rather it means "to give soul to," from the Latin word, anima...To breath soul into an object, does not mean making a perfect copy of it...An artist makes us believe that any object he touches is alive, and 'ensouled', that is, it contains a living soul.

The puppet may be the product of the imagination of the person who made it, but once created it exists in its own right. The relationship between puppet maker and the puppet cannot be totally separate.

## The Freedom of Puppets

"Puppets, though normally associated with gross buffoonery, are poetic. They are, because they are not human, immediately metaphors" (Bass, 1992, p.1). Puppetry, as seen as metaphor, can be differentiated from other art forms; it has zaniness and a style of oral communication that is at once strongly visual

and persuasive in terms of involving the spectator. A puppet is made to speak. Whether or not the mouth has a movement mechanism or is glued shut or painted on, whether the puppet is symbolic or abstract in shape and design, it has a function that involves communication. This aspect of puppetry is intrinsic to it.

When a particular puppet character comes to mind, there is often a slight twitch in the hand. If a puppet is put on one's hand, it is impossible to keep it quiet. It has a mind of its own. If it wants to interrupt, it does. Its personality comes from some part of the puppeteer that is dominant enough for it to have been created as a concrete visualization. It is a statement of thoughts that may not have been consciously expressed; here, those thoughts are not only stated, but stated strongly. This aspect of puppetry makes it a dynamic tool for developing language communication skills with both children and adults. A puppet is an extension of the personality, but it has greater freedom to express this personality. It can go where the person is afraid to go; it can speak with mistakes without worry. It can fly. It can sing.

**Magical Interactions**

Whether the puppet is realistic, abstract, or a functional object used as an animated object, its role is to make a statement. It is given life through the puppeteer and is used to entertain or to present the viewpoint of the puppeteer to others. It exists through interaction with an audience, and only the imagination of the spectators gives it life. The puppet and audience interact, the puppeteer interacts with the audience, and the puppet and the puppeteer interact. The participation of the audience has an effect on the movement and action of the puppet.

Bil Baird (1973) described the feeling of the puppeteer on stage. He's very conscious of how he's "coming down the strings." The puppeteer sees himself through the eyes of the spectators and reacts through interaction with the puppet. Baird wrote:

> Further, and perhaps more important, there is the almost magical interaction of puppets and puppeteer. Never get the idea that the puppet stands independently between the audience and his manipulator. The puppeteer can feel the response of the audience through this extension, this part of himself, as much as the actor on the stage. (p.17)

In a theatre project focusing on animated objects at the Sao Paulo University Department of Theatre, Ana Maria Amaral worked with object theatre in terms of the sensorial and mystic aspects of the object. In terms of the first project, the object was viewed first within its natural environment and later, away from it. Away from its natural environment, it appeared autonomous, if somewhat odd. The next step was to work with the object as animated and magical.

The infusion of a magical or supernatural element into non-living objects is not new in human history. Part of the belief system of primitive man is that there is a live being within both animate and inanimate things. In terms of the puppeteer, the relationship between the object and the life it develops through animation is akin to the relationship between the concrete idea and the abstraction. The additional element that is native to puppet drama is the strong psychological connection between the animated object and the puppeteer.

## The Puppet is Oral

The basic nature of the puppet is oral; its orality differentiates it from other art forms such as sculptural objects or dolls. However, the natural zaniness of this inherently performance-based media, allows for the free flowing of ideas that can digress and move into the past and future time without adhering to any particular form and code. The lack of set conventions is one of the conventions of the puppet world. Puppetry has been associated with oral language in primitive cultures. Aboriginal culture shows string figures, which are used as adjuncts to songs that are passed down orally. Audience repetition of songs and parts of predictable stories are parts of oral culture often associated with the use of puppet theatre. Sometimes the puppets have no speech of their own, but act in concert to a ritualistic presentation of a story in which the audience serves to vocalize the words.

Speech, then, is what separates this art form from others. Walter J. Ong (1982) wrote of the power of speech in his book, *The Orality of Language.*

> Speech is inseparable from our consciousness, and it has fascinated human beings and elicited serious reflection about itself from the very early stage of consciousness, long before writing came into existence. Proverbs from all over the world are rich with observations about this overwhelmingly human phenomenon of speech in its native oral form, about its powers, its beauties, its dangers. (p. 9)

Puppetry adds another dimension to speech. It gives the speaker a way to state a thought in a strong way before a word is uttered. It reaches into the psyche of the speaker to find the words that reflect emotions and thoughts that are central to the speaker. It searches for the stance, the mood, the set to transmit feeling and receptivity to the anticipated listener. The power of the puppet is the power of a person to connect with others. It provides a way for connection that is direct because it travels indirectly, through the puppet, within the human understanding that is universal.

In *The Shoemaker and the Elves* (1983), Lewis Hyde wrote about the shoemaker who finally succeeded in making his work live. He likened this to the artist who succeeds in making his work real by its reflection of his spirit. The "gift," this creation of the artist, may be passed along to the audience who must enter a kind of state of "giftedness" in order to receive the creation of the artist. "Let us just say that the suspensions of disbelief; by which we become receptive to a work of the imagination are in fact belief, a momentary faith by virtue of which the spirit of the artist's gift may enter and act upon our being" (p. 48). In the case of the puppet drama, the puppet, once having developed a life of its own, seeks to continue the relationship and turns it in directions that often have not been consciously intended by its creator.

In a discussion of the nature of metaphor, Ellen Winner (1982) referred to the use of the word, candle, by Macbeth upon hearing of the death of his wife. ("Out, out brief candle, life's but a walking shadow, a poor player that struts and frets his hour upon the stage and then is heard no more." [Act 5, Scene 5]). Winner wrote about its metaphoric use to present human life and then discussed the fresh insights that metaphors offer the reader. We are invited to look and process information in a new way. In Winner's in-depth discussion of metaphoric language, she differentiated between "good" and "bad" metaphors. "Finally, good metaphors are more apt to be based on dynamic, changing properties of two elements, such as the way they move or the sound they make, rather than on fixed properties, such as their shape and color" (p. 54).

In Heidegger's sense of recollection as thinking, which attempts to "approximate" the experience of being at the beginning of history, we might say that the person, through the puppet, is going down into him/herself, into the "innermost" of individual depths of him/herself and bringing forth the potential to be developed. The process of recollection is not dependent on the puppet, but the puppet is a way of crystallizing ideas and bringing a participation between a person's inner and outer self that is tuned in to a basic "primordial" understanding.

When we think of puppet drama in terms of metaphors, we go beyond movement, sound and/or shape. If Macbeth's candle is thought of as puppet drama, the problems facing the puppeteer would involve the whole concept of the image, the transient status, the fading of what once was vital. If the puppet looks like a candle, how does one evoke the image of Macbeth's wife? The technical problems to be explored might involve the projection of the image of the wife's face onto the flame of the candle. The question of transient status might be built into the movement of the candle as it connects with the audience. The candle, as puppet extension, has a life of its own. It is a personality. It has to deal with the issues involved and to present itself as a statement, for that is in the nature of the visual quality of puppetry. The problems evoked by the media are part of its fascination. The audience must "see" into the character for the drama to be successful. This is true of all drama, but the nature of the stated visual metaphor adds power to the portrayal of idea.

The basic dynamic is one in which the emotional response of the members of the audience is high, but is also tinged with the awareness that they are responding to a bit of fabric or fluff. Before the audience response, there is a dialogue between puppeteer and puppet. This dialogue reflects many subtleties of thought that are stated in a simple outward shape with relatively stilted movement. This crystallization of thought and idea from simple to complex and back again refines the ideas being presented, and there is a point when audience and puppeteer connect that contains the moment of "poetic buffoonery" that Eric Bass speaks about. Issues of life and death, man's fleeting glimpses of his gods, loneliness and isolation, and moments of ecstasy are analyzed, portrayed and commented on by pieces of fabric put together in all sorts of ways. The temptation to clown and to show both sides of an issue, to make fun of human frailties and to use a touch of the absurd, is overwhelming; it is part and parcel of the medium of puppetry.

## References

Arnheim, R. (1954,1974). *Art and visual perception.* Berkeley & Los Angeles: University of California Press.

Baird, B. (1973). *The art of the puppet.* New York: Bonanza Books.

Bass, E. (1992). *Breaking boundaries: American puppetry in the 1980s.* Atlanta: Center for Puppetry Arts.

Hyde, L. (1983). *The gift.* New York: Random House.

Kodicek, H. (1992). Excerpts from an interview with Joseph Krofta conducted by Hannah Kodicek. In *Conference papers: The theatrical inanimate: A conference on changing perceptions in the New York Shakespeare Festival.*

Ong, W. J. (1982). *Orality and literacy.* New York: Mathuen & Co.

Winner, E. (1982). *Invented worlds.* Cambridge, MA: Harvard University Press.

[A version of this article first appeared in *The Journal of the Imagination in Language Learning and Teaching (1993, Vol. I).* It is reprinted here with permission.]

# CHAPTER 3

## CREATIVITY AND THE TALENTED AND UNTALENTED CHILD AS IT RELATES TO THE ART OF PUPPETRY

### Bruce Chessé

It has long been a practice in this country to identify the artistic and creative student by the talent he or she expresses. It is often the ability of the individual to draw two-dimensionally, or sing on key, which becomes a primary criterion in determining this talent. In addition, the teacher or person making this determination often has no qualification for making this decision. As a result, in the educational system it is the talented individual who is first encouraged to explore their creativity to the detriment of the so-called untalented child.

Because of this, many of us go throughout life with strong negative feelings about our creativity. We are discouraged from exploring our creative urges by others and ourselves and end up never developing the creativity that lies inherent in all of us. In addition, there is an inherent fear of failure that comes into play, which prevents us from even trying.

I make this assessment based on my own experiences, being brought up in an artistic family, and the forty years I have spent in theatre and puppetry as a puppetry in education specialist in many school districts. As such, a majority of my lifetime has been taken up putting students and teachers alike in touch with their own creativity. It is my personal belief that we are all creative and that finding a form of artistic expression that works for you will put you in touch with the talent we inherently all have and something we can view passionately. It is through the art of puppetry that I feel this can be accomplished.

But first let us talk about creativity itself or the facility we all have for creative invention or fantasy. The ability to fantasize is directly related to the experiential level of the individual. It crosses all social and economic levels. In my work with children of all age groups, it is the person with the most experiences who develops the freedom to fantasize freely. Fantasy, in short, is the luxury of the experiential child. If children are raised in an environment where they are read to everyday and are taken out to the zoo, the aquarium, or the theater, involved in creative playgroups, or anything that expands their view of the world, then creative play will be broadened. If a child is raised in an environment that is limited in experiences, then the creative play of the child is very concrete.

For example, when I watch the puppet shows created by my students with limited experiences, the shows are about everyday happenings, concrete experiences, like going to school, falling off a bike, etc. If I take students with more experiential backgrounds and combine them with the less experienced, their stories and plays take on a broader context. The puppets themselves made by the less experienced child are also less inventive and more concrete in their design. The puppets and their stories will always reflect the environmental experiences of those who make and perform them.

A more profound example can be found in working with Eskimo children in Alaska. On the West Coast, in Lower Kuskukwim and Yukon River areas where Yupik speakers live, there is a tradition of storytelling that is highly valued and practiced. Children have story knives that they use to draw house floor plans and this is a game they regularly play in groups, out in the snow or in the mud. There, the Aurora Borealis can be seen with great regularity. Mask making, art, sculpture, and doll making, too, are highly valued. The economic base in a majority of these communities is very low. Reading is not always well established. However, the puppet shows and the puppets they made were very innovative and abstract and reflect the influences of the Eskimo art that is very colorful and overtly abstract. Are the children abstract thinkers? Not always. Are they rich in experiences? Yes, but not in terms of children in the lower 48 states.

When I first went to bush Alaska in 1976, the sixth grade field trip was to Anchorage where visiting a supermarket was a primary experience for them. Television consisted of two educational stations whose reception and programming was extremely limited. Today, however, all this has changed with most of the villages having satellite programming and a multitude of stations at their disposal. The puppet experience with the Yupik speakers was often very different from the Athabascan communities found in Central and Eastern Alaska, where conditions were harsh and experiences limited. All of this had a direct effect on their creativity and their comfort level with expressing it.

This brings me to how and in what way puppetry can put you in touch with your creativity. Puppets stand alone as magical images. They evolved out of religious and mystical ceremonies because, like a magic trick, they are illusory in nature. When manipulated, they take on an individuality all their own and are accepted as distinct personalities and as such are highly prized by their makers. In addition, puppets may take responsibility for their own actions. To criticize or argue with a puppet figure makes you look foolish and ridiculous. Therefore, children readily accept a puppet and it is a safe house for them when they use them.

The art and craft of puppetry itself is a positive and highly accommodating one as well and that makes it a perfect medium for motivating children and involving them in the artistic process. Puppetry is theater. As an art form, it encompasses the entire spectrum of the arts and it involves individual choices that allow one to be selective.

It involves design, sculpting, writing, acting, improvisation, and painting skills. In addition, all the technical theater skills such as set and prop building, music, and the production of audio and videotaping can come into play as well. In your involvement in the craft and performing art of puppetry there will always be one area or aspect of it that you can excel in. Success is the key and with puppetry, it is always a positive experience for the individual as we consistently learn from positive experiences.

In addition, the puppet itself is self-motivating in that it creates its own life as it is being built. It is an evolutionary process that on completion exists as a reminder of your successful and positive accomplishments. Secondarily, it involves social skills that demand interaction from both performers and audience. It gives the timid or uncommunicative child the opportunity to express himself or herself through a middleman, the puppet. The aggressive child can find an acceptable outlet for aggressive behavior by acting out concerns in puppet shows. Puppetry facilitates cooperation and this interaction is rewarded by a positive response from the audience. In short, it becomes a self-gratifying experience that in turn motivates and reinforces discriminating positive behavior. This in turn enhances the individual's self-image. It allows the child to fit in and/or to find a way to fit in.

Puppetry provides a role-playing approach to social growth and problem solving, sequencing, and the organization of ideas, whose validity is tested and proven in the performances. I say performances because it is from the process of performing that the individual learns what works and what doesn't and is rewarded instantly. And finally, all of this activity involves a continual series of individual choices that personalize one's creative efforts (choice becoming the most important factor).

Now I would like to talk about what brought me to these conclusions and offer some concrete examples. In the 1970s, I was married to a special education teacher with whom I collaborated on a number of projects, but it is the first one that sticks most prominently in my mind. Jeanne was working with a group of children who were designated as EH or educationally handicapped. These were children in regular classes who were having difficulty learning in a large class setting and were sent to the EH class for remedial work in a variety of subjects with an emphasis on reading. They were pulled from class each day for a certain number of hours. My wife came to me one day and asked if I had any ideas on teaching the concept of "when two vowels go walking one does the talking." My idea was to illustrate the concepts with puppets. Together, we made up a story with puppets representing the five vowels I E A O and U. There was nothing special about the puppets except for the fact they each had their representative vowels attached to their shirtfronts. The story went as follows:

E wanders in from the right side of the puppet stage and crosses to the center of the stage. I enters stage left and crosses over to E. E tries to speak to I and is subsequently hit on the head by I who then exits stage right. A sign then comes up with the word TIE pictured on it. Confused, E watches I leave as O comes in from stage right and confronts E by hitting him and tying him up with a rope. Subsequently, as each vowel comes in, E is met with more restraints. E is now completely immobilized and gagged. Each time this happens, a sign is raised with the word, which indicates that E must remain silent. Finally, the letter A arrives, crossing over to E, and slowly begins to remove all the restraints. E then tries speaking to A. A says nothing. E then looks out at the audience and a sign with a lit light bulb appears. E then turns to A and begins to tie and gag up A. He then looks at A and as a sign comes up with the word DEAL on it, E turns and walks off the stage as another sign comes up reading THE END.

Once the story was worked out, we got the students together and had them learn and perform it for each other. This they took great pleasure in and the performance was repeated many times, each with a great deal of enthusiasm. This enthusiasm was so great, in fact, that as a group, they decided that they had to perform it for the Kindergarten classes. Next, they had to perform it for all the classes in the school. This was done with a great sense of fun and accomplishment. This took place over several weeks.

During this time, several things happened. First, the students received a lot of positive recognition. Their peers then singled them out positively and instead of teasing, kids wanted to know how they could get into the EH class and do puppets. Their self-image was improved 100% and this was important since many of the EH students had a problem with self-image. Secondly, it illustrated the concept in a visual, audio, and tactile sense, accommodating most learning disabilities. Finally, we were able to drop the whole project and return to it months later and totally evaluate it. The same students were given the puppets and asked to improvise the show. They were able to repeat it instantly. They had learned the concept and I would venture to say it was something they will never have forgotten to this day.

One of the most interesting facts was that this show was primarily non-verbal. It didn't require any great verbal skills and as such was an easy project to involve the students in. There was no risk for them but many rewards. This set them up for more adventuresome puppet projects with which Jeanne was to follow up.

It was this project, which initially established my direction in Puppetry in Education because the effectiveness of what we were doing was irrefutable. I went on to establish a method of construction that involved choices on the part of the students, which enabled them to create a puppet that was truly of their own making. Their shows, too, were individualized and a reflection of their own ideas and concerns.

(Author's Note: For a more detailed picture of the techniques I employ in the classroom, see the Oregon Puppet Theatre's video, *Making and Using Puppets in the Primary Grades,* ISBN: 0-96-28355-2-8. Copies can be ordered from Puppet Concepts Publishing, P.O. Box 15203, Portland, OR 97293-5203 (503) 236-4034.)

# CHAPTER 4

## THOUGHTS ON PUPPETRY FOR THE VERY YOUNG

### Suzanne Down

I believe in a renewal of puppetry where it opens the heart and brings, through visible story, a picture of the possibilities of humanness. The movements and gestures of the puppets, the colors, quality of storytelling voice and music, choreography, staging and story content, lifts us out of the "everyday" and connects us all with a story world.

How we approach puppetry for the different ages, of course, must follow the development of the child. For the last 10 years, part of my puppetry research has been for the very young. This has centered on 2-4 year olds as well as birth-2 year olds with their mothers. I am often sitting on the floor with a close circle of little ones, silk over our laps and legs – our story space!

We all stand in awe at the achievement of the child's first three years of life. To gain uprightness is the first fundamental achievement the child must gain in the first year to then begin their "doing" in the world. We stand with our feet gaining the balance and strength to hold our weight. The muscles of the back and neck develop enough to hold our spine and head up straight. This frees our arms and hands for activity. Then the first steps are taken when we experience the left and right sides of the body used in our human walk, with our uprightness held in the middle. We begin to orient our upright self in space and move in space. We can propel ourselves from here to there. Our free hands are eager to pick up something from a greater distance than ever before. How exciting are all the possibilities to do more! Add the huge acquisition of speech, memory, and first thinking, and we see the miracles of the first three years of life. How can puppetry enhance the child's early development? Very much, by supporting these three major accomplishments.

When a Wee Willie Winkie small table puppet or finger puppet goes through the town, we as puppeteers can be conscious of the puppet's uprightness, the human left and right of Wee Willie's walk – mirroring the child's. We surround the little ones with musical speech, the singing quality of consonants and vowels, together with the wonderful gestures of Wee Willie moving in space. The gesture and movement quality in our own imagination will support the inner processes of the very young.

Imagine a mother lovingly holding her one or two year old on her lap, delighting in the rhythm and sounds of the nursery rhyme words. Then here comes Wee Willie Winkie over their laps, going upstairs (up a child's leg) and downstairs (down the leg), peeking through the lock, and running along the lap and folds of cloth, creating joyful closeness and playful pictures and song story sharing.

The child will want to see it again and again; the rhythm, repetition, and language reassuring and confirming uprightness, walking into the world, and formative speech. The young child's whole self will be twinkling in the wonder, love, and fun of it all, and so importantly, the soft sense experience is in harmony with his own accomplishments. We can ask ourselves, with an understanding of the stages of childhood, what kind of puppet story will bring meaning to the child's development.

For the **six months to one year olds** I would suggest the introduction of puppets to be much like this Wee Willie Winkie, accompanied by the love and holding of a mother, a father, grandparent, or caretaker. Song and story, told with attention to language, being "lifted" out of everyday speaking into storytelling voice, will enhance the child's experience of speech and give the child clear, beautiful consonants and vowels to imitate and form his/her own first words with.

What kind of puppet would you use? Something made from natural material to support the child's growing healthy sensory relationship to his surroundings. The puppet of choice is by far the soft wool roving finger puppets and lap and table puppets. The wool roving puppets are soft in colors, and natural in material for the young senses to absorb with their eyes and their touch. In fact, the porous quality of the wool invites them to sink into the story, poem, or song, so they are held there, and listen deeply. There is air in the gently wrapped wool puppets to help the viewer breathe. The gestures and movements are full of rhythm and wonder. They move slowly so the child's senses can take in the depths of the gesture. The puppets have a living quality because the puppeteer enlivens them with understanding and love. It is a powerful medium to help the youngest ones sit in peace, find stillness, and take in a beautiful visual story. For the one year olds that will hold the puppet, and perhaps put them in their mouth, I use wool felt, cotton velveteen, or soft silk puppets.

The **two year olds** have come a long way. They have had a year to step out and explore their world. Their hands are much more capable of doing things, and the verbal communication with people in their immediate lives is leaping forward. Hearing well told storytelling, song stories, poems and nursery rhymes will help build their language skills.

We can help them build language through the visual pictures of puppets accompanying their growing listening ability. When we add movement and meaningful gesture to our puppets we are bringing rich living pictures, as opposed to the fixed pictures in picture books and technological movements in children's videos. We cannot underestimate the human heart of the puppeteer that enlivens the puppets for little children.

At this age I love to bring puppet experiences that flow in harmony with a child's actual daily life and growing experience in the immediate world around them. A story about picking apples with grandpa; using a grandpa and child puppet can meet a true experience of apple picking in autumn. Bringing the apples home to puppet grandma, who bakes the pie, can mirror real ideal life. Even better, add celebrating autumn with a real apple pie after the puppet show!

Here the puppet story can add meaning to the real practical event. The warmth of relationship in the puppet characters' gesture to each other, the reaching and picking, the carrying of a basket, the rhythm and life of real activity can be made visible and even more conscious in our puppet movements. We can mirror the healthiest of daily life. By adding the rhythm, repetition, and breath of a song or story to the gesture of the puppet, we support the potential for health of movement in the daily tasks.

One of the greatest contributions of puppetry for this age is bringing the cycle of the year to children with visual seasonal stories, songs, and poems from their day to day experiences. Stories about building a snowman, the birds weaving their nest, caterpillars becoming butterflies, the pumpkin patch, the squirrel gathering nuts, all bring seasonal pictures to help integrate a child within their environment. For this age, we want to bring beautiful puppet stories that are still within their experience, stories that bring a further joyful connecting to their seasonal world.

We want to bring the seasonal tone and color into their story time, creating simple open stages on tables, our laps, the floor, using colors representing the changing seasons. I use solid colored silks, cotton gauze, and soft fabrics. Collecting leaves, acorns, feathers, berries, and flowers from the children's walks to add to the puppet "stage" will add to their interest in the story world you bring. Use puppets they can hold and touch. Strong wool felt small table puppets and finger puppets welcome touching.

When we are enlivening the puppets with a little story, how important it is for these little ones that absorb everything with their senses and imitation, that we bring puppet gestures that are true; so that a butterfly will move in the element of air and levity, and the bunny will have a rhythmic hop, the chickens will peck, peck, peck, the pony will trot, and the human characters will have uprightness, and walk with an awareness of the left and right of a human walk. A human does not walk like a bunny hops!

We aim for the archetype of the movement, and then capture its unique rhythm and mood in a soft slower timing that the youngest senses can sink into. Puppetry can capture the purest of gesture, which can be taken inwardly by a child's imitation. What fun to go outside after a nature puppet story and run and fly like that butterfly, hop like that puppet bunny, or scurry like the mouse. The observation in nature, the deep absorbing of the puppet pictures in the story, the taking hold of the story so that it can be re-enacted in the child's play, this is a healthy child!

I put out a basket of small bunny puppets for children to use after I have presented a bunny story. Try this and watch the story be re-enacted to the detail through their powers of imitation. Imitation is the building block toward the development of their imaginations.

Then something remarkable happens, starting at **three years old**, which continues on until around five years old. There is a blossoming imagination, and the activity of the child at this age can be engaged to transform objects in play with a quality of <u>fantasy</u>. The child creates out of the memory of things he has experienced. A basket of pine cones can become the people in a child's story village. Poppy seed pods become salt and pepper shakers in the sand kitchen.

A child experiences a wonderful puppet show such as Elsa Beskow's "Ollies Ski Trip," a story about King Winter, Mrs. Thaw, and the coming of Lady Spring. The child opens heart and receives the story portrayed with meaningful gestures, movements, colors, and puppets appropriate for this age. Then, as if by magic, in free play time the children play Mrs. Thaw. A brown cloth becomes her cloak, a stick becomes her broom. Lady Spring arrives cloaked in a green cloth, wool roving flowers at her feet! The healthy child will re-enact the story. The engagement of their own activity to recreate the story strengthens the children's budding fantasy capability.

When I perform this story to 3-5 year olds I make wool roving puppet characters while they are in free play, and they all end up watching me and wanting to make their own Lady Spring or King Winter. I have colored wool in baskets beside me available and ready for them to create their own simple characters. They then later use their own "puppets" to retell the story over and over.

For the development of fantasy to be alive in children, we as adults can help guide their activity. Sometimes the children are full of chaos, or don't know how to create play. They are the watchers on the sideline. Neither of these kinds of children knows how to have meaningful play. Trust the regular rhythm of children experiencing your puppet plays, and encourage their fantasy by having simple props and puppets available for them to use. They will start to imitate you, and with the spark of outer objects will find a pathway to their own creative fantasy play.

Children this age still benefit by living into the seasons and the cycle of the year through puppet stories. Now they can begin to have a little more complexity to the plot. One of my favorite seasonal stories for this age is for the darkening days of autumn turning into winter. I have a rod puppet character that has a puppet size lantern that really lights with a candle, and he lights up his way home. The children love this puppet, and know that he is real. And to their imaginative selves, he is as real as the sun, moon and stars.

Puppetry, for the first few years of life, embraces a simplicity so the child's own imagination can be fully engaged. This imagination is the building blocks to later creative thinking. We are doing more than bringing joy to the children with our puppetry. We are welcoming them to their world through stories that ring true for their profound steps of development.

# CHAPTER 5

# TEACHER EDUCATION THROUGH THE KENNEDY CENTER
## Hobey Ford

Hobey Ford and a rod puppet from Animalia.

I have worked with The Kennedy Center Professional Development for Teachers program since 1989. The program utilizes artists of various fields in training teachers to incorporate the arts into the curriculum as a tool for enlivening non-arts related topics. A dancer might use movement of the body to recreate the movement of the heavenly bodies of the solar system, or in my case, puppetry is employed to teach folktales and monarch butterfly metamorphosis. I will explore the processes, which the Kennedy Center uses in developing workshops with artists, looking also at their justifications and reasons why the arts are so effective in teaching. I will describe my own workshops and how I have structured them to be as beneficial as possible for the teachers with whom I work. I will also share my experiences along the way.

Many make the assumption that if you are an artist, you can teach art. This is not always true. When I came to the Kennedy Center with a workshop idea, I thought that I was ready to go. I had led the workshop on shadow puppetry numerous times. What followed was unexpected. My mentor at the Kennedy Center led me through a maze of details and preparations, which I had not considered. There were many questions to ponder. What are the needs of teachers? What is their world like? What concrete goals will be reached in the workshop? Will they feel intimidated by these new techniques? Will they be able to use these educational tools in the classroom? Will these techniques help their students learn? In addressing these questions, I had to learn about the methods of teaching, curriculum standards, and the different ways people learn and absorb knowledge.

My three-hour workshop was planned down to the minute. The topic I was working with was shadow puppetry. I needed to make a curricular tie-in, so I chose folktales. Shadow puppetry was a useful technique for it is so easy to learn and create, yet so versatile. In refining the construction techniques, I looked for easy to find, affordable materials and tools. Over the years I have refined these aspects of the workshop, which brings up one of the core disciplines of being a Kennedy Center workshop leader: evaluation and improvement. Artists involved in the program are constantly looking at what areas of their workshop can be improved. It can be a little thing like refining the introduction or adding humor or reflection time. It could be a simplification of the project to allow more time to absorb what is presented. Evaluations are collected from participants as to the usefulness and effectiveness of the workshop. This re-evaluation of the workshop is thought of as an upward spiral. We constantly try to elevate the level of quality in our workshops.

The Kennedy Center has focused its education department's mission on utilizing the arts in other areas of the curriculum. While it is understood that there is implicit value in the art form itself, they are striving to demonstrate the arts as a teaching and learning tool. The ideas of Howard Gardner's (1983/1993) multiple intelligences are at the heart of this emphasis. Gardner has shown that we all have different fundamental ways of learning. Some of us learn in the traditional methods of verbal-lingual communication that has been the hallmark of our educational system up to recent years. But there are other types of learners whose learning styles are not engaged.

Gardner points out several other learning styles including: kinetic, mathematical, visual-spatial, musical, interpersonal and intra-personal. A kinetic learner for instance can be more readily able to absorb knowledge through body movement. This type of learner will benefit by learning situations that get them out of their chairs. By incorporating dance and creative movement into a lesson, the student will absorb information in a way that they could otherwise not as readily comprehend and retain. The visual-spatial learner will be more successful when projects and lessons include visual media and art. The interpersonal learner will do best when working in groups with social interaction built into the lesson. The arts by their very nature offer opportunities to every one of these learning types. By incorporating the arts into the educational system in a meaningful and purposeful way, students are offered new opportunities to succeed. As an art form, puppetry uniquely meets these goals. Puppetry is fun and accessible.

In working with shadow puppetry I try to alert teachers and students to puppetry's core strengths and requirements. The heart of puppetry is action and animation. While puppetry also can utilize speech and music, it falls flat without action. Action is to puppetry, what a verb is to a sentence. I encourage my students to look for the action in the puppet. If they are interpreting a piece of folklore, I ask them to think about what their characters must "do." What is the essential action they must perform to satisfy the story. In "Hey diddle diddle..." the cow must jump over the moon. A moving mouth or wagging tail, are beside the point. Using first, the simplest means of animation, I have them create the action in their puppet. Once they have achieved this, the puppet's range of action can be expanded.

I offer also the technique that I employ in my own work: "storytelling with puppets." I give my teachers/students free reign to edit their stories so that they feature the action of the story. I encourage them to use humor, sound, music, participation, ensemble work, and imagination as they tell their stories. I emphasize allowing the puppets to fully come alive and not to burden them with lengthy text. I ask them to make the animation come first and to marry it to the story. I try to teach them what "good" puppetry is like.

To these ends I must lead them through their tasks and steps in a way that builds their knowledge as they proceed. I start with simple skills and build on those skills as we go. I must offer encouragement and positive critique. I must be on the lookout for those who are having trouble and guide everyone along the way toward our end performance. This requires much organization of materials and ideas. I have to make my instructions clear and simple. I use a handout which has illustrations where needed. A picture is worth a thousand words. I include in this study guide all the information they would need to do the project if I weren't present. They won't have to take as many notes.

At the beginning, my twenty teachers divide into groups of four to six per table and choose a folktale. Then they go about creating puppets and a simple script or outline to perform a scene, synopsis, or brief telling of their tale to last five minutes or so. The results are always fun. Their work always impresses me. Sometimes a group's effort will pale to the efforts of another group. I try in these cases to applaud their efforts and stress the positives. The ways in which they miss the mark are usually obvious to all and are most always avoidable if they are paying attention. During their rehearsals, I try to move about and nip these pitfalls in the bud. Their mistakes are often turned into comedic triumphs. I encourage them to have fun and not to let on when something goes amiss.

I find that the energy at these workshops builds toward the finale. I offer other workshops as well as my "Telling Folktales with Puppetry." My other favorite is "Teaching Metamorphosis and Migration of the Monarch Butterfly through Puppetry." I teach the participants how to build foam rubber rod puppets of the monarch caterpillar and butterfly. As we build the puppets, I tell them about the science of the monarch and run a video presentation of a monarch's metamorphosis. The teachers go away with puppets and knowledge with which to use in teaching this curriculum.

In choosing my workshop themes, I try to find an area of curriculum, usually elementary level, but multileveled if possible, which interests myself, and then tie it in with a particular puppetry style, which is doable in the classroom. My association with The Kennedy Center has been very beneficial professionally and has brought out my potential as an arts educator.

## Reference

Gardner, H. (1983/1993). *Frames of mind: The theory of multiple intelligences.* New York: Basic Books.

(**Author's Note:** The Kennedy Center offers training workshops for artists who are interested in their techniques. A sample of workshops and information on training can be found at <u>artsedge@Kennedy-Center.org</u>.)

# CHAPTER 6

## FROM PHONICS PALS TO PECOS BILL:
## TEACHING LITERACY TO SECOND LANGUAGE AND SPECIAL
## EDUCATION STUDENTS THROUGH PUPPETS

### Elizabeth Freeman

Three Billy Goats Gruff puppets. (Grade 3 English Language Learners)

Puppetry has been called the "ultimate disguise" (Latshaw, 1978). For centuries, puppetry has been used to entertain young and old, but is it also a viable pedagogically sound method to teach literacy?

Good teaching techniques for reading and writing are essential to all students, especially for second-language learners and special education students with language-learning disabilities. For these students I have observed that more attention needs to be paid to develop their oral language skills. If a child cannot say IT, he will not be able to write IT or read IT successfully. Generally children who successfully learn to read in the primary grades entered kindergarten with excellent communication skills. Oral language skills are considered a reliable prediction of success in reading comprehension.

Since 1989, I have begun to use puppets in my classroom after attending a week of workshops at Puppets: Education Magic, sponsored by the Boston Area Guild of Puppetry and which was part of the Puppeteers of America's national festival. This led to my research strategies to improve literacy skills and to determine if puppetry could be used to implement my findings.

Intervention activities for students with language-learning disabilities should have the following characteristics:

- The instruction should focus on function rather than grammatical form.

- Students should work collaboratively with one another.

- Activities should incorporate themes, experiences, and/or events that have meaning to students.

- Activities should acknowledge students' backgrounds and experiences, and should promote the development of self-esteem. (Roseberry-McKibbin, 1995)

Some conditions necessary for language acquisition are comfort, risk taking, nurturing environment, communication, meaningfulness, non-correctiveness, and a positive attitude. The puppet stage and a variety of puppets in my classroom invite the students to play informally, at first, individually, and then together, improvising dialogue.

Some mascot puppets, like Dino the Dinosaur and Squeek the Monkey, help introduce the class to routines, offer friendship, and participate as characters in class plays. Max the Bear has his own journal which models writing styles such as narrative, poetry, reflections, and dialogue. Senora Nerviosa provides comic relief for such hesitant students who may inquire if a new lesson is going to be difficult by declaring frantically that, "Oh, my! Yes, this is going to be extremely hard and absolutely impossible to learn." Even the most reluctant will laugh and be more ready to attempt the task.

Jennifer McMaster described using drama to build literacy as she observed a third grade class in Syracuse, New York (McMaster, 1978). She described drama as "an invaluable tool for educators because it is one of the few vehicles of instruction that can support every aspect of literacy development." It is an effective medium for building decoding words, vocabulary, grammar, conversation, and knowledge. Students are provided multiple opportunities for social interaction, feedback, and problem solving. Drama is thinking out loud, developing oral language skills as the child defines, articulates, expresses, and verbalizes thoughts in the structure of an improvised activity. By participating in drama activities, children develop listening skills while waiting for cues, and also evaluative skills while in the audience.

Faceless cloth hand puppets, practice puppets, have been used in my classroom to teach students how to manipulate puppets as the professionals do. At the same time, students are listening and following directions such as, "Puppet One, enter crying, looking for something. Puppet Two, enter, see Puppet One, inquire about the problem and help him find the lost object." They learn about verbs and how to change their voices and words to match the character and situation, a skill that can transfer later to oral reading.

Groups of two or three students work on the same scene for a few minutes before volunteers perform their version at the puppet stage. Rarely is there a group, which does not want to perform. Being behind a puppet stage curtain is great for the shy, more introverted students, who may want to be more extroverted. The short two-minute skits become longer as students are more comfortable with language and performing.

Drama can also teach basic sight-words and decoding of word families (it, at...) through the active engagement of students. Students need to internalize that alphabet letters are symbols representing sounds, as puppets represent people and animals. Bilingual and special education students often need more time to develop decoding and encoding skills. Many years ago I noticed that most of my bilingual and special education students had difficulty distinguishing the short E and short I sounds. Project Read materials suggested making a sock puppet named Ed to teach the short E sound (Greene & Enfield, 1986).

I looked over my stock of puppets and chose five to become The Phonics Pals: Abigail the Cat, Mr. Ed, Mr. It, The Odd Frogs, and The Lucky Ducks. Oslo and Tupper have also been included. The appropriate puppet introduces each new short vowel sound. Labeled pictures of the puppets and their sounds are also displayed near the reading table. I have observed children when writing, saying a word they want to spell and checking it with the /I/ for IT and /e/ for ED. Other puppets have been added to represent the "R-controlled" vowels: Charlie, Irwin, Senora Nerviosa, and Ursula. To keep the individuality of the sounds distinct, the Phonics Pals are a hodgepodge of puppet styles.

To improve fluency, English as a Second Language (ESL) and special education students need frequent review and repetition. "We've read it already!" students often cry when a teacher wants a story reread for better fluency and comprehension. Research has shown that these students need opportunities for repeated readings of the same material (Bidwell, 1990). Students reread when they choose a piece of literature to perform, decide on characters and dialogue, and while they practice. By giving them a real purpose to read, they do so eagerly.

In my class, we rarely use a prepared script, but several times a year, we will use a Reader's Theatre script or poem to practice fluency, looking for interesting vocabulary and phrases, punctuation, and character traits. One group may read the script while the other group listens and manipulates the puppets.

To become a successful reader, knowing how to decode is not enough. Students need training in strategies to promote comprehension. Story retelling appears to be a technique that enables a child to play a large and active role in reconstructing stories. Results of studies suggest that guided story retellings with interactive discussion result in significant improvement in comprehension and recall. Retelling does not mean memorizing, but telling the story in your own words. If a story includes special catch phrases crucial to the story, children should be encouraged to use them.

Stories can be retold with props such as stuffed animals, paper cutouts, and found objects. The use of puppets also encourages children to use stories. Shy children tend to feel more secure retelling stories with puppets. Stories with dialogue and a limited number of characters are best suited for this type of retelling (Gambrell & Almasi, 1996).

Another way drama can be used is for assessment. It provides useful and immediate feedback about the students' understanding of new material. Students can summarize what they have learned by acting. Reviewing stories with the faceless practice puppets are a quick and easy assessment of a group's understanding of the story's main idea and important events. Teachers can assess if there is a discrepancy between what children comprehend and their ability to express that comprehension (McMaster, 1998).

With longer stories, the practice puppets can be used to have small groups predict the ending of a story before it has been completely read. Often, students will learn to reread the original story, skimming for important information and appropriate dialogue. These higher-level thinking skills are all needed for overall comprehension of text. On occasions when I observed a complete lack of understanding of a reading passage, I have used puppets to act out the scene for the children before they reread it together.

Portraying a character requires students to think about the character's walk, talk, and other important details of his personality. Students must read between the lines and beyond the lines. The art of becoming a character seems to free children from their own self-conscious selves as they explore the story beyond the basic plot. Discussions among the players arise naturally during the rehearsals. Incorporating music, mime, movement, and art can enhance the dramatization of historic events, stories, and poems (Robb, 1994).

After reading a number of tall tales, I have had students work in pairs to create large parade puppets representing the main characters such as Pecos Bill and Paul Bunyan. After discussions of the characters' personalities and special occupations and events in their lives, the students were able to write "self-portraits" of their characters in the first person. In a parade around the school, children were able to introduce "themselves" and answer questions from the other students and teachers, staying in character.

The use of classroom themes built around curriculum requirements but centered on students' needs is one mentioned by many authors as an effective method to organize classroom learning. Through themes, students are able to improve their reading, writing, speaking, thinking, and research skills. With themes, a typical class with varied reading abilities can find books to use on a well-chosen topic. Note taking skills, searching for important vocabulary and concepts, can be done in cooperative learning groups. Although a topic might be scientific, such as the water cycle or volcanoes, children often enjoy the opportunity to create a play based on their research. Parents can be asked to send in fabric scraps, yarn, plastic flowers, or anything that can be made into a puppet or prop (Robb, 1994).

It is important to recognize and support the cultural background of the students. Through the thematic units and interaction with other students, the second language learners learn more about the "American Way," vocabulary and attitudes. Using multicultural materials is important, reminding all students that some of the folk clothing and housing might be from the past. Children might think that people in Japan only wear kimonos or the Dutch only wooden shoes. Someone representing the United States today would not be dressed up like George Washington or buffalo skins going to work or to his job, but would be dressed in a modern business suit or blue jeans. Not all of those in Southeast Asia live in rural bamboo huts. Many live in the bustling cities such as Bangkok and Saigon. Shadow puppets were common in Southeast Asia and the Middle East. To celebrate Cambodian/Laotian New Year with another class, my students borrowed traditional puppets and used them in an abbreviated version of "The Ramayana."

Teachers are often reluctant to use drama in their classrooms because of the lack of time in the school day. To most, planning a school play is a big production that lasts for weeks. For use in a language arts program to develop and support literacy skills, the use of mini-performances is much more effective (Morado, Koenig, & Wilson, 1999).

A program in Ann Arbor, Michigan was developed through the school's Title One program for their at-risk kindergarten, first, and second graders. The mini-performance program provides different rather than remedial instruction in which literature, drama, music, and movement are woven together creating stars from students who are struggling academically.

The mini-performances invite the students into literature, to have them interact with the text, and to help them transform what they see and hear into action and words. A small group of children work together for six thirty-minute sessions over three weeks to turn a story into a performance. They hear the story during their first time together and perform it on the sixth. During those sessions, story elements of characters, setting, and plot are discussed and considered for inclusion in the performance. Repetitive phrases from the text may become chants, songs, or poems. An important part of working with the story is its retelling in the child's own words. Scripts must come together quickly.

During the practice and performance, the teacher serves as narrator to convey the story not spoken by the characters. Scripts are typed in large type and given to students to read (or be read to them) at home. Simple props and costumes can be added for performances. Mini-performances are videotaped for students and parents to borrow. Each child receives a copy of the original book used and one is presented to the school library and the classroom library.

I have used a similar format with children at school and in a library setting. With three two-hour sessions, groups of a dozen children have been able to go from start to finish producing a puppet play that they presented for parents and friends on the fourth afternoon. Most students did not memorize the scripts, but were so familiar with it that they were able to be more genuine in their delivery and able to improvise appropriate lines as needed. Performances were not always the same, but often more effective than when children tried to recite memorized lines, which are often more stilted, and without inflection.

For some groups, we made sentence strips with important scene information that could be used as prompts. Again, when the teacher acted as narrator, the play kept moving, especially in transitions from one scene to another. There seems to be more spontaneity in such performances.

With the adoption of the Massachusetts Curriculum Frameworks for Language Arts, Social Studies, Mathematics, and Science, all teachers must plan lessons based on the learning standards. Most other states also are using state curriculum standards based on National Frameworks. To implement the standards, teachers may use puppets to teach language, literature, and composition.

From my research and classroom experience, I would conclude that using puppets in the bilingual and special education classrooms is an appropriate and significant teaching strategy when they are incorporated into classroom lessons to improve literacy skills across the curriculum. A whole language program must include oral language development, decoding/encoding strategies, and strategies for reading comprehension. Students of all ages like "doing" and the drama of puppetry provides students the opportunity to "do" literature and other classroom subjects. Everyone's involvement and contribution is important. Puppetry gives all of the children a chance to be successful and to work collaboratively with others, and it promotes the development of self-esteem.

## References

Bidwell, S.M. (1990). Using drama to increase motivation, comprehension, and fluency. *Journal of Reading, 34,* 38-41.

Davidson, R. (1995). The linguistic environment of early readers. *Journal of Research in Childhood Education, 10,* 5-21.

Gambrell, L. & Almasi, J. (1996). *Lively discussions! Fostering engaged reading.* Newark, Delaware: International Reading Association.

Greene, V. & Enfield, M. (1986). *Phonology guide.* Bloomington, MN: Language Circle Enterprise.

Latshaw, G. (1978). *Puppetry: The ultimate disguise.* New York: Richard Rosen Press.

McMaster, J. (1978). "Doing" literature: Using drama to build literacy. *The Reading Teacher, 51,* 574-584.

Morado, K., Koenig, R., & Wilson, A. (1999). Miniperformances, many stars! Playing with stories. *The Reading Teacher, 53,* 116-123.

Robb, L. (1994). *Whole language, whole learner: Creating a literature-centered classroom.* New York: Quill, William Morrow.

Roseberry-McKibbin, C. (1995). *Multicultural students with special language needs.* Oceanside, CA: Academic Communications Associates.

# CHAPTER 7

## COLONIAL LIFE IN MINIATURE: HISTORY BROUGHT TO LIFE THROUGH PUPPETRY

### Ronni Gerstel

"How can I make this unit on the "Early American Colonies" more interesting for my students? They find it so boring, and frankly, so do I!" This was the dilemma that Marge Norris, a 5th grade teacher at Hammock Pointe Elementary School in Boca Raton, Florida posed to me at our initial meeting. As an artist for the Center for Creative Education (CCE), I was used to just this sort of question. CCE is a non-profit organization that promotes arts integration in the curriculum by placing artists: painters, dancers, musicians, actors and more, in the classroom. It is precisely my job to collaborate with teachers on arts-based lesson plans in my area of expertise - puppets!

After just a couple of hours planning, we had designed 10 one-hour arts-based lessons for her students. On my first visit, the class used their history books to brainstorm the cast of characters one might meet in the colonial days. We came up with an impressive list, including a preacher, plantation owner and his wife, slaves, dog-whipper (who controlled dogs that slept on their master's feet for warmth at church), shop keepers, and many more. Next, the students broke into three groups representing the New England, Mid-Atlantic and Southern colonies. Each group decided on an appropriate setting for their puppet play. The New England Colonies decided a church was the most important setting in the lives of these devout colonists. The Mid-Atlantic Colonies group wanted a street full of shops where their characters could sell or trade goods. And the Southern Colonies students chose a cotton plantation that was home to the wealthy owner, his family and his slaves.

In our next session, students worked in groups to write their scripts. The teacher and I circulated, assisting students with the writing process and keeping them on task. Marge set the criteria for each script: each student had to introduce his or her character, make sure the character's job or role was clear in the context of the story, have all the characters interact, and describe their daily life. Marge also required that each group have a narrator to tell the name of each colony and where it is located, and describe the geographical region. Beyond that, it was up to each group's discretion as to what type of script they wrote.

The New England Colonies students wrote a clever piece about a church meeting, full of humor that contradicted the serious setting. The Mid-Atlantic Colonies students brought a bustling street scene to life, demonstrating a typical day in that region. The Southern Colonies students developed a poignant piece about a runaway slave who was captured and returned to the cotton plantation. Marge reviewed the scripts, made suggestions to improve them, and had the students type them out before my third visit.

In the next lesson, students created rod puppet characters from wooden cooking spoons. The energy in the room was palpable as they researched and created costumes appropriate for each group. (For example, the deeply religious New Englanders wore dark, somber colors, while the Southern plantation owner's wife embellished her wardrobe.)

In lesson four, the groups designed backdrops for their puppet production to establish the setting. They sketched their designs onto large sheets of butcher paper and colored them in with acrylic paints. Now that the scripts, characters and backdrops were ready, it was time to rehearse!

The fifth lesson was all about puppet manipulation. The students practiced bringing their characters to life and telling their stories. Before getting into the scripts, each puppet character made a solo appearance, introducing himself or herself and describing their role in the colony. Then they proceeded to work on lines and manipulation. At this point, some of the performers decided to incorporate props. For example, the Mid-Atlantic group wanted to show how bartering took place in the shops. We brainstormed ways the puppet carpenters, blacksmiths and silversmiths could pass goods between them. The solution: magnets applied to the puppet's hands! Before long, the Mid-Atlantic "folks" were busily trading their wares on the street.

Several rehearsals took place over our next four sessions. As the groups grew more confident, we had each perform for their peers. The audience gave a positive critique: What was good? What could we make better? We practiced vocal projection through fun exercises. Then we sent invitations home to family members, inviting them to attend the culminating performance and celebration.

The program looked like this:

Welcome to our Presentation:
"The Early American Colonies"

1. The New England Colonies
   Introduction of Residents
   Sunday Church Meeting

2.  The Mid-Atlantic Colonies
Introduction of Residents
Everyday Life in the Colonies

3.  The Southern Colonies
Introduction of Residents
Life on the Southern Plantation

As part of our participation in the CCE program, our class learned about the first American colonies. Under the guidance of "Miss Ronni", our resident artist and professional puppeteer, we made puppets, and wrote character description and scripts.
All puppets were hand-made by the boys and girls in Mrs. Norris' class. All scripts and speeches were written BY THE STUDENTS also.
Thank you for attending!

On performance day, the room resounded with the buzz of happy parents, siblings and school staff members. The students were nervous but confident. Finally, after weeks of work, it was "show time." The audience listened, laughed, and learned as their children brought history lessons to life. After the show, Marge and I sat back and enjoyed the scene as happy students excitedly accepted accolades from their "fans."

In fact, once the buzz about the student puppet production got around, other classes wanted a share in the excitement. So, Marge sent around a sign-up schedule, and by the following week, her group had presented the "Early American Colonies" Puppet Show a total of *fourteen times*!

But our collaboration was not over yet… Marge's class and I still had one more session together. We decided to use this time to reflect on our work and assess the project. For part of the session, the students wrote me letters about their experience. Here's what one of them had to say:

Dear Ms. Ronni,

I think that this puppet show was probably the highlight of the year. I liked being in the show, and I think that my group, the New England Colonies, was funny. I liked being the narrator and the town tickler.

The puppet show was a better way of learning as to just reading it out of a book. Everyone learned a lot about the three chapters. I also liked getting to physically learn a chapter instead of just reading it.

I loved making the puppet. I also learned a lot, which was probably what the point was. Anyway, thank you for teaching us how to make the puppets and helping us do the shows.

Sincerely, Brianna

"A better way of learning"..."physically learning a chapter instead of just reading it"... Well said, Brianna. That's what puppetry in the classroom is all about.

# CHAPTER 8

## HOWARD GARDNER'S THEORY OF MULTIPLE INTELLIGENCES AND THE ART OF PUPPETRY WITHIN THE CURRICULUM

### Joy Gwynne Ginther

Elroy and Joy.

Howard Gardner, a professor at Harvard's Graduate School of Education, developed a theory about intelligence that argued that there are distinct sets of processing operations, which define separate intelligences (Berk, 1998, p. 301). Rather than accept the standard, more limited view of intelligence usually addressed by intelligence tests and in the schools, Gardner combined ideas that laid groundwork for inclusion of the arts within the curriculum (Smith, 1996).

Gardner initially listed seven, and more recently, eight, separate intelligences. These include the more traditional intelligences of linguistic and logical-mathematical intelligences. The use of language skills to communicate and express ideas has almost always been part of the concept of intelligence. Logic and mathematical ability has also been commonly addressed when speaking of general intelligence. Gardner's theory adds to these more common aspects of intelligence the following six additional divisions: spatial, bodily kinesthetic, musical, interpersonal, intrapersonal, and naturalist.

In his theory of multiple intelligences, Gardner begins by describing the sorts of processing skills with which a person with linguistic or verbal intelligence operates. Strength in this area may make a person a poet, or a journalist or other type of writer, or a teacher, a lawyer, a politician or a translator. People whose strengths lie in this area may develop expertise in foreign languages. The may be great orators or debaters or perhaps storytellers or puppeteers.

People with spatial intelligence may become artists or architects, interior designers, navigators or engineers. Their special ability to perceive the visual may lead them to think in pictures and to create mental images. They may particularly enjoy looking at maps or charts, videos and movies, drawings and paintings.

People whose strength lies in a bodily kinesthetic intelligence may have the ability to use their whole body or a part, hand, fingers, feet, etc. to solve a problem or to create something. This skill may lead them to handle objects skillfully. These types of learners may enjoy all kinds of hand eye coordination, playing ball or balancing on a beam. These learners may become athletes, dancers, actors, physical education teachers, firefighters or artists.

Musical intelligence refers to the ability to think or hear musical patterns. This includes the ability to produce and appreciate music as well as the ability to recognize and manipulate patterns. These learners may think in sounds, rhythms or patterns. Possible careers for these types of people are musician, disc jockey, singer, and composer.

Two of the most interesting of Gardner's categories are interpersonal intelligence and intrapersonal intelligence. People who have strong interpersonal skills may have a deep understanding of other people while those with strong intrapersonal intelligence have a clear understanding of self. A person who has strong interpersonal skills may make an excellent teacher or counselor or politician or even sales person. A person with strong intrapersonal skills may be a researcher or a theorist or a philosopher.

The newest addition to Gardner's list is the naturalist intelligence. This intelligence refers to those people who have a certain kind of sensitivity towards the natural world, plants, and animals, as well as geological features and clouds, etc. Gardner speculates that people strong in this intelligence may have been gardeners and farmers and hunters, but he also speculates that this intelligence, today, may aid consumers in brand recognition when shopping and some kinds of pattern recognition.

A professional puppeteer since 1981, I have often been called upon to defend the reasoning behind including puppetry within the curriculum. I agree with Gardner's theory of multiple intelligences. It seems quite obvious to me that people think and learn in many different ways. The inclusion of aspects of Gardner's theory within lesson plans and the curriculum in general may help reach those learners who are not benefiting from programs which address only a more narrow view of intelligence as being only logical and verbal.

> The important point is that all seven intelligences are valuable and can be developed within a comprehensive educational program. The traditional emphasis in schools on the linguistic and logical-mathematical intelligences, in Gardner's view, is too narrow and leaves many potentialities undeveloped in students. This broader view of intelligence recognizes contributions of the arts for significant learning in schools. (Hurwitz, 1995, p.17)

Model programs have been developed trying to address all of Gardner's intelligences, "for example, linguistic intelligence might be fostered through storytelling or play writing, spatial intelligence through drawing, sculpting, or taking apart and reassembling objects" or puppets (Berk, 1998, p. 310).

An art educator for many years, I often witnessed children who were known as "trouble makers" or "difficult" succeed and excel within the open classroom of my art room. I believe that the study of the art of puppetry could add much to the general curriculum. All students could share in the benefits of studying puppetry.

Most learning styles and all eight of Gardner's intelligences could be addressed. Linguistic intelligence can be addressed through the creation of a script for a puppet play. Improvisation and experimentation in puppet manipulation can also draw upon skills inherent in language arts. But, not only can students strong in this intelligence benefit from a study of puppetry. For example, the pre-recording of a soundtrack for a show can provide an excellent opportunity for children who are poor readers to be motivated to practice and re-record over and over again. Throughout the process of talking about, writing and reading a script, students are practicing their reading and writing skills as well as developing dialogue and exploring all aspects of language.

Students creating puppets and developing a puppet performance address all sorts of spatial challenges. The actual creation of three-dimensional puppets will draw on the spatial expertise of the students. Staging and the creation of scenery and props also use this intelligence. Those to whom this comes easy will excel and add much to the total performance, but those who are more spatially challenged will have an opportunity to experiment and experience the spatial reality of a puppet show. The whole body is used during the performance of a puppet show. Students with strong bodily kinesthetic intelligence will excel at puppet creation and performance, but those less talented will still experience plenty of opportunity to achieve success. Fingers are used to create puppets and props and scenery, but the whole body is active in puppet manipulation and performance.

Students who have particular musical abilities sometimes emerge as leaders within their groups when given an assignment to develop a song sketch. Not all sketches make the final cut for the main performance, but all students exercise some musical intelligence. During one workshop I led at Explora, I discovered that one of my students was a piano player. She developed improvised material to perform between our sketches in the final presentation.

Most of all, the participation in the creation of a puppet performance, offers students an opportunity to develop and refine their interpersonal skills. Students must communicate with each other at all points in this pursuit. They must work together in their groups developing sketch material and they must work together in the actual performance. The students must choose which among them will perform various bits and also who will be stage manager, dim the lights, etc. The students must address each other's strengths in order to facilitate the creation of a successful show.

The students must also assess their own strengths when they choose how to be a part of the development of a puppet performance. Each student uses his intrapersonal skills when he or she volunteers an idea or a character for our show. A child who is weak in this area may need direction in order to develop sketches, which are actually possible for him or her to perform. I do believe that everyone involved in the creation of a puppet presentation inevitably learns something new about him or herself. Gardner's newest intelligence, naturalist intelligence, could be particularly useful when developing puppet shows with an environmental or ecological message.

Puppetry is accessible to nearly all students in some form. Special students who may be weak in some intelligences may be strong in intelligences related to the art process. Henley (1992) noted that,

> Howard Gardner presented the idea of multiple intelligences in which visual /spatial abilities are seen as discrete abilities, which may function a part from other cognitive domains.... Gardner concludes that the capacity to create art is not wholly dependent upon intact intelligence. (p. 272)

A puppet making workshop culminating in a public performance will address all aspects of Gardner's theory. Regardless of students' individual strengths, all eight intelligences and the inherent learning styles associated with them are used. It is my sincere belief that by giving students an opportunity to make their own puppet show, we give students an opportunity to explore their own individual learning styles and intelligences as well as to hone skills using all eight of Gardner's multiple intelligences.

**References**

Berk, L. (1998). *Development through the lifespan*. Needham Heights, MA: Allyn & Bacon.

Henley, D.R. (1992). *Exceptional children exceptional art*: Teaching art to special needs. Worcester, MA: Davis.

Hurwitz, A. (1995). *Children and their art*. Fort Worth, TX: Harcourt Brace.

Smith, P. (1996). *The history of American art education*. Westport, CT: Greenwood Press.

# CHAPTER 9

## SHADOW PUPPETS THAT HIGHLIGHT INDEPENDENT LEARNING

### Farryl Hadari

In order for there to be a shadow, there must be light. The interaction between light and shadow is a theme of a new educational project at the Seminar Hakibbutzim College in Tel Aviv, Israel. In this project, shadow puppets are being used to shed light on the path to independent learning.

Seminar Hakibbutzim is a liberal arts college. Most of their faculty members are connected to the field of education. There are a number of different learning centers on the campus, each specializing in a specific educational aspect. Examples include: the Center for Academic Literacy, the Center for the Use of Multi-Media in Education, and the Workshop for Designing the Educational Space. Dr. Gissi Sarig created a new learning center, which encompasses all of the existing ones. This enables a student to come to one central place to explore a variety of venues of research for a selected topic. The new center is called PRODESC, which stands for the Professional Development Support Centers, and Dr. Sarig is its academic director.

Dr. Sarig felt that in order for PRODESC to be an effective and viable center, it needed to offer a new approach to teaching and learning. She invited Farryl Hadari, chairperson of the Art Studies Division and puppetry teacher at Seminar Hakibbutzim, to collaborate with her on the creation of a PRODESC educational unit. They decided to design the module for two groups of first year Creative Education students. Creative Education is a branch of the Elementary Education Department, and it stresses the use of the arts as educational enhancements.

Learning is acquiring and owning knowledge. Sarig and Hadari aimed at providing their students with a framework for attaining knowledge and with methods for processing, expressing, and passing this knowledge on to others. The students would determine the depth into which they would delve into this framework. They would receive the tools to become independent learners and the pedagogy of defining an educational goal for the presentation of material that they would want to teach.

Another essential element in the PRODESC educational unit was to stress the importance of creating an avenue to experiential learning. The teacher and the students must be partners in the discovery process. The teacher needs to be open to individual ways of learning and to learning about and from students during the various stages of an educational unit.

Creativity is a facilitator of the impetus toward independent learning. Teachers must come in touch with their own creativity in order to value it and help their students discover their own creativity. Puppetry provides an excellent tap to various fountains of creativity.

Farryl Hadari and Dr. Gissi Sarig had a goal of translating the totality of puppetry production into the creation of experiential learning and teaching. Both disciplines required: researching a topic to be presented, defining specific research questions about the topic, developing an innovative way of looking at the topic, enlisting creativity in the process, presenting the material to an audience and creating a dialogue with them, and providing a fun, enjoyable experience for everyone involved.

The course that evolved from Hadari and Sarig's collaboration had the stated goal of teaching students how to design educational contents in the framework of a shadow puppetry production. It aimed at integrating the following types of knowledge:

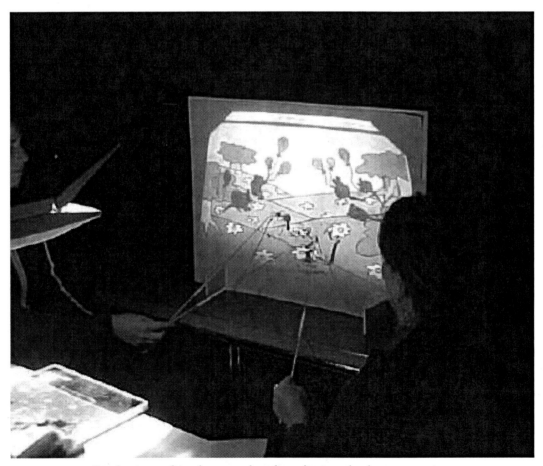

Students performing overhead projector shadow puppetry.

a. Theoretical and practical knowledge about shadow puppetry; Designing a shadow puppetry show for educational requirements.
b. Theoretical knowledge about literacy; a model for story creation as a basis for creativity.
c. Disciplinary knowledge concerning the topics of expulsion, foreignness, and non-belonging; the disciplines to be explored were literature, Bible, history, Israeli culture, and psychology.

The topics covered in the class included:
1. Story construction as the basis for creating educational material.
2. Adapting disciplinary material to the form of a story.
3. Shadow puppetry history, construction, manipulation, and production.
4. Creating an educational unit which uses puppetry as a teaching and learning tool.

The students in the two classes were to create a shadow puppet show based on theoretical and practical knowledge, which they acquired on their own about one of the predefined topics. They were to choose one of the disciplines as a defining framework for their presentations. The shadow puppet show was to be one element of the proposed educational unit.

Since PRODESC is the integration of the various learning centers, the initial stage of the course was to introduce the students to some of the potential uses of a number of the individual centers at the Seminar Hakibbutzim College. The first station was the library. There, the students were given an intensive workshop on how to research the topics of expulsion, foreignness and non-belonging. They were instructed how to use the book and journal catalogues and how to conduct Internet research. They were also taught how to adapt the phrasing of their search in order to apply it to different disciplines. Finally, they were introduced to the Frieda Katz Center for Children's Literature. This center offers referrals to children's literature based on titles, authors, and topics.

In the next lesson, the students were introduced to Salor, a center founded by Dr. Sarig for the advancement of academic literacy. Here, the students were introduced to Dr. Sarig's model for story creation, and they started to develop and practice their skills in this art. They were also taught how to take factual material and adapt it to the narrative form. Finally, they were given guidelines for researching a given topic. Dr. Sarig told them that they should start by asking, "What do I want to know about this topic?"

At this point, the focus was returned to the specific goal of creating an educational unit. The members of the classes divided into groups of three or four. Each group selected one of the following disciplines:

1. Expulsion in history
2. Expulsion in the Bible
3. Expulsion in children's literature
4. Expulsion, foreignness or non-belonging in Israeli society

5. The process of expulsion, feeling foreign or not belonging and methods of dealing with these phenomena from a psychological or educational viewpoint.

They also composed one research question about their chosen topic and discipline. One group chose to work on expulsion in the Bible; they wanted to focus on the story of the expulsion from the Garden of Eden. Their original question was, "Was the expulsion from the Garden of Eden an effective punishment?" After a week of research, they returned to class and notified Farryl Hadari that they wanted to change their research question. They said that Adam, Eve, and the snake had each received individual punishments for violating the ban of eating from the Tree of Knowledge. Adam was to suffer the hard labor of working the earth; Eve would suffer the pain of childbirth, and the snake was forever doomed to crawl on its belly. The expulsion was a second, collective punishment. The new research question was, "Why was the second punishment, the group exile, necessary? What did it achieve that the other individual punishments did not?" The students pondered the thought that this may have been the first group expulsion in history. They decided to further research the theme of expulsion in the disciplines of history, sociology, and psychology.

Another group chose the topic of non-belonging in the discipline of children's literature. Their initial research question was, "How is it possible to become integrated into a group without losing one's special uniqueness?" They began their research by reading a number of children's stories that dealt with an outcast character. The students developed a curiosity as to the defining traits of these characters. They developed a new research question that was, "Do the outcast characters in the different stories have something in common?"

The members of the group decided to create a shadow puppet project where each of the fictional characters was portrayed as a shadow puppet. They planned to have their production begin by having each character introduce itself to the audience and to provide them with the background information from their story about his or her self and about the details of their being left out. The members of the group would then proceed to interview each of the puppets, in front of the audience, based on their further research questions. Thus, the audience members could formulate their own theories about the major research question.

The group members were curious about queries such as:
1. Is the outcast character responsible in any way for his or her being cast out?
2. How does the act of casting out effect the outcast character and the characters that cast out him or her?
3. What elements of human nature support the act of expulsion?

The next step in the process was to guide the students to understand how to translate the knowledge they had gained from their independent learning into the language of puppetry. They had already researched their topics and decided what material they wanted to present. These elements are basic both to puppet production

46

and to the creation of an educational unit. Shadow puppetry was the designated means of creating a dialogue between the audience, or members of the class, and the students who had conceived the various educational units.

At this point, Farryl Hadari taught the students the history, construction, manipulation, and production of shadow puppetry. She began by illustrating simple shadow puppets made from poster board and scenery drawn on overhead transparencies.

She continued the instruction by introducing her classes to the college's Center for the Use of Multi Media in Education. Here, the students learned how to search for music and sound effects in the center's audio library. They also learned how to use the center's recording facilities to create a taped playback for their puppet productions. They were taught a variety of methods for using computers as a tool for puppet and scenery creation. For example, scenery for the shadow puppet stage can be designed by searching the web for a desired background picture. When located, the picture can be printed on a color overhead transparency. The result is an exciting scenic effect on the shadow screen.

Different scenery, together with music and sound effects, can be compiled as a power point presentation. A Bartol projector was used to transport such power point projects onto the shadow screen. The result thrilled the audience.

Clip art pictures can be collaged together to create scenery, and they can also be used as a basis for constructing a shadow puppet. The Multi Media Center has a very large clip art collection, and the students were taught to search for different visual elements by looking for specific items or for general definitions of the required scenic effect. Each creative use of multimedia in the shadow productions was essentially a means of educating the audience in the potential applications of multi-media in shadow puppetry and, hopefully, in other disciplines.

Farryl Hadari had created a shadow puppetry site at the Seminar Hakibbutzim web page. It contains a short history of shadow puppetry, instructions for stage and puppet construction, a brief justification for its use in education, pictures of student shadow puppetry projects, and recommended Internet links. The students were encouraged to visit the site in order to augment their independent search for knowledge.

While the students were creating the shadow puppetry productions, it was possible to come to Farryl Hadari's class and discover that some of the students were at work in her art room while others were in the Multi Media Center or in the library or in the Center for Academic Literacy. They were transforming the knowledge offered by these centers into tools for highlighting the knowledge they wanted to present through the medium of shadow puppetry. They learned to appreciate their own intelligence by discovering and getting in touch with their own creativity. Allowing an outward venue for creative energies is truly a joyous experience; it is an experience, which should ideally accompany the act of learning.

The shadow productions took various forms. Some were adaptations of existing stories, some were original stories based on facts gathered from research, and some took characters from diverse disciplines and presented them in a new light through shadow puppetry. For example, one group researched the character of the undesired supernatural being in different cultures. They found similar traits but different methods of dealing with it. They discovered that this demon would inhabit a human body and cause it to behave in strange, unconventional manners. In Moroccan and European cultures, a process of exorcism was employed to cast the unwanted being out of the human body and to send it away.

In African culture, there was a different approach. The members of the community would perform a ceremony where they would invite the demon inhabiting the human to sit with them. Their goal was to try to understand and get to know it. They aimed at establishing a means for coexistence.

The students who researched this topic created a very touching shadow performance. They made one puppet called, The Shed, or The Demon. It appeared in a scene of a Moroccan exorcism, and then it appeared as a dybbuk in a Jewish European exorcism. It finally appeared in its African form. In this scene, it found a peaceful way of living with the members of the community. The implications of this show were immediate and poignant for the audience. Acceptance and mutual understanding, instead of rivalry and out casting, may truly lead to coexistence. This is a topic that is constantly in the Israeli consciousness.

The members of each group prepared a written summary of their work to accompany the presentation of their shadow puppet shows. This included: the topic, the discipline, the major research questions, a brief summary of the shadow puppet production, and a short bibliography. These summaries were Xeroxed and compiled into a pamphlet for each student. The students essentially created their own activity book illustrating the use of shadow puppetry as an educational tool.

This shadow project shed light on alternative methods of teaching and learning. Although, perhaps its most exciting sensual effect was audio. It was the thrilling sound of deep thinking!

# CHAPTER 10

## VALENTINE AND ZOPHIE:
## PUPPETRY USED FOR CHARACTER EDUCATION

### Sheila K. Harris

Sheila, Valentine and Zophie.

My childhood was enriched by characters such as Howdy Doody, Kukla, Fran and Ollie, Lambchop, Mr. Rabbit, and Mortimer Snerd. I witnessed these characters being treated with respect by their human partners. That respect for the characters made me feel safe enough to enter into their world. They engendered trust to suspend disbelief. There is a "magic" in the animation of puppets.

No matter how plain or simple a puppet may be, it can become a familiar character to children engaging their attention and active participation in learning. Valentine was just a figment of my imagination, as I sat at my kitchen table one morning with some faux fleece, scissors, needle and thread. By late afternoon Valentine had taken on a form and a personality. She began as a simple sock style puppet with a working mouth; she grew arms and legs and demanded clothing. She grew out of my imagination into a being so much more than I ever could have envisioned.

In fact, her image is a bit of an insult to my aesthetic and artistic sensibilities. Ostensibly a little girl, Valentine has fleecy skin, a pompom nose, tacky googly eyes, and garish neon red braided yarn hair. Her mouth is an exaggeration with contrasting calico prints for lips, tongue, and uvula. She looks child-made.

If Valentine's appearance wasn't enough to give me second thoughts, some of the things she has said when activated by my own hand have filled me with trepidation. I often had no conscious thought for some of the things she would say. She is stubborn, impulsive, and she speaks openly about the injustices she perceives in being a puppet. Nevertheless, something about her invites children into her world. Could it be that she shares some of the same desires, fears, etc. that fill their world? Valentine can ask questions children might be hesitant to voice. She can say things to them that would not be believed if spoken by a 50-something year old teacher. Since that spring day nearly 20 years ago when Valentine was conceived, she has been my partner in visiting children in hospitals, telling stories to people with severe disabilities, entertaining preschoolers, and in being the in-house storyteller at the elementary school where I am a special education teacher.

At morning program, Valentine's appearance is a visual cue signaling a time set apart for story. She also acts as the cue for listeners to join in the storytelling by repeating phrases with her. When we begin, she frequently is in an off-mood and the children join me in encouraging her and reassuring her that she can do it. For example, every Christmas season, she brings up her wish to become a real little girl and her anxieties about Santa not fulfilling this wish. The children help me reassure her that we all love her just the way she is and that it's okay if you don't always get what you wish for. She likes to do our King Wenceslas bit wearing a miniature page's hat, feather and all. Valentine helps demonstrate to the children that there is a story to listen for in the familiar song. Her voice helps to differentiate the characters that are speaking/singing. Sometimes, she even reminds me to tone it down, and that we are cooperating.

Valentine is invaluable in character education. In our dialogues, we can discuss misconceptions, conflicts, coping skills, etc. Through the metaphor of our stories we can make abstract concepts such as responsibility and respect concrete. Valentine easily wins hearts (she wears hers on the front of her dress) wherever she goes, but as much as I love her, I have to admit she has limitations.

One day I felt another puppet in my head trying to get out. A school snow day afforded me the time to bring her into being. She is an earth spirit - a creature such as might live under a tree stump - part elf, part gnome, and part fairy with a little gypsy thrown in. She's not at all what one would call pretty, with a sculpted and wrinkled cloth face, penetrating German glass eyes, and seaweed-looking, greenish hair. She has a very old soul in contrast to Valentine's naiveté.

Zophie, a combination of Zoe (life) and Sophia (wisdom), will be going to school with me soon. She can be a voice for those things of this creation that we do not normally see or hear; things we need to honor and respect. An earth spirit can express concern about the importance of trees, rivers and lakes and fresh air, and the delicate balance and interconnectedness of all life.

Valentine has a role in teaching social skills and acceptance of ourselves, and others who may be different from us. She can help us to understand ourselves, and others better. Zophie will take us beyond that to enduring issues, from self-consciousness to mindfulness and consciousness of the greater world.

# CHAPTER 11

## ENHANCING A 5ᵀᴴ GRADE MULTICULTURAL UNIT WITH THE ART OF PUPPETRY

### Marlene Joyce

*What do I love about puppetry? I love when I get to talk and play my puppet and to move it around like it's real. I love making animal stories, making my animal do things nobody would ever think of. I feel good inside and happy and cheerful to be playing along in my imagination and just saying great ideas I have in my head. I never get shy or embarrassed, there's nothing embarrassing to say, nobody's gonna start laughing at you; they'll only laugh with you if you say something or do something funny. And that's what I love about puppetry. (Fifth grade student in Florida)*

The opportunity to bring puppetry to the fifth grade class in a Florida school came to me because their teacher wished to have a "fun" activity to balance the intense intellectual preparation for the state evaluation test. When we met to get acquainted, exchange information, and plan our work together, she explained that her goal was to integrate puppetry into a multicultural study of six countries: Nigeria, Egypt, Ireland, France, Italy and Korea. Students were to select a culture, learn about the lifestyle and select a folktale to enhance this understanding. In addition, recognizing and creatively working with the elements of a folktale was the subject of their literature study. We considered the personality and abilities of her class, predominately the children of Hispanic migrant workers, as we discussed how puppetry could enhance this work. I wanted the puppetry to fit harmoniously into the curriculum the teacher planned.

Creativity, dedication, and flexibility are qualities that make a successful partnership and I was pleased to be working with this kind teacher who possessed them all, including a love for her students. She felt it was important that every student make their own puppet to give them a sense of ownership for their own learning, so we decided to make felt table puppets, which added teaching sewing to our list of new endeavors.

I planned to work with students two hours, twice a week for two months. At other times during the school day the class integrated geography, science, health, culture and social behavior into their study. With the help of the librarian, the teacher had chosen several traditional folktales from each country. After reading them together, each group had decided upon their story and chosen which character they would make. The teacher was now ready for me to work with the students.

When I arrived, they were enthusiastic about getting started. For my first meeting with the class, we jumped right in with a performance. The previous summer, I had traveled to Kenya and while there, I performed *The Land with No Story* (Down, 2000) with marionettes for school children. I presented slides of my trip followed by the marionette show with the help of two teachers.

The teacher had been reading the modern fable, *Mufaro's Beautiful Daughters*, an African Tale by John Steptoe (1987), so the teachers and I chose to illustrate this story with a marionette performance for the children, also. Knowing they were going to do their own show, their interest was focused on details as well as the story. Many questions were asked about setting up the scene, making puppets and moving them. Each child took a turn holding the stringed marionettes and playing with the movement. We laughed as the puppets danced to life with their control.

Now it was the students' turn to become puppeteers. We began by bringing finger puppets to life. The students were seated in a circle with chairs placed close together. I walked around the inside of the circle with a very long rainbow-colored silk I had plant-dyed (4 ½ feet wide by 44 feet long) and covered the knees of each person. Then I offered a variety of finger puppets from a basket and each student took one. We placed the silk over our arms and hands and I showed the students how to position the finger puppet over the silk to "ground" it. To demonstrate, I moved my "pelican" puppet and he spoke to the person next to me, "I'm hungry, do you have a fish for me?" Most children sat blank-faced not knowing how to reply. Going around the circle, our puppets each spoke to their puppet neighbor and each puppet was the center of attention for a moment. Awakening the spark of imagination that is inside each child, this exercise was easy for some students, harder for others.

At our next session, we again put our chairs in a tight circle. However, this time, each child chose a separate colored silk scarf and a finger puppet, which we positioned as before. Keeping the elements of a folk/fairy tale in mind, my "princess" puppet interacted with each one in the circle, searching for three special things to prevent the witch from casting a spell over her, which would cause her to fall into a deep sleep forever! Imaginations had grown and the story easily kept everyone's interest. The teacher remarked that the shy children seemed less reluctant to speak and there was laughter and a lighthearted-ness to our work.

I left my basket of finger puppets with the teacher, and during my absence she used them for a writing exercise. When I arrived, she met me at the door smiling and told me that the children were changing. They had always been polite and done their work, however, now there was a new vitality and interest in their work. She explained that as they wrote stories, they put the finger puppets on the tops of their pencils and had conversations together. The stories were imaginative and students were asking her to spell words that she was unaware they even knew.

By now all of the materials were purchased: a variety of colors of felt, cotton knit fabric for the head, stuffing, thread and needles, so we eagerly began to hand make our puppets. Most boys and many girls needed sewing instruction, however they learned quickly and the puppet heads and bodies began to take shape. Everyone had a bag for their materials, but as each story character began to develop with unique colors and embellishments, some students kept them out on their desks throughout the day.

Fern Sloan (1985) expressed the unsung value of handwork in the classroom as follows:

> In the making of something complicated and beautiful, there comes to the growing child a deep sense of competence and ability. The sense of accomplishment, which students have at the completion of a project, is one of the important gifts handwork gives. Hands, which felt awkward and clumsy, have become skillful. Obstacles and difficulties have been overcome with great patience and perseverance. Wonder and enthusiasm have been born with the hands' marvelous skillful capacity.

Within a few days, the table puppets were ready, so we began to discuss ways to set up the landscape. Each group made a list of the colors of silk needed for their background and of the props they would use. The teacher made tape recordings of each story and when time permitted, each group met to listen to the story and move their puppet. This allowed the students to analyze the characters in their tale, and delve deeply into understanding the story.

Once we had our scenes and props prepared, we practiced moving the puppets and illustrating the story. We worked to "feel" the character of the puppet, moving a giant with a heavy, earthy gait, while a king walked majestically upright, and a sad young girl kept her eyes downcast as she moved slowly. Finally, we added some finishing touches influenced by my work as a Waldorf teacher: we placed a long sky blue silk over our scenes, billowing it as we took it off before the story, and replacing it at the end for our "curtain" going up and coming down.

As the day of each performance arrived, the students were excited and a little "nervous." A "speaker" announced the title of the story. The silk was billowed and placed on the floor in front of the chairs, which served as our stage and backdrop. I read the story, keeping pace with the movements of the puppet characters. Each story had a unique feature, which provided a surprise for the audience and a challenge for the students to perform. When the story was finished and the "curtain came down," the puppeteers made their bows.

As each story was performed, I watched the members of the audience sitting on the edge of their chairs listening and watching intently. I, too, saw a new attitude in these students. They were engaged and actively enjoying these simple stories performed by their own handmade table puppets. It appeared to me that these students had found that place in themselves where the eternal child resides!

I returned once more to the class to thank them and ask them for their comments about this experience with the following questions:

1) What did you like about this Folktale Puppetry project?
   Most of the students in the class liked learning to sew and creating the puppets. They expressed that it was "fun." Several students liked the action of the story and the way it was performed.
2) What did you find difficult about this project?
   Almost everyone said the sewing was difficult. Moving the puppets like people, and knowing what to do with them, as well as where to go themselves was difficult for some.
3) What did you learn from studying folktales, making the puppets, and performing the stories?
   Almost everyone learned how to sew. Many students learned that they needed teamwork to do a puppet presentation. Some students mentioned they learned to treat the puppets as if they were alive, like real people.

Other comments were expressed. One student said, "I loved it so much I might do it at home and teach my family." Another said, "I liked doing these very much." A third comment was, "They were the best."

I thanked them for their cooperation and commended them for their work by giving them each a "Certificate of Success in Puppetry Arts." I also asked the teacher for her comments. She felt the $50.00 she paid for materials was well spent for this two-month project, although initially she did not expect it to take this long. When asked if she would do it again she replied, "Absolutely, my students loved creating their own puppets. This would be a great unit to begin at the beginning of the year and build on throughout the year."

## References and Folktale Resources for Puppetry

Climo, S. (1992). *The Egyptian Cinderella* (adapted). New York: HarperCollins.

Down, S. (2000). The land with no story. In *Multicultural stories: A resource book for teachers and parents* (collected, adapted and written). Boulder, CO: Juniper Tree School of Story and Puppetry Arts.

Gerson, M.-J. (1995). *Why the sky is far away: A Nigerian folktale* (retold). Boston: Little, Brown & Co.

Ginsburg, M. (1991). *The Chinese Mirror*. New York: Harcourt.

de Paola, T. (1975). *Strega Nona* (retold). New York: Simon & Schuster.

Perrault, C. (translated by Arthur, M.) (1990). *Puss in boots*. New York: Farrar, Straus, & Giroux.

Sloan, F. (1985). *Why handwork?* Unpublished manuscript.

Steptoe, J. (1987). *Mufaro's beautiful daughters: An African tale.* New York: Lothrup, Lee, & Shepard.

Unknown. (1986). Cylinder standing dolls. In *Homespun Patterns* (p. 14). Unpublished manuscript, The Waldorf School, Lexington, MA.

# CHAPTER 12

## MUSIC EDUCATION THROUGH PUPPETRY

## Mary S. Mazzacane

It is my pleasure to share my knowledge and experience during the many years of teaching music using puppets. My students and I made and used puppets for the entire music curriculum which included Music Theory and Instruments of the Orchestra (The String Family, the Brass Family, the Woodwind Family, and the Percussion Family) which resulted in a puppet play called "The Magic World of Musical Instruments."

Music Appreciation also culminated with a musical play in 12 scenes depicting the development of music in America relating to the Pilgrims and Indians, George Washington, Betsy Ross, Francis Scott Key, the Gold Rush, the Circus, The Pony Express, Abraham Lincoln and the Civil War, Billy the Kid, Marian Anderson: The Spiritual, The Statue of Liberty: Music of Other Cultures, Dr. Martin Luther King, Jr.: Civil Rights Songs and Uncle Sam. This play was called "Spotlight on America."

We also performed puppet adaptations of orchestral works such as "The Carnival of Animals," "The Sorcerer's Apprentice," and "Peter and the Wolf." In addition, puppet composers were made and studied along with various styles of music such as opera, jazz, rock, etc. Entertainment and musical variety shows along with the other plays were presented for the whole school. The "Magic World of Musical Instruments" play was partially televised on WTNH, New Haven, Connecticut.

There are numerous skills in the music curriculum that a music teacher is required to cover. So to get to specifics, I will zero in on the teaching of music theory which includes the recognition of the treble clef and the bass clef, names of lines and spaces, pitch, keyboard, rhythm and melody. The basic concepts are taught directly through the use of puppets. This helps the student retain the knowledge acquired. If the puppet comes alive, so does the lesson.

The puppets made to teach these skills were musical note puppets: the whole note, the half note, the quarter note, the eighth note, and the sixteenth note. The notes were made out of car sponges or hamburger boxes painted white for the whole note and the half note and black for the other three notes. The stem was made out of cardboard. We also made a large wooden desk-top treble clef which allowed the students to place a note either in a space or grasp a line with the mouth of the puppet. The student and the class would identify the line or space by number or by the proper syllable - do, re, mi, fa, sol, la, ti, do. To indicate a ledger line below the staff, another student would hold a ruler under the staff to indicate middle C on the line and D in the space between C and E of the first line of the staff. The bass clef would be taught in the same way.

Half note puppet on treble staff.

When this skill was mastered, a piano chart was placed behind the piano keys and as a student placed the puppet on a line or space, the class would identify the line or space and the student at the piano would play the note identified as the class would sing the note on "Ah" or the syllable of the note (do, re, mi, etc.).

An enjoyable activity is to sing the Do, Re, Mi song from "The Sound of Music." You can use a note puppet for indicating the different pitches in the song on the staff and another puppet to characterize "Maria" (or the teacher) who stands on the side of the staff to help sing.

An even bigger staff can be made to accommodate eight students. It can be made simply by stretching five pieces of rope across a section of the classroom or from two stands or ladders. Hang a black cloth behind the ropes and cut holes big enough at each line and space for the note puppets to come through at the proper time. This activity allows for students to manipulate the puppets and the whole class to participate as well. Therefore, this activity reinforces the concept of recognizing the pitch interval as well as the vocal and rhythm skills.

Teaching music with puppets is a way of stimulating the student's creative imagination that results in minimizing the resistance to learning. Puppetry in music instills confidence in a student and enables him to establish a better rapport with his teacher and peers. Puppetry in music helps to develop better listening habits, encourages cooperation, motivates interest and participation, provides a greater sense of security, and generates enthusiasm in the learning of musical skills. Puppetry can reinforce the basic musical skills because it elevates the learning process to the point where the student is free to think creatively as an individual without inhibitions.

Mary Mazzacane and her music education puppets.

# CHAPTER 13

## PUPPETS IN EDUCATION: PROCESS OR PRODUCT?

### Judith O'Hare

Straw rod puppets.

Puppets have a special appeal and attraction for children, and they have power and magic to enhance and stimulate learning. When puppets are put into the hands of children in the classroom, it is very important that the teacher, director, or puppeteer carefully determine the goals for the puppet project and the expectations for the children. Planning, performing, and producing puppet theater is one goal, and the prime goal for the professional puppeteer, but it is one of many possible goals when working with children in an educational setting.

It is important to distinguish between puppet theatre and puppets as a form of creative dramatics, not for the perfection of the performance, but for the growth and development of the child/puppeteer. When the goal is either creating theatre, recreating original stories or stories from literature, or making a statement on the human condition, the puppeteer works for perfection in: manipulation, staging, technical theatre, and overall aesthetic and artistic presentation of the theatrical piece. When the goal is education, the puppets become a vehicle for expression of the child's understanding of life, literature, social studies, etc. Puppets become foremost a vehicle for communication and personal interaction through child drama, and the theatrical performance becomes secondary.

In planning a puppet project with children there must be a clearly defined goal. The goal could be to present a wonderful piece of theatre or the goal could be to use puppets to improvise a story from literature or a scene from history, or develop voluntary language, or work cooperatively to create a story or act out a scene, or practice writing skills, or construct an original puppet from a variety of materials, or illustrate what has been learned by restating it through the drama of puppets, etc.

Puppetry in education is very different from puppetry in theatre. Puppets offer educators a unique vehicle for expression. According to George Latshaw, former editor of the Puppeteers of America's *Puppetry Journal*, and author of *Puppetry: The ultimate disguise* (1978), puppetry offers children the "ultimate disguise," the opportunity to communicate through an inanimate object; to use puppets and props to tell a story or recreate a scene from life, literature, history, or imagination. The puppet becomes an extension of the child, yet separate from the child. The puppet speaks loudly, forcefully, aggressively, angrily, kindly etc. It offers the child anonymity and provides an imaginative environment for shaping and reshaping experiences and accumulated information into a dramatic presentation.

When I work with children in a classroom setting, I discuss with the teacher what he/she wants to accomplish. Is the goal to recreate a story from literature? To discuss the story, understand the plot, characters, theme, and setting and make the story come to life? Or is the goal to create an original story from life experiences or from the imagination? Is the goal to stimulate language, explore ways to get children to be expressive verbally, to use language appropriate to the character or situation? Or is the goal to explore a topic such as social studies, cultures, mythology, composers, science, ecology, social issues such as drugs, abuse, etc.? Or to explore feelings and social interactions and express what has been discovered through puppet drama? Is the goal to give children an opportunity to speak through an alter ego, the puppet? All of the above and more provide the material for classroom puppetry. The puppet characters and puppet dramas become the art form through which the children express their understanding of what they have read, talked about, experienced or imagined.

There are many skills that children need in order to use puppets as a means of expression. When children are introduced to puppets in the classroom, they see them out of the theatrical world, without lights, sound, and theatrical settings. I start with a bare slate: the children assisted by the teacher and me create the puppets, story, characters, setting, music, and even the theater. They go through the same process that a professional puppeteer does, only they have to learn all the steps. The process requires them to use a variety of skills they have already acquired in school, apply these skills, add to the skills, and blend all the skills into a unified whole, the final production.

The production, culmination of their combined efforts, is important because it reflects how much they have learned and grown. It may not be a polished piece of theater. I judge a final production on how well the children learned the process, how well they were able to work together, to come to consensus, to construct puppets that reflected the characters, to solve problems which arise in trying to make a story come to life with puppets. I also look for personal effort and involvement. Every child must have input and every child must have an opportunity to make the puppet talk and move as agreed upon in the production plan, the outline or map.

A puppet play requires understanding of the topic to be portrayed, sequencing of events, dialogue, props, movement, articulation, volume, expression, sharing, thinking quickly, and using bodies and voice simultaneously. It also requires listening, responding, reacting, sharing and supporting one another. It requires constructing puppets and learning new ways to use familiar materials to make an inanimate object, which can move and talk. It requires fully understanding the topic which is being presented and internalizing the events and characters so that they can be recreated with conviction with puppets.

Learning how "to make puppets come alive" is part of the process and it is a learned skill. Children will not manipulate the puppets very convincingly when they first begin. It takes years of training and skill in puppet construction and manipulation to become a puppeteer. Each time the children are presented with an opportunity to work with puppets, they should be given more opportunity to develop skills in manipulation. As I watch the children perform with puppets, I see many ways they could make the puppets move more realistically. This and other performing skills will come with teacher coaching, experience, discussion and evaluation.

Children need time to talk about what was good and what could be improved. Always include evaluation and keep it positive. The teacher/puppeteer/coach is the facilitator who helps the children to repeat what was good and to explore and experiment with new ways to solve script and manipulation problems. The more experience the teacher can get in puppet manipulation, character development and voices, the more he/she will be able to guide the children in making the puppets come alive. The more skills the teacher develops, the more he/she will understand the unique "LANGUAGE OF PUPPETRY."

When working with preschool and early primary children it is essential to keep the age and developmental level always in mind. Young children use puppets as an extension of themselves and their play with puppets should always be in the realm of creative dramatics. The puppet play can be as simple as making puppets move in a variety of ways such as dancing, walking, jumping etc., and adding the movements to a song or action poem. This can lead to telling simple repetitive stories such as "The Gingerbread Boy" where each child can respond to the gingerbread boy in his/her own words.

Embellishing a story with lots of character "extras" can give all of the children a chance to make the puppet talk and be part of the dramatic play. Young children should never be asked to develop story lines and dialogue which are above their developmental level. They should NEVER be asked to memorize lines. When they play with puppets, the play should be improvised child drama, from their hearts and heads. Doing formal plays with little children is often cute, but seldom good educationally or psychologically.

Carol Sterling, former educational consultant for the Puppeteers of America and director of Arts Partners for the City of New York, was part of Puppets: Education Magic at the Puppeteers of America's Festival in 1989. She suggests the following:

Puppetry provides children with opportunities to achieve the following educational goals:
- to develop creative expression
- to stimulate and enhance imagination
- to develop spontaneous oral expression
- to improve speech, enunciation, and voice projection
- to practice writing skills, become more fluent in oral reading
- to gain appreciation of literature
- to develop coordination and a sense of timing
- to enhance a child's feelings of self-worth
- to gain self-confidence and personal satisfaction
- to release fears, aggressions and frustrations in acceptable ways
- to develop social interaction skills
- to create and use manipulatives in an integrated, purposeful way I would like to add to that list the following:
- to gain skills in problem solving
- to improve fine motor skills
- to sharpen listening skills
- to come to consensus, give and take of ideas
- to observe the world through the senses, to remember what was observed, to process what was observed and remembered and to recreate it with puppets
- to evaluate
- to polish, improve on what was done

Working with puppets requires students to apply all of the above educational goals. When children work step by step to create the puppets, develop the story line and script, decide how and when characters will speak and move, solve problems, and present the play, they are involved in an educational process. The success of the process will affect the quality of the product.

The process is more important than the product. Putting all the steps together is essential. The artistic quality of the product will reflect the age, developmental level, and accumulated experiences of the children presenting the play. In working with puppets and drama with children the most important element is the growth of the child. When puppetry, drama, and the arts are viewed as a "one night stand," or "the play is the thing," we run the risk of having people say, "Plays are nice, but we don't have time for them. We have so much to cover in the curriculum; we don't have time for all that rehearsing and memorizing of lines."

However, children who are fully engaged in planning and implementing a puppet play are immersed in the curriculum. They don't need to memorize lines because they have created the play, they KNOW what comes next, they KNOW what the person would say and do in that situation, and they KNOW how the character would feel. When the puppet play is created by the children working together, it reflects their understanding of the topic, the characters, the setting, the plot, the thematic concepts, etc., and there is a high probability for success. Good child drama is one of the most powerful ways to build self-esteem. Children with good self-esteem have a greater possibility for overall success than those who do not.

While I do not espouse putting all the emphasis on the final product at the expense of the growth and learning which takes place during the process, I do urge and encourage children to become involved in puppet theatre. It is important that they see good puppetry by talented performers and that they strive to achieve the highest level of puppet construction and puppet drama, as they are capable of.

Puppets are a creative expressive accessible art form and the learning that takes place when children are involved in puppet drama can reinforce and add to the educational process in the classroom. We cannot teach children all the facts they need to know to go through life. At best we can teach children how to learn, how to be open to learning from their environment, from people around them, and from living life to the fullest, and how to express what they have learned in words and actions. If we only focus on the product, they may not learn and internalize the steps it took to get there. When we give children the tools to create a puppet or a puppet play, they can continue to explore the creative and artistic possibilities of puppetry as they grow. Maybe one or two will even choose to become puppeteers, but more important, we hope all will become literate inquiring educated adults.

Bottle-head rod puppets.

## Reference

Latshaw, G. (1978). *Puppetry: The ultimate disguise.* New York: Rosen.

# CHAPTER 14

## RATIONALE FOR INCLUSION OF PUPPETRY IN THE MIDDLE SCHOOL PERFORMING ARTS CURRICULUM

### Marianne Parr

Near the end of the school year 1996-1997, I noted the need for new curriculum for my middle school, grade 6 students. Previously, the focus had been on music theatre. With new Washington State education guidelines focusing on communication, I felt that my curriculum should shift to a communicational art form. Having received information on puppetry courses offered through Central Washington University, I decided to enroll in an introductory course during the summer of 1997. After completing the challenging course, I was "hooked." I had experienced first-hand just the curriculum I needed.

I needed and wanted a project-based curriculum that included the following:
- creative problem solving
- communication (oral interpretation skills)
- increased self-esteem
- pride
- fun

Puppetry in the classroom seemed like the perfect solution to my needs and the needs of my largely, low-income students.

### The Project Overview

Approximately 180 grade 6 students study puppetry in our middle school elective nine-week rotation. These students belong to all ability groups. During their daily 43-minute classes, they observe the teacher demonstrating the sequential steps needed to complete a rod puppet and a simple marionette. They spend six weeks building a sophisticated rod puppet from a teacher-made puppet kit. They spend one week building a simple bottle-head marionette. The remaining two weeks are spent in rehearsal for two, teacher-written puppet shows. This curriculum originated during the school year 1997-1998 and is on-going. To date over 1200 rod puppets and 1200 simple marionettes have been constructed in my classes. The student success rate of puppet completion is phenomenal. Only a dozen students total experienced little or no success with the project.

Prior to building the puppets, the students read (aloud) a puppet script whose theme focuses on typical middle school problems such as peer pressure. The students audition for at least three characters with whom they identify. After auditions, three teachers carefully cast the play and students begin creating their puppet characters.

## Project Results

During the puppet-making process, I have observed the following:

Pride in a tangible project. As students build their puppet, they invite their parents, friends, and teachers to view the daily process in making the puppet. These people stop by before, after, and during school to view not only the puppet itself, but to watch the students in the process of puppet building. These supportive observers can watch the proud faces of the puppeteers, hear their words of praise for each other's puppets, and daily observe the students' intent focus on the task of puppet building. The studio classroom is alive with activity yet orderly and surprisingly quiet. Discipline issues are nearly nonexistent. Outside observers marvel at the success of students of varying abilities. Indeed, puppetry warms the hearts of all my students. It captivates and motivates. It offers heightened levels of success for special needs students as well as gifted students. The quality of puppets produced by a 6th grade student is phenomenal. Setting and achieving high standards results in pride in a job well done. This pride yields the student success and nothing succeeds like success. Indeed, puppets have been very successful in my classroom.

Team-building. Each of the students performs as a member of a cast of 22-28 puppeteers. They work collaboratively creating a cast that works together to tell a story and present a sophisticated message. During the shared workshop time in class, students can be observed helping one another in puppet assembly and in making creative decisions on costume and hair design. They often offer praise and encouragement to fellow classmates. Often a more accelerated student assists a struggling student with no intervention from the teacher. The positive sense of togetherness created by the teamwork of cast members yields a sense of oneness. This unity allows students to produce an excellent show because the students trust one another to trouble-shoot any production problem that arises and solve it effectively. I marvel at the scene saves I have observed. The cast's (team) pride in presenting a serious message together yields a sense of togetherness (belonging) and the wonderful feeling of pride.

Increased self-esteem. My students have seldom, if ever, had the opportunity to perform and be recognized for an excellent performance. The opportunity to audition for at least three characters, be cast in a role, build a puppet character, and perform in two shows seems like a dream come true to my students. My students have the opportunity to build a beautiful puppet and become its voice. The simple, easy to memorize script dialogue creates a sense of security in that students of all abilities can easily memorize their lines and cues. With ease of dialogue mastery, student puppeteers are more willing to take risks in creating unique voices for their puppets. The end result is an excellent show enjoyed by both performers and audience. Students who earn the respect and admiration of an audience become more confident. With this confidence comes increased self-esteem. When my students do a curtain call, one need only look at their faces and the way they smile, maintain eye contact, and stand proud, to know that puppetry has enhanced their learning experience. Puppetry in the classroom is truly a worthwhile experience.

<u>Personal enjoyment</u>. It is no wonder that students have fun in my classes. They feel good about themselves and want the class to never end. After leaving the middle school, many return to tell me that they still have their puppet. I smile at their desire to stay connected with the middle school, puppetry, and me.

## Project Summary

Washington State currently requires testing for student mastery in the area of communication. Puppetry in the classroom offers students the opportunity to become better communicators. Students feel pride in the accomplishment of building a quality puppet. They thrive in a group and they have fun doing it. The life skills they acquire through puppetry are invaluable. I have fun watching my students grow and bond with their puppets. I smile as their parents sit aghast in the audience. Truly, puppetry is a wonderful medium for student success and should be a part of every middle school elective curriculum.

Puppets warm the heart and stimulate the creative genius we all have inside. Puppets are an effective learning project that taps into the affective and the cognitive domain. I feel strongly that puppets need to be a part of everyday learning so that we become more than just an intellect. Puppets belong in today's classroom to enhance student learning. Whether one reads the word puppets from left to right or from top to bottom, I know that...

**P**uppets

**U**nilaterally

**P**rovide

**P**erformers

**E**steem

**T**hrough

**S**uccess

Felt puppets.

# CHAPTER 15

## PUPPET POWER:
## A DISCUSSION OF HOW PUPPETRY SUPPORTS AND ENHANCES READING INSTRUCTION

### Sharon Peck

Sharon Peck and mouth puppet.

**Abstract**

The purpose of this essay is to inspire teachers to incorporate puppets into their classroom literacy instruction. The content discusses the powerful medium of puppets and how it can enhance curriculum. Vignettes of puppetry use in classrooms are highlighted to show both how puppetry fits in the curriculum and the literacy research that supports it. The essay concludes with considerations for teachers and possible puppet instructional ideas are highlighted.

## Puppetry in Education: Why Bother?

Puppetry is a powerful medium with the ability to communicate with all ages, cultures and levels of language. It can be done easily with little expense or great, it can be elaborate and rehearsed or simple and improvised. It is also a lot of fun. But to the elementary teachers that I speak with, it is above all, a challenge. Some teachers have suggested that with the many constraints on curriculum and time, using puppets, although they love the idea, becomes an after thought. The purpose of this essay is to substantiate the reasons why puppetry is such a powerful medium in the classroom, and more specifically, in the teaching of language and literacy. The essay begins with rationale for using puppets in the classroom. It then provides vignettes of the possibilities, and ends with suggestions for teachers and considerations for specific ages/grade levels. This essay takes on the stance that there are many important reasons why teachers should use puppets in education.

## Why puppets?

While I tackle this question, the more apt question is why puppets aren't used more in classrooms. In 1947, the New York City School District put out a publication to encourage classroom teachers to incorporate puppets into their instruction. The publication suggested: An educational program, which includes the type of experiences offered by puppetry, will help the pupil to:

- Discover and develop his special aptitudes and talents.
- Express and use an effective vocabulary, recognize the need for learning and practicing improved speech patterns, and for speaking with poise.
- Extend manipulative skills.
- Gain improved knowledge of manual, industrial, and fine arts.
- Gain increased skill in work-study techniques.
- Experience the feeling of satisfaction and success that accompanies achievement.
- Develop individual security by releasing inner tensions through dramatization of experiences related to personal, family or school problems.
- Share worthwhile information and special skills.
- Develop self-control and consideration for others in the pursuit of a common purpose.
- Participate in vitalized experiences in the various major curriculum areas.
- Understand and practice meaningful and orderly audience listening and participation. (Wade, 1947, p. XI)

Now, nearly sixty years later, the same warrant applies, yet puppets do not have a strong presence in classrooms. Each of the above objectives remains as needs and aspects of today's school curriculum. Using puppetry in the classroom can effectively meet these goals, while building students' motivation in learning.

I would extend the above objectives to past and present curriculum needs in literacy education. Puppets provide a powerful medium that transcends learning styles and student backgrounds to engage and motivate students in active learning. And, using puppetry in teaching literacy, reading, writing, listening, speaking, and thinking, will also help the pupil to:

- Improve their reading fluency through rereading of puppet scripts.
- Improve their spoken and receptive vocabulary.
- Improve student's reading comprehension.
- Improve student's listening comprehension.
- Increase number of sight words, or words students can recognize instantly.
- Develop strategies for decoding new words based on context, meaning and phonic and word awareness.
- Increase student engagement with text.
- Build motivation for reading and writing fictional texts.
- Provide meaningful and purposeful opportunities for writing.
- Provide opportunities for students to explore point of view and characterization.
- Develop understanding of imagery and detail to improve writing and extend reading experiences.
- And, promotes language learning for English Language learners.

Wow…let's review. Puppets are easy to use, inexpensive to make, and using them with literacy instruction can meet the above curricular goals. Puppets are effective for reaching audiences of all ages. Using puppets has many purposes, which directly link to curricular and instructional goals. Puppets are already used in a wide variety of settings beyond entertainment. Puppetry use can develop key literacy skills, enhance literature engagement, and make learning experiences more meaningful. What is the catch you say? There is no catch. In the next section, vignettes of puppetry use from real classrooms are presented, followed by a discussion of how the above goals are met. All of this is supported by research. The essay then concludes with suggestions for teachers and students.

**Vignettes from Real Classrooms**

In a kindergarten classroom, a teacher led circle time with the help of Wanda, a little girl puppet who continually needed help in matching her letter sounds. Students in turn made suggestions of words beginning with a certain letter, and then helped Wanda decide if the letter and beginning sound matched. Later in the morning, students had the opportunity to work with other puppets, friends of Wanda's, to work in pairs on matching letters and beginning sounds of words.

In a first grade classroom in a large urban city, students were engaged in reenacting the story of the "Three Billy Goats Gruff" using puppets and masks they have created using paper plates. Students worked together to read and reread the story. With teacher guidance, characters were assigned and students developed puppets based on their character. Then, the teacher led them in recreating and retelling the story with their puppets. Students chose actions for the characters, and set up the play area so that the troll could be lying on the floor hiding under the bridge of chairs, which popsicle stick goat puppets trip trapped across. Students decided that a narrator would help tell the story, and that the dialogue would be performed by each character. The teacher helped students think about what the voices of each character might be like, and all participants tried on various voices, from meek high-pitched littlest goat gruff, to the rough, deep growl of the troll. Students also worked together to make pieces of stand up cardboard scenery, one depicting a barren brown field and the other lush green pastures and hills. Some students chose to develop posters and signs to publicize the show at the writing center. Other students wrote about the story and their puppets in their journals. Students performed the show for their classmates and invited other classes in to see the performance. Shy smiles beamed from the actors as they bowed at the end of the performance.

In a second grade classroom in a suburban school, students enthusiastically invited parents and other classes in to see their puppet rendition of an Irish Folk Tale, the story of Finn McCool. Students began with the story in script form, then read and reread it until all understood and related to the story. They chose large puppets made from cardboard and placed on dowels, and created a set by stringing a blanket on wire suspended across the classroom. This allowed students to hold the puppet up over their heads while holding the script in their other hand. Students again studied their characters to create their puppets, developed appropriate voices, and worked on timing and inflection as they worked together to present the script. They also problem solved how to create sets and scenery with the raised set up. Students also worked during writing time to respond to their characters and connect with the story. Students also compared this story to other versions of the folktale, and studied the characters of giants in folk and fairytales. The show came off with out a hitch, and even the quietest of student voices was audible as students participated in their play.

In a fourth grade classroom, students chose to make more developed puppets using Styrofoam balls and dowels with large squares of fabric. To these puppets they added shortened dowels to create a simple rod puppet with arms. Fourth graders chose to depict various historical events with their puppets. One group of five students depicted an immigrant family making the difficult decision to leave their home country for the opportunities in America. Another group chose to depict the trial of Benedict Arnold as he was tried for treason in the revolutionary war, and another chose to depict travelers on the Louis and Clark expedition. These simple skits were performed with the puppeteers in view, against student created backdrops. Due to the detailed context of their subjects, students told their stories through main characters to reveal and review the most significant aspects of the historical experiences. Each student delved into research on their character and topic, and made several high level decisions as they planned the best way to tell their story through puppets.

In a sixth grade classroom in a rural school, students chose to depict Greek myths through the use of shadow puppets. Each team of students read through several myths to decide on one to depict. They worked to understand the possibilities of shadow puppetry, which can be done (amazingly) through use of a classroom staple, an overhead projector and a sheet or shower curtain. Students studied scale and imagery as they brought the snakes on Medusa's head to life and depicted the labors of Hercules. Here, students were concealed by their staging and worked carefully through their scripts to maneuver their puppets without blocking the light source, while projecting clearly to their audience. This was particularly enjoyable for the students who enjoy participating but don't enjoy the spotlight.

These vignettes display an array of possibilities for puppetry use in the classroom. In each case, students chose or were guided to appropriate texts to work with to create a story based on facts. Before one can bring a puppet to life, or decide how a character might act in a certain situation, they have to adequately comprehend the story. They have to be able to not only know how the character acted in the story, but also why, and how that might relate to another action. One cannot do this without sustained engagement with texts, a goal of literacy education.

Students worked with texts, developed texts, read, reread and memorized texts. Their initial work in text reading and thinking helped develop strategies for decoding new words based on context, meaning and phonic and word awareness (Goodman, 1965, 1996). They worked with language and fluency, paying particular attention to voice, intonation, expression, projection and timing, key aspects of fluency (Opitz & Rasinski, 1998).

For students who are learning English, these valuable language interactions provided purposes and opportunities for English language learning (McCauly & McCauly, 1992). They became fluent readers of appropriate texts, and gained confidence through re-reading, another critical aspect of literacy programs (Reutzal, Hollingsworth & Eldrige, 1994). Through re-reading and performing the scripts, students developed their reading comprehension and listening comprehension (Elley, 1989).

Further, through developing their puppets, and again applying their deep understanding of their characters, they added another dimension to their thinking and learning (Martinez, Keehn, Roser, Harmon & O'Neal, 2002). They didn't have to be center stage, but had a character through which to present their understandings. They had an opportunity to develop and practice their literacy and learning skills through a project that they chose to participate in. And, because each participant developed their own puppet and character, their ownership of the project and their learning added to the experience (Tovani, 1999). Finally, and most importantly, students deepened their engagement with texts and strengthened their skills because they were motivated by the medium of puppetry.

## Considerations

While use of puppetry adds so much to student learning, and is supported by research, teachers may still be searching for ways to make it happen in their classroom. In the next section, I suggest possibilities and considerations for teachers and students.

**Pre-Kindergarten and Kindergarten Considerations.** In the early years, it is important to consider developmentally appropriate practices when using puppetry in the classroom. Pre-kindergarten and kindergarten students see puppets as real characters, even though they can see you manipulating them. This means that puppets must be used in a consistent framework, such as having puppets with distinct characters, which do not change, and only carry out certain roles. It is important that each character has boundaries and acts in predictable ways. For instance a puppet of a little old lady should not one day turn into a monster. Due to the developmental needs of preschoolers and young learners, puppets should be introduced in frameworks that recognize and respect shorter attention spans. Suggestions include acting out short stories, having puppets chant and sing songs, interacting one on one with students, promoting touching so that students become comfortable with the puppet, choosing stories with repetition which students can act out or chime in on with puppets, and developing language thorough conversation with puppets. Of course, an important role of puppets at this level is "just" play. Here it is worth introducing how puppets should be treated so the puppets' feelings, and those of other students, aren't hurt.

**Elementary Grade Level Considerations.** As students progress developmentally and move through concrete to symbolic stages of thought, more possibilities open up for puppetry in the classroom. Students can create simple or skillfully developed puppets, all the while increasing their own manipulation and artistic development. Varieties of puppet types should be explored from found objects, to hand puppets, rod puppets, shadow puppets and simple marionettes. While one aspect of puppet use at this level can be creating puppets, other considerations should focus on the notion that elementary students still see the puppet as real. They will tell you that you are making the puppet move, and then converse in earnest with the puppet. Again, it is important to be true and consistent with puppet characters, and to model this as children learn to develop characters. We wouldn't expect the Gingerbread Man to give up and say, "I'm tired, go ahead and eat me," so we need to convey that to students as they bring puppets to life.

Due to increased developmental and cognitive levels, students are ready for more types of puppet interaction; they can take on the perspective of a character. And they are ready for more traditional notions of performance. They are also at a stage where they can present performances in small groups. Here there are many details to consider, and elementary students enjoy the details of sets, staging, puppet blocking and developing script, voice, and character.

**Intermediate Grade Level Considerations.** As students progress in their academic and developmental achievement there are even more puppet possibilities. A wider variety of puppet choices for making and manipulating are available including hand puppets, rod puppets, marionettes, and shadow puppets. Shadow puppets tend to be popular at this grade level as they meet the degree of detail that this level enjoys, and they keep students out of the spotlight. Older students can take on more ownership roles in reviewing texts and adapting scripts or developing scripts based on research and non-fiction sources. They tend to get quite caught up in the details of characters, developing lengthy scripts and the development of sets and staging. They are also developed enough to create more challenging puppets in terms of manipulation, including traditional marionettes, rod puppets and Bunraku puppets. Of course, with this age level more time will be necessary in establishing group roles and experimenting with play and improvisation so that students will be comfortable working together in small groups.

**Considerations for Teachers.** Many teachers are concerned about making puppets come to life, about the quality of their voice and mannerisms. Just like teaching, puppetry is a skill that you improve upon with practice and time. If you never step up and try it, you won't improve. However, with a little risk taking and a smile you will soon feel comfortable asking the sock on your hand for advice on revising a story, or spelling a word. Here are some ideas for starting out.

There are a few basics that make puppets come to life and they can be remembered as "The Three E's," *Energy, Exaggeration*, and *Establish a Mood. Energy* refers to how one might bring a puppet to life. One might consider how the puppet and corresponding character would breathe, walk, run, etc. You might ask if the old man puppet would move quickly, or with the constraints of age is he moving slowly with more deliberation. *Exaggeration* refers to the notion of expressing emotion.

Since many of the puppets that students will create will not have moving eyes or faces that can change greatly to show emotion, the puppeteer must work to find other ways to do so. One way, is to make each of the movements, although in character, exaggerated. So a puppet wouldn't nod his head casually; he might nod vigorously, or with a very wide range of motion.

And the final E suggests, *Establish a Mood.* This speaks to the integrity of the puppet. To flesh out a puppet's character, what mood will you create? Will my old man be a frenzied worried individual who tries to move faster than his body will allow, or will the Little Red Riding Hood puppet skip through the forest happily? This consideration of mood will help puppeteers develop movement that fits that character.

The final consideration that teachers must consider is voice. Some teachers when using puppets with children choose to not speak for the puppet, but have the puppet whisper in their ear. That is a fine choice. When considering voice though the same concerns apply, it must be consistent with the character. Little Red Riding Hood will not have a deep gruff voice, and the troll will not speak in falsetto. Many puppeteers just keep trying on different voices until one fits. For students, it can be helpful to brainstorm possible voices. Then they can repeat a phrase or poem with each voice until they find a perfect fit.

**More Possibilities.** The ways in which puppets fit into the classroom are too numerous to mention, and ultimately you'll know what is best for your classroom, curriculum and students. Here are some other possibilities for incorporating puppets into literacy instruction from real classrooms:

Reader Response: Puppets can enhance students' reader response as they write in response to texts. Students could respond to puppet shows and texts. Students could respond to inform a puppet character about how they connected with the text. Students extend their understanding of the text through acting out a favorite part with puppets, or developing a puppet based on a character.

Read to a Puppet: Recently, educators have been reminded of the importance of rereading of known texts to build reading skills, comprehension and fluency. What could be more motivating than allowing students to choose a classroom puppet to read aloud to or with? Students could even take on the character of the puppet as they reread a text to a friend.

Write a Script: Students enjoy taking their own stories and writing them as scripts for performance. Also, with increased awareness of the value of learning from authors' writing styles (Harwayne, 1992), it can be very motivating to take a known or read story and turn it into a script. It could be an actual adaptation of the text, or could be extended to allow students to rewrite characters, events or endings.

Classroom Climate: Puppets can be a motivating way to help develop communities of learners. Puppets can serve as peers to turn to for ideas on how to handle difficult situations. Puppets can serve as unbiased judges in cases of student squabbles. Puppets can also be good encouragers. In one first grade classroom where I observed, there were several puppets that held different roles in the classroom. One puppet was an encourager and students who were challenged or were struggling with their work could choose to ask the puppet to sit with them as they worked.

Poem Master: Recent work has demonstrated the importance of using poetry in the classroom, and the effectiveness of reading and reciting poetry to develop reading and fluency (Raskinski, 2003). A puppet can serve as the poem master, either as a master of ceremonies to lead students in sharing selected poems, or in providing a way for teachers to remember to include poetry by having weekly performances by the puppet poem master. Also, students could sign up to share their poems using the puppet.

Book Reviewer: Students could also create book reviews to be shared by a puppet character. Imagine students consulting a puppet as they select books, or taking a turn in bringing the puppet reviewer to life to suggest other books to peers.

Roving Reporter: The venue of news holds so many possibilities. Students could share daily news through Muppet casters, or interview peers on reading skills or book topics.

And of course...

Free Choice: It is so important to build choice and play into all levels of instruction. Think about the value of play as an area to explore, expand and extend current issues that students are learning. Retelling a story or thinking through a student written story through puppet play gives students a chance to own their learning, to think things through in a non-stressful setting, and helps them think more creatively.

These ideas for including puppetry in the classroom represent a limited range of ideas. When you begin to consider your teaching, your curricular and instructional goals and your students, many ideas will spring to mind.


**Why now?**

Now more than ever it is imperative that we embrace the use of puppetry in the classroom. This essay has taken on the goal of presenting rationale for puppetry use in the classroom and to support literacy instruction. Through reviewing vignettes of puppet use in real classrooms and addressing the research and possibilities for puppet use, it is the hope that teachers will find the courage and support to bring puppetry into their teaching. There is no time like the present, and with current initiatives for instruction and assessment, which limit the types of instruction that teachers are allowed to present to their students, puppetry provides the tool to bridge between skills, practice, and the arts. Now more than ever, puppetry has a role in building student motivation, providing opportunities to develop a love of language and literature, and so much more. Teachers should be excited by the possibility and the power of puppets.

## References

Elley, W. (1989). Vocabulary acquisition through listening. *Reading Research Quarterly, 24*, 174-187.

Goodman, K. (1965). A linguistic study of cues and miscues in reading. *Elementary English, 42*, 633-643.

Goodman, K. (1996). *On reading: A common-sense look at the nature of language and the science of reading.* Portsmouth, NH: Heinemann.

Harwayne, S. (1992). *Lasting impressions: Weaving literature into the writing workshop.* Portsmouth, NH: Heinemann.

Martinez, M., Keehn, S., Roser, N.L., Harmon, J., & O'Neal,S. (2002). An exploration of children's understandings of character in grades 1-8. In *51st Annual Yearbook of the National Reading Conference, Inc.* Oak Creek, Wisconsin.

McCauly, J. & McCauly, D. (1992). Using choral reading to promote language learning from ESL students. *The Reading Teacher, 45*, 526-533.

Opitz, M. F. & Rasinski, T. V. (1998). *Good-bye round robin: 25 effective oral reading strategies.* Portsmouth, NH: Heinemann.

Reutzal, D.R., Hollingsworth, P. & Eldridge, J. (1994). Oral reading instruction: The impact on student reading development. *Reading Research Quarterly, 29*, 40-62.

Tovani, C. (2000). *I read it but I don't get it: Comprehension strategies for adolescent readers.* Portland, Maine: Stenhouse.

Wade, J. E. (1947). *Puppetry in the curriculum: Board of Education, City of New York, Curriculum Bulletin No.1.* New York: NYC Board of Education.

# CHAPTER 16

## SOCIAL COMPETENCY SKILLS THROUGH PUPPETRY

## Lesley Smith

What kind of miraculous medium could appeal to an age range of two to eighty years and everything in between? The ancient art of puppetry and the newer art of television puppetry have been this fantastic education vehicle. Puppetry has the capacity to reach across cultural and social barriers and into the minds and hearts of all the world's children. It can be used to introduce sophisticated social competency skills that are as enjoyable to two and three year olds as they are to adults.

### "Edutainment"

I have been teaching complex concepts under the guise of educational entertainment for over twelve years. It is through the medium of educational puppetry that has enabled artists like myself to make a difference in the personal life of the audience member and in their community. Written pre and post evaluations give educators feedback as to whether the children are learning and retaining concepts. Many performers also create an opportunity for immediate feedback and a "check in" with the audience to be sure they have grasped the program's message at its conclusion. The "check in" might include introducing the main character and as a ventriloquist, answering questions and "testing" the audience in the concepts taught that day.

### Conflict Resolution Skills

In a performance on conflict resolution, children five years of age through adults are taught, "I statements," active listening, anger management, and problem solving with win-win resolutions. This is done through interactive music to sing and sign language the concepts, role modeling the positive social competency skills through a puppet show, and having the audience assist the puppet characters in brainstorming solutions to their common problems.

The traditional classroom style of learning social competency skills such as "I statements," includes an instructor writing an example of an "I statement" on the board and then having students practice filling in the blanks. Through an engaging puppetry performance, the entire audience learns by observing the puppet's actions and through musical repetition.

By the conclusion of a one hour show, the students have learned the structure of an "I statement." "I feel__, when you__, because___. What I want you to do is__." By observing the puppets, they have learned that a "You statement" can put people on the defensive. For example, "You are messy. You don't keep your room clean. Why don't you clean it up?" As opposed to an "I statement": "I feel angry when your room is messy, because I think I'm going to have to clean it. What I want you to do is pick up your room today."

## Puppets Help the Audience Focus

Adults with strong conflict resolution skills are empowered to enhance their relationships at home, at work, and in the political arena. Children that are learning these skills at an early age are better prepared to address the complex issues of our time. The key to making these critical educational concepts accessible, fun, and delightful, is the vehicle of puppetry. It is true that a professional puppeteer can make learning opportunities an "extravaganza experience." Anecdotal evidence indicates however, that after placing a puppet on a teacher's hand and with the right intention, they can emulate the professional and no one will be the wiser. In puppetry workshops, participants always marvel that once the novice puppeteer put the puppet on their hand, the audience no longer looked at the human. The audience member watched the puppet. If the voice was uninteresting, and the movements were sloppy, then the audience didn't care. Their eyes were "hooked" on the puppet. Children are even more forgiving.

## A Lesson on Teaching Empathy

One of the foundation concepts in acquiring social competency skills is developing empathy. Theater games and puppetry performance skills increase students' ability to identify others' feelings and perspectives and to respond empathetically to others. Empathy requires the identification of others' feelings through verbal and physical clues. Acting and puppetry skills explore these clues in depth. A puppetry workshop on empathy promotes learning about body language, identification of feelings, similarities and differences in others' feelings, and predicting and communicating feelings.

A workshop on empathy begins by asking children, "How do puppets communicate a story?" Children identify that it is through movement, expressing emotions, and the dialogue. The presenter then asks children to name "feeling words" that describe emotions. Children are asked to physically dramatize the "feeling words" through theater games and movement. The presenter comments on the body language the children are using and states how body language helps to recognize and identify the feelings of others. The presenter then demonstrates with a puppet the "feeling words" that the children have been dramatizing.

Children are invited to "guess" what emotion the puppet is expressing. The goal is to increase the students' ability to identify others' feelings, take others' perspectives, and respond empathically to others. The presenter then passes out hand puppets to each child. A game of "Simon Says" allows each child to express different emotions and movements with the puppets. The presenter calls out, "Simons Says: sad, mad, angry, shocked, surprised, frightened, shy, etc."

The presenter states that physical signs alert us to our feelings. Children are asked to describe the physical clues that help us to identify the different feelings. Children are then introduced to creating character voices, lip synchronization, and stylized puppet movements. The presenter asks one child to act out an emotion with a puppet while the group is encouraged to name the emotion in "Guess the Emotion" game. A discussion of similarities and differences in feelings develops from this exercise. The presenter explains that people may feel differently about the same situation at different times.

Another game is "Predicting Feelings". The presenter dramatizes simple skits with a puppet that would lead to predictable feelings that the children can guess. For instance, the puppet goes to get his lunch but the cookies are missing; the puppet gets lost, the puppet is called a name, the puppet forgets her homework. A requisite for social perspective taking is the ability to predict others' feelings. This game is an easy method of developing this skill through a delightful and engaging exercise.

## Conclusion

Children readily identify with the teaching puppets that have taught them complex social competency skills. Their minds are open and receptive during the "teaching moment." It allows the teacher to take advantage of the relationships that the students have created with the teaching puppets. The teacher can immediately remind students of the skill sets they developed by bringing out the puppet or revisiting any of the puppetry games. Most importantly, they have learned from an ancient art form that has taught them skills for a lifetime. And all the while they were being taught there was laughter in their hearts and a smile on their face!

Lesley Smith and friends.

# CHAPTER 17

## EDUCATIONAL PUPPETRY AND TELEVISION PROGRAM FORMATS

### Carol Sterling

**Rationale**

As an arts educator who has experienced firsthand the power of puppets to enrich all curriculum areas, one of the most common concerns K-12 teachers share with me is that their students watch television in a passive, uncritical way. They also confide concerns about the importance of students learning how to work cooperatively in groups. In response to these concerns, here is a lively educational puppetry activity that will tap what students know about television programs and stimulate them to develop original puppet skits that reinforce curriculum concepts. It will also provide them with an opportunity to learn many valuable and practical skills, attitudes, knowledge and techniques as they work together to engage in problem solving, divergent thinking and spontaneous creative thinking activities and critical viewing skills.

In addition to sharing specific classroom activities, this article also addresses the importance of documenting the impact of educational puppetry as it contributes to fulfilling Core Curriculum Content Standards for the Visual and Performing Arts. These Standards, as developed by State Education Departments in each of the United States, provide a framework for educators to demonstrate how all learning activities they undertake will help students achieve mastery at developmentally appropriate levels for K-12. Please see the Appendix for how curriculum goals can be achieved using this project.

The goal of inclusion of these Standards is to help justify how theory, philosophy and practical projects of educational puppetry, such as outlined in this article, can help to meet the curriculum requirements of respective state departments of education. They can also be used to assist educators in crafting language that may be useful in lesson plans for planning and implementation as well as for submission to administrators and/or supervisors.

It is hoped that this article will inspire educators, special education colleagues, therapists, librarians and administrators to adapt the ideas and share their experiences with puppetry in education colleagues in future articles.

## Example of an Educational Puppetry and Television Program Format Implemented in K-12 Classrooms

Step 1: Getting Started: Motivation

a. Begin by "brainstorming" with students. Brainstorming is an activity, which encourages an expansion of ideas, arouses curiosity, captures, engages and involves all students.
b. You will need to have at least five pieces of large white brainstorm paper and a colored marking pen. Place at least five sheets next to each other in a horizontal line on a wall or blackboard.
c. Write the heading, "Favorite TV Shows" on the far left and top of the first piece of paper.

Step 2: Brainstorming TV Shows

a. Ask students, "When I count to three, tell me the names of your favorite television shows. Ready? One, two, three!"
b. As students call out their favorite shows, list them under the heading:

**Favorite TV Shows** (Sample responses)

| | |
|---|---|
| American Idol | Oprah Winfrey |
| Charlie Rose | 20/20 |
| The People's Court | News/Weather |
| SportsCenter | Seinfeld |
| Lizzie McGuire | Days of Our Lives |
| Who Wants To Be A Millionaire | As the World Turns |
| Sesame Street | Arthur |
| Barney | Teletubbies |
| Rugrats | This Old House |
| Caillou | The Wiggles |
| SpongeBob | SportsCenter |
| Hollywood Squares | The Price is Right |
| Survivor | Fitness Fantasy |
| Food | Etc. |

Step 3: Brainstorming Types of TV Shows

a. Next, write the heading, "Types of TV Shows" to the right of the listing of Favorite TV Shows. Say, "Take a good look at the programs you have listed. Tell me what types of television shows they are." Encourage students to just call out the types of shows, rather than identify the type for each of the shows mentioned. (You want to keep the upbeat momentum going.)

b. As students identify programs, indicate what categories they fall into by matching the names of the programs with the types of shows they are. Reinforce directions by asking students questions such as, "What do these shows have in common?" or "Which of them seem to go together?"

| **Favorite TV Shows** | **Types of TV Shows** |
|---|---|
| American Idol | News/weather |
| Oprah Winfrey | Talk/interview |
| Charlie Rose | Documentary |
| 20/20 | Reality TV |
| The People's Court | Game shows |
| Any News/Weather | Sports |
| SportsCenter | Comedy |
| Seinfeld | Cartoon |
| Lizzie McGuire | Soap Opera |
| Days of Our Lives | Crime Show |
| Who Wants To Be A Millionaire | Science/Nature Show |
| As the World Turns | Drama |
| Sesame Street | Children's Show |
| Arthur | Superhero |
| Barney | Talent/variety Show |
| Teletubbies | Physical Fitness |
| Rugrats | Food/Nutrition |
| This Old House | House/Decorating |
| Caillou | |
| The Wiggles | |
| SpongeBob | |
| SportsCenter | |
| Hollywood Squares | |
| The Price is Right | |
| Survivor | |
| Fitness Fantasy | |
| The Food Show | |
| Etc. | |

(Tip: Don't erase or remove the suggestions after brainstorming each idea. Keep all ideas on view. Once the group catches on to this technique, the enthusiasm will be contagious and ideas will flow naturally.)

c. Encourage responses by reminding students of additional programs.
d. Ask, "How about (<u>Name of program</u>)? What type of program is that?

Step 4: Draw a Line from Favorite TV Show to Type of TV Show

a. Ask students to draw a line from each of the favorite TV shows to the type of TV show it is. This reinforces categorizing and analysis skills.

Step 5: Select One Type of TV Show

a. Now, select one type of television show that provides opportunities for development and reinforcement of specific skill areas. A television news program format is especially effective for strengthening improvisational as well as writing skills while addressing themes and concepts related to social studies, language arts, science, health and physical education, and the visual and performing arts.
b. Ask students to brainstorm. "When I count to three, tell me every idea or word that comes to mind when I say, "Television News Show. Ready, one-two-three."
c. Under the heading "One Type of TV Show", write "TV News Program" and list all suggestions.

## One Type of TV Show
**TV News Program** (Sample responses)

| | |
|---|---|
| reporters | sports |
| weather | international, national, local news |
| microphones | commercials |
| graphs | desks |
| films | images |
| logo | maps |
| scripts | screen to interview "guests" not in the |
| studio | |

(Note: A similar brainstorming approach can be used with each type of television program [e.g., soap opera, drama, documentary, game show, etc.])

Step 6: Brainstorm "What a Puppet Can Do"

a. Write the heading, "Puppet" to the right of the "One Type of TV Show" and "TV News Program".
b. Ask students to brainstorm.
c. Say, "When I count to three, tell me all the words, actions that come to mind when I ask, "What can a puppet do?" Ready? Set, one-two-three."
d. Once again, write all suggestions under the heading PUPPET.

(Your brainstorming documentation will look like this:

| Fav. TV Shows | Types of TV Shows | One Type of TV Show<br>TV News Program | Puppet |
|---|---|---|---|

**Puppet** (Sample responses)

| | |
|---|---|
| run | sing |
| jump | sneeze |
| cry | fall |
| read | dance |
| disappear | bow |
| snore | talk |
| fly | clap |

    e. Help students along by reminding them that puppets are make-believe and are capable of outlandish and super heroic actions.

Step 7: Classroom Management

    a. Announce to the students that they are going to do a "live" television news show using puppets as reporters, in commercials, etc.

    b. Organize students into small groups so everyone gets a chance to be involved. Usually this includes approximately three or four students. Students can choose the part of the show that they would like to do and make the puppets for their favorite parts. Possible choices for a three or four member television news show might include:

| | |
|---|---|
| Anchor Puppet: | Reports on current events, international, national and local news. |
| Anchor Puppet: | Reports on school news; can also be an "on the scene" reporter. |
| Sports Puppet: | Reports on international, national, local sports including school sports. |
| Environmental/<br>Science/Technology<br>Puppet: | Reports on trends in environment and computers, science and health, etc. |
| Weather Puppet: | eports on the weather. |
| Interview Puppet Host<br>And Puppet Guest: | This could be an author, TV or film celebrity, VIP, newsmaker or local spokesperson such as a school principal, drama or sports coach, school mascot, mayor of the town---anything that relates to timely news. |
| Consumer Advocate Puppet: | Provides advice on best buys in computers, software, cell phones, school and sports items. |

Film/TV Critic Puppet:  Provides advice on best flicks, shows, etc.
Commercial Puppets #1 and #2:  Provides testimonial for products or public service
announcement.

(Note: The older the students, the more independently they will work. You might consider encouraging them to include additional reports than the ones listed.)

(Tip: Keep the show VERY SIMPLE in the beginning! Three newscasters are enough to learn the format that works best.)

Step 8: Motivation for Making the Puppets: Brainstorming Puppets as Newscasters

   a. Encourage students to create puppet newscasters from inexpensive scrap materials into distinctive personalities. This technique helps students think about and focus on what the puppets will say even when they are in the creation stage.
   b. To stimulate visually interesting puppet characters as newscasters, help students brainstorm a wide variety of possibilities. For example, try a free association of ideas to expand on the idea of a "Puppet Weather Reporter."
   c. Say, "When I count to three, tell me everything that comes to mind when I say "TV Weather Reporter."
   d. Encourage the students to express key words and images from which to later develop the weather report.
   e. Remind students that puppets can be objects and made from anything.

**<u>TV Weather Reporter</u>** (Sample responses)

| maps | temperature | | |
|------|-------------|------|------|
| rain | thermometer | warm/cold | galoshes |
| person | thermostat | windy | boots |
| umbrella | degrees | wet/dry | floods |
| clouds | Fahrenheit | cats and dogs | drought |
| duck | Celsius | hat/glove/scarf | "travel advisory" |
| puddle | ice sleet | snow | |
| sun | windshield wipers | | |

   f. To stimulate the creative juices, you might say, "Take a look at some of the ideas that have been suggested. Do any of them give you an idea of how a weather reporter puppet might look?"

   g. Can you imagine making a puppet in the form of any of the brainstormed ideas? You might ask questions such as, "Could a weather puppet be a <u>(Select any idea that was brainstormed, e.g., Boot?  Cloud?)</u>"

h. Or, "Have you ever thought about a <u>(Select any idea from the list, e.g., umbrella)</u> as a weather forecaster?" Students will catch on and probably come up with terrific ideas such as a fluctuating thermometer, footwear such as a rubber boot predicting rain or a talking cloud. This technique will encourage students to make the connection that puppets can be anything under the sun, including the sun!

(Note: Once students have learned the free association techniques of brainstorming, they can apply this activity to other puppets in the television news program. Here's how brainstorming for the Sports Puppet Reporter might look.

## TV Sports Reporter
| | |
|---|---|
| football | scores |
| soccer ball | team uniform |
| man/woman | photographs |
| basketball | banners |
| tennis racquet | rivals |
| cheerleaders | stadium |
| megaphone | |

## Commercial Puppets
food: potato chips, cookies, yogurt, soda, cereal, candy household products: toothpaste, shampoos, baby products, medicine, detergents, furniture polish, toilet bowl cleanser, paper towels, tools toys cars

i. To generate original puppet ideas you might ask, "Can you fill in the answer to this question? "A commercial puppet could be a <u>(Select from objects from the brainstormed list.)</u>."
j. After brainstorming ideas for other newscaster puppets (anchor, local interviewer, sports, environmental/science, health, school news, consumer advocate, film/TV critic, etc., encourage students to complete the phrase: "A <u>(type of newscaster puppet, e.g., sports)</u> could be a <u>(idea from brainstorm list, e.g., talking football)</u>."

For example:
- A current events puppet could be a <u>(newspaper, town landmark, etc.)</u>.
- A school events puppet could be a <u>(school building, principal, mascot)</u>.
- A consumer advocate puppet could be a <u>(price tag, search engine on the Internet)</u>.
- A film/TV critic puppet could be a <u>(person made from film products)</u>.
- An interview puppet could be a <u>(microphone, mouth and ears, or eyes)</u>.

k. Now it's time to ask the students to select the type of newscaster puppet they like best. Ask them to make an original puppet with a unique personality and voice. Encourage them to create the puppet's appearance and voice so that it will be so compelling to look at and listen to that it will engage the audience with compelling news that is interesting to listen to and watch!

To make unique newscaster puppets, try including one of these puppet tips!

Tip 1: Make sure that the newscaster puppet has something on it that moves!

Tip 2: Make sure that the puppet has an exaggerated facial expression (that can reflect the mood of what he/she is talking about).

Tip 3: Encourage the use of scrap, inexpensive recycled materials that in themselves can stimulate original personalities and unique visual and oral qualities.

Step 9: Creating the Puppet TV Show: Improvising a Television News Program with Younger Students

a. Start simply. Once the members of each group have made their puppets, ask each team to write a brief television news show with the following segments:
   - An opening greeting to the audience.
   - One report.
   - One commercial.
   - Thanks for watching and goodbye.
b. As students become more experienced, add more news puppet reporters.

(Tip: To begin, the only criterion for the students to follow is that they develop a TV news show with a beginning, middle, and an end. At first, for younger children especially, do not encourage script writing in the formal sense. It may inhibit creative, spontaneous expression at an early stage of development. If you feel a script is important, it can be developed after the first try at improvisation.)

c. At this point, assist students in making sure they each understand how to improvise a 30 second news report (perhaps highlight a school or local event), weather or sports story. Try and include a commercial since all students are very familiar with this format. Try and provide your assistance as director.

Step 10: Critiquing the TV News Program

a. After each group has presented its news program, ask the students to respond to the following questions:

   - What did you like about the way the puppets looked?
   - What did you like about what the puppets did?
   - What parts of the news program did you especially like?

b. Encourage students to be very specific by asking questions such as:
   - Did you like the voices they used?
   - What did you like about the way the puppet moved? (Indicate or refer to a specific action.)
   - What was so effective about the way the puppet did that?
   - What do you think might have made the program better?
c. To make the critique as constructive and positive as possible, elicit responses that are specific such as, "Did you think that the puppets could have spoken louder?"

Step 11: Critiquing the Group Process

a. After each group has presented its news program, ask students to "debrief" how they think their group worked as a cooperative unit. To help students evaluate their interaction, here are some questions that might help each group discuss it in an informal and individual way:
   - How did you feel about being in this group?
   - How did you feel about the group's accomplishment of the task?
   - What did you do most in the group----talk or listen?
   - Who talked the most? Who listened? How did people show they understood or agreed?
   - What role or roles did you play? Leader? Follower? Contributor? Comedian? Peacekeeper? Withdrawer? Other?
   - Did the group compromise making use of the varied ideas of the members or did the group stick to the ideas of one person who served as leader?
   - What would you do differently as a group if you had the chance to do the puppetry TV format over again? Be specific.

**Final Notes**

The foregoing example is illustrative of how puppetry can be incorporated into a TV program format in the classroom. After students have tried one type of TV format, encourage them to experiment with puppets with others: situation comedies, soap operas, drama, documentaries, game shows, etc. All TV formats can be put to beneficial use in strengthening students' skills in the visual and performing arts as well as in all subject areas. Once students have tried this technique, encourage them to perform their skits for students in other classes and grades. Students who are given the task of looking at their favorite television shows with an eye and ear for adapting them for curriculum development, will more likely develop skills that turn what is often a passive, uncritical situation into an active learning experience. And, they will learn to get along with their peers in what promises to be a mutually gratifying social experience.

**Appendix**

**How Educational Puppetry and Television Program Format Lessons Support State Core Curriculum Content Standards for the Visual and Performing Arts**

The importance of demonstrating how educational puppetry helps to achieve academic goals as noted in the State Department of Education's curriculum frameworks will help to validate its inclusion in all subject areas. To demonstrate how the article, *"Educational Puppetry and TV Program Formats"* can help to fulfill curriculum goals, here are examples of language that refers to how specific skills, attitudes, and knowledge relate to each of the Standards in the Visual and Performing Arts. Educators are encouraged to review their respective states' performance standards and analyze how each educational puppetry project they do meets these standards. Inclusion of these references in reports as well as in lesson plans will help to strengthen the rationale for the importance of educational puppetry for administrators, principals, curriculum coordinators and other supervisors.

**Sample:** Core Curriculum Standards in the Visual and Performing Arts (New Jersey). Please note that many states have similar standards.

**All students will acquire knowledge and skills that increase aesthetic awareness in dance, music, theater, and visual arts.**

Students will:
- use a variety of visual arts materials, techniques and processes in the production of two and three dimensional artwork and puppets.
- engage in self-expression, and the creative process.
- become familiar with educational arts resources culled from critical review of television programs.
- become familiar with use of inexpensive and recycled scrap materials to create puppets and artwork.
- compare the life experiences that appear in images on television to their own experiences.
- be exposed to how the visual arts can illustrate themes in all subject areas, including English/language arts, social studies, mathematics, science, and the visual and performing arts, including music, theater, dance and media.

**All students will refine perceptual, intellectual, physical, and technical skills through creating dance, music, theater, and/or visual arts.**

Students will:
- improvise and/or write an original script that identifies basic facts and essential ideas that relate to aspects of the curriculum.

- locate, access and evaluate resources to identify appropriate information on the Internet and beyond for reenactments of the television program format.
- pose questions and contribute their own information or ideas in large and small group discussion in order to create a TV program format.
- strengthen brainstorming, planning, thinking and discussion within a classroom and small group setting.
- make oral presentations that demonstrate appropriate consideration of audience, purpose, and information to be conveyed.
- use problem solving and thinking skills in the planning for and creation of puppet action and movement.
- use listening skills to ensure cooperation of all points of view in group setting.

**All students will utilize arts elements and art media to produce artistic products and performances.**

Students will:
- be exposed to visual arts materials, techniques and processes for creation of puppet projects.
- use the art elements of line, shape, color and form.
- use performance elements of character and story creation.
- interpret how form, symbols, techniques and medium construct meaning in works of art.
- develop skills in the use of a variety of art materials, processes, mediums, and techniques, and create and perform puppet skits as related to the curriculum.
- create works of art that connect to diverse curriculum areas and address a wide range of topics, themes, and concepts related to television program formats.
- be exposed to selected vocabulary of contemporary art and the ways in which it can be brought together to create an effect in the creation of a television program.
- work independently and in teams to create artwork.
- cooperate and collaborate.

**All students will demonstrate knowledge of the process of critique.**

Students will:
- engage in individual and group critique and will describe the strengths and areas to be developed in the creation of puppets and puppet action.
- reflect on their work to determine appropriate choices to strengthen final product.

- analyze how their own experiences influence their critical judgments about their works and the works of others.
- understand ways in which creation and performance of puppet works reflect and/or parody societal values.
- have access to questions to assist in analysis of their artwork.

**All students will identify the various historical, social and cultural influences and traditions which have generated artistic accomplishments throughout the ages and which continue to shape contemporary arts.**

Students will:
- learn how puppets can be created from recycled materials and/or objects.
- be exposed to social commentary as a forum for the creation of puppets and puppet action.
- learn how the visual arts can reflect social/historical issues and recognize relationships between the arts and cultures.
- create puppet and art works that reflect concepts of diverse curriculum areas including development of historical and/or fictional characters, topics, and themes.

**All students will develop design skills for planning the form and function of space, structure, objects, sound and events.**

Students will:
- use the elements and principles of art to communicate specific meanings in their puppet work.
- learn how designing puppet projects teaches about the principles of design.

# CHAPTER 18

## PUPPETS IN CYBERSPACE:
## THE USE OF TECHNOLOGY IN THE PERFORMING ARTS AND EDUCATION

## Jo Tomalin

My latest interest and challenge is the use of technology in education with online teaching. Online or distance education has rapidly grown as a viable alternative to traditional classroom teaching in the last two decades. Online courses are available nowadays to fulfill K-12 home school, undergraduate and graduate degree programs. Students enjoy the asynchronous nature of logging on to study any time, any place with a computer and Internet connection. The principal reasons for the rapid growth of distance education are the freedom of being able to study when and where one chooses without having to travel to an institution combined with the increase in quality and recognition of online programs.

Online education content is posted on the course Web site which participants access with a user name and password. There are several popular online course management software packages which contain, organize, and password protect the content such as WebCT and Blackboard. Faculty who embrace technology in education appreciate the advantages of easy communication through email, the ability to manage and post course documents, interactive multimedia, handouts, assignments, and attendance, and to carry on meaningful discussions online. However, there are disadvantages to classes conducted online such as when faculty and students miss the face-to-face contact of a traditional classroom.

The performing arts are often deemed an inappropriate match for technology or distance delivery. However, we all know that technology is here to stay. Therefore, arts educators and entertainers will need to consider producing performances and learning opportunities with storytelling, puppetry, theatre, and music via the Internet.

A few years ago I jumped into the unknown and developed a fully online three unit upper division course at San Francisco State University called Theatre in

Education. As a member of a large university with over 1,000 faculty, I am one of a handful of early adopters who has developed and taught a fully online course, and I am currently the only one in the entire College of Creative Arts. In my online course, students learn theatre techniques and how to integrate them into K-12 curriculum. While no one is actually acting on the Internet in my class - yet - students do learn acting, improvisation, story telling, and puppetry techniques through discussion, handouts, images and assignments.

It is surprising how much can be achieved online, but I took a deep breath before assigning students to build a puppet based on a character from a story in the text book or of their own choice. Students had to write a brief report of their construction techniques, describe the story they based their character/s on and upload a photo of their result! It was wonderful when students actually fulfilled all these requirements. And although the hardest part of this assignment (to them) was learning how to upload a photo of their puppet, the results were worthwhile.

A memorable photo of puppets from my Spring 2004 online course, Theatre in Education, was by Ava Miedzinski. Ava asked her husband to take the photo with her two sock puppets, and it not only provided me with a face to one of my online students but also a genuine sense of fun and achievement. Ava described how she started with two old socks, planning to make a boy and girl character which evolved into the characters of Mordechai and Queen Esther from a story based on a Jewish holiday called Purim. Ava used fabric remnant and beads she had in a box and glued on the character details. She also described how she spontaneously performed her first version of the characters interacting to children at the Purim festival which was so successful that she took them along to the next gathering.

Ava Miedzinski and her Purim sock puppets. (photo by Yitschak Miedzinski)

As an educator, creative artist, and director with an interest in puppetry, instructional design and technology, I want to delve into this new territory to help bring the art form of puppetry into classrooms as an entertainment, learning and teaching tool. The next step is to apply interactive media and teaching strategies to create streaming video of student puppet performances via distance education so participants can watch in their own home even if they live thousands of miles from each other!

## Interactive Multimedia

Media such as slides, 16mm film, and audio have been superseded in classrooms by new technology. Wang (2000) stated, "Traditional media technologies can no longer meet the needs of our classrooms' teaching practices and learning processes, as the direct result, and they have been rapidly replaced or are going to be replaced by multimedia and its technology" (p. 303). Multimedia in education includes video, text, graphics, sound, the Internet, and interactive computer learning objects. Waldrep (1998) observed that a classroom lab of VHS machines was "sterile" (p. 46) when compared with the mobile sophistication of digital video. The older style media such as film and slides is used less and less, but their applications in teaching techniques are the foundation for the integration of new multimedia into the curriculum.

Digital video (DV) has rapidly grown in use for educational, training, and entertainment purposes. Dessoff (2001) observed that "In just a few short years, *digital video* has gone from an expensive, unattainable dream for educators to a mainstream, invaluable tool that can allow students to do everything from conduct videoconferencing events to prepare multimedia presentations" (p.46). Nowadays, it is more common to find digital video camcorders, PCs equipped with digital editing software, DVD burners, and DVD players in K-16 classrooms due to the lower costs, relative ease of use, and high quality results.

Bassoppo-Moyo (1997) observed that "Education and training have been the first large-scale universally understood multi-media submarkets which have successfully attempted to utilize the compressed full-motion, full screen digital video attributes of DVI" (p. 307). Digital video equipment is smaller, more convenient to use, and produces higher quality results than cumbersome 16 mm or VHS equipment, which makes DV a natural fit with education, entertainment, and training.

## Streamed Video

One of the most powerful applications of interactivity in distance delivery is streamed digital video, which is also called video-on-demand. Streamed video can be live video from a digital camera to a participant's monitor; a captured and edited file for download on a home computer; or a captured and edited file contained on a server for viewing without download on a home computer. Streamed video files are large and need to be compressed using editing software. Cable and DSL Internet access provide wide bandwidth which results in the fast download of large multimedia files. Dial-up Internet connections have a narrow bandwidth and it may take over 30 minutes to download a short video clip compared to minutes or seconds with DSL or cable.

The cost of video editing programs varies widely from $50 to $1500 depending on the features. There are several low cost programs which do a good job. The more expensive programs produce high end professional results but are more complicated to learn. I suggest that anyone interested in learning how to edit and compress digital video start with the software that comes with the camera or is included in your computer operating system. Another option is to compare several software programs and features online to find a product that suits your needs. Some computer magazines provide comparisons of price, features and reviews which may be helpful.

Streamed video of the performing arts via distance delivery is a wonderful tool for demonstrations and performance techniques. Puppetry performances and puppet construction demonstrations can be streamed for live or asynchronous peer group, individual, or instructor feedback online.

## Digital Video and the Performing Arts Curriculum

How teachers integrate digital video into the performance curriculum depends on the content area, learner needs, and teaching strategies. Technology is the tool that drives the learning and acquisition of knowledge. Waldrep (1997) stated that "Schematic visuals, coupled with sound go a long way toward cultivating new knowledge. But the real breakthrough comes when you present these elements interactively. The greater the degree of engagement by the student, the greater the chances for meaningful learning" (p. 46). Interactive simulations provide rehearsal of skills and real world experience to provide for diverse learner styles. Learning takes place when the near-transfer skills are far-transferred by critical thinking, analysis and synthesis (Clark, 1999). It is important to reflect on the value and application of digital video in education as technology alone does not provide learning. Well designed interactive learning activities produce high rates of retention by encouraging practice, modeling, and in turn, comprehension of concepts.

The following examples demonstrate the application of interactive technology in teaching music, art, acting and storytelling:

## Digital Guitar Instruction

Waldrep (1997) developed a fascinating guitar playing program for Boston's Berklee School of Music. The interactive DVD format allowed students to customize training according to needs by skipping or selecting in-depth demonstrations. Waldrep's focus on this project was that the integrity of the music-training program should be enhanced by the technology. Audio tracks could be repeated easily for practice and camera angles zoomed in to detail fingering techniques. Images of chord symbols were added digitally to the video for visual learners, as a supplement to the existing textbook; not simply a reprint. Waldrep's innovative extensions of digital video included animations of finger and chord positions, slow motion video of challenging passages, DV Camera Internet connection for tests, teacher evaluations, and dynamic Web site resources. This entire program and instructional design with integrated digital video technology sounds innovative, motivational, and excellent.

**Multimedia and Creativity**

The Vermont Web Project of a Junior High School developed an art and music program enhanced by technology (Hamilton & Smyth, 1999). The main strategy was that multimedia should be integrated and that "students not 'play' on the computers" (p. 33). Although the multimedia used was simple at first, students progressed to digital techniques. Another goal of this project was for students to produce collaborative and expressive music composition, images, or video. The results of the learner-centered curriculum driven project were regularly showcased on a school Web site.

**Digital Shakespeare**

Steven Marx, a California Polytechnic State University professor at San Luis Obispo, used digital video to capture, archive, and stream student performances of Shakespeare scenes (Read, 2002). The mobility of the digital camera equipment and the excellent sound and image quality enabled Professor Marx to shoot scenes at night in low light forests and daylight beach shoots. Professor Marx' students were involved in planning the filming of scenes, performing, and reflecting on their streamed video performances in online discussions.

Marx presents this project on a Web site called Shakespeare Triangulation (http://cla.calpoly.edu/~smarx/Shakespeare/triang/). The interactive site provides students with three ways to learn about the work of Shakespeare: reading, viewing and performing. Read (2002) stated that, "In papers Mr. Marx has posted on the Web site, students discuss their performances, describing stage fright, the boundaries between scholarship and performance, and a host of other concerns." "When students can reflect on their own experiences," he says, "they give you some wonderful angles of perception" (p. 44).

The Web site is an excellent experiential resource for past, current and future acting students. Read (2002) noted that Terry A. Gray, academic-technology supervisor at Palomar College calls Mr. Marx's online work with Shakespeare "a fine model for Web-coursework integration" (p. 44). The streamed video clips are formatted and play in RealPlayer, which is an inexpensive way to store footage for online delivery (http://cla.calpoly.edu/~smarx/Shakespeare/triang/performing/339films.html).

**Digital Storytelling**

The Black History Makers group is an oral history project in Chicago seeded with funds from the National Endowment for the Humanities (Roach, 2003, p. 32). The eight-year project entails a projected collection of 5,000 digital videotaped interviews of prominent Black Americans. The digital video collection will be available in a digital archive in Chicago accompanied by an online catalog. In 2007, the completed project will be available for viewing through several university research libraries at no cost.

The Web site currently lists interviews with "notables, such as novelist Terry McMillan, physicist and Morehouse College president Dr. Walter Massey, former U.S. Senator Carol Moseley-Braun, and performers Ossie Davis and Harry Belafonte" (Roach, 2003, p. 32), although the general public recommends individuals for inclusion via a link on the Web site (www.thehistorymakers.com). This huge project is possible through digital video. The high quality and compression for streaming can be archived perfectly on DVDs, which do not decompose like other video formats such as 16 and 35mm, or VHS.

Another innovative use of streamed video is The Storyteller of the Year 2004 contest sponsored by the Creative Arts Institute in Ohio (http://www.storytelleroftheyear. org). The Web site provides 3 - 5 minute examples of each finalist's storytelling performance in small and large download formats as well as an audio file of the 2003 contestants (http://www.storytelleroftheyear.org/stream.htm). Viewers watch the streamed performances and then go to the home page to vote for their favorite. It is also interesting to note the quality of sound and image of the storytellers in this contest and their use of lighting and microphones to enhance the video of their work.

## So What about Puppetry and Technology?

How can puppetry be presented or taught using any of these interactive techniques?

- Puppet construction techniques can be demonstrated on a DVD, or even a CD ROM if the file is small enough. The file could also be streamed into a student's home or school from a Web site or online course.
- Puppet performance techniques and actual performances can also be disseminated by DVD, CD ROM, and streamed video.
- Auditions for puppet festivals and other performance opportunities could be conducted by the company providing a link to a Web site of a streamed digital video file to view.
- Students can perform or demonstrate "live" their puppetry projects using a camera on their computer to videoconference with an instructor or group in different locations.
- Students can discuss, rehearse or direct a puppetry performance project by "live" videoconferencing, with participants in different locations.
- Web sites of puppet companies can be enhanced by including a brief video clip sample of each show to share the style and dynamics of the puppet characters and story.

## Copyright Issues

It is important to consider copyright issues of ownership before uploading performances of your work on the Internet for the entire world to see. Is the story or dialogue of the puppet show written and published by someone else? If so, you would need to ask for permission to publish digitally and chances are that permission may not be granted. If the text or puppets are original and created by you or commissioned for your company, then do you want to share the performance which others may copy? If you produce a "how to build or manipulate puppets" video, do you want to provide streaming access for free or sell your expertise on a CD ROM or DVD? It is vital to consider the ramifications of posting images, text, sound, and video online, even if the site is password-protected. Don't forget to get signed release forms from any actors, presenters or participants agreeing to their likeness and work being filmed for reproduction.

## Advantages of Digital Video

The advantages of digital video according to Dessoff (2001) are: reduced cost, ease of use, video conference capability in distance learning, training, easy editing with programs such as iMovie, high quality image and sound, professional results without a steep learning curve, and far superior to analog film and equipment. Wang (2000) noted that digital video "may offer a unique environment for interactivity, learner control and student interest and motivation" (p. 313) and that video-on-demand is a significant multimedia tool.

## Disadvantages of Digital Video

Disadvantages of digital video according to Reed (2003) are: high cost, bandwidth limitation, content challenges and digital rights, accessibility, teacher training, and security problems. Fritz (1999) noted additional disadvantages when transferring digital video to DVD storage media: learning curve, expensive authoring and MPEG encoding systems, incompatibility between authoring and productivity software such as Director, QuickTime, and DirectShow.

## Conclusion

Technology in the form of distance education and interactive multimedia is rapidly evolving as an effective tool for entertainment, teaching and learning. Digital video is a principal tool of new media due to its high quality, ease of use, low cost, and superior features to analog film. The applications of digital video in the performing arts and education are varied, innovative, and should be explored. Technical expertise is less important than the creativity and imagination to provide a rich learning experience through interactivity. Technology is a powerful tool if used with creativity, imagination and integrity. I enjoy being challenged and will continue to connect my main interests of technology, education, and performance. However, I also enjoy loading my home made puppet theatre and bag of glove puppets into the back of my car and driving off to entertain a small group of young children with my fuzzy animal puppet show!

## References

Bassoppo-Moyo, T. C. (1997). Digital video interaction (DVI) technology: The world's new frontier in education, training and development? *International Journal of Instructional Media, 2*(4), 10.

Clark, R. (1999). *Building expertise: Cognitive methods for training and performance improvement.* Washington, D.C.: International Society for Performance Improvement.

Dessoff, A. L. (2001). Kids, teachers and videotape. *Curriculum Administrator, 37*(5), 46-49.

Fritz, M. (1999). For training & education. *Emedia Professional, 12*(5), 7.

Hamilton, A. & Smyth, M. (1999). Technology enhances the arts. *Curriculum Administrator, 35*(3), 33-34.

McLellan, H. (2000). Experience design. *CyberPsychology & Behavior, 3*(1), 59.

Read, B. (2002). Professor's Web site "triangulates" Shakespeare through students' performances. *Chronicle of Higher Education, 48*(3), 1-4.

Reed, R. (2003). Streaming technology improves student achievement. *T H E Journal, 30*(7), 14-20.

Roach, R. (2003). Oral history project preserves stories of black history makers. *Black Issues in Higher Education, 19*(25), 2-3.

Waldrep, M. (1998). DVD-video: An unlimited training and educational format. *EMedia Professional, 11*(10), 46.

Wang, S. (2000). Multimedia and some of its technical issues. *International Journal of Instructional Media, 27*(3), 303-313.

# PART TWO:

# PUPPETRY IN THERAPY

# CHAPTER 19

## INTRODUCTION TO PUPPETRY IN THERAPY

### Matthew Bernier

Puppet Therapy, Puppetry in Therapy, and Therapeutic Puppetry are terms which usually refer to the use of puppetry as an aid in physical or emotional healing, remediation, or rehabilitation. The use of puppetry in therapy capitalizes on the innate expressive and therapeutic value and benefits of puppet making, puppet play, interaction with puppet characters, and observation of, and response to puppet shows.

Therapeutic puppetry combines verbal and nonverbal modes of expression through the intrinsic artistic and dramatic elements of puppetry. Therapeutic puppetry is most often thought of as being used with children, but it can be adapted to a variety of people of all ages, to meet various treatment goals. Therapeutic puppetry techniques can be applied with individuals, couples, groups, and families.

In medical hospital settings, in the hands of trained nurses, child life workers, etc., puppets serve as therapists in pre- and post-operative situations. They assist the frightened, sad, frustrated, angry, or confused patient (usually a child) to express, explore or contain emotions and to better understand the medical procedures, environment, and personnel (Aronoff, 1994; Cassell, 1965; Linn, 1977, 1978; Petrillo & Sanger, 1980; Schneider, 1976).

In many cases, ready-made puppets are used by the therapist to perform for the individual or group in an effort to entertain, instruct or interact (Bender & Woltmann, 1936; Cole, 1993; Oatman, 1981; Renfro, 1984; Sullivan, 1982). For example, Diana Chiles (2001, 2005), a pediatric therapist in Tennessee, finds that puppets can provide trust, comfort and friendship. They can help children and their families cope with the fears and emotional stressors of illness and hospitalization.

Chiles uses a puppet character named Bernard as a mediator, with the potential to reach the child and to provide an acceptable and alternative outlet for expression of fears, feelings, and frustrations. Bernard assumes the role of a patient on the pediatric unit and shares the hospital experience with the children. Bernard creates a trusting relationship with the child by having the same fears and illnesses as the child. Chiles' (2005) effective work can be seen in the documentary videos, *A Boy Named Bernard* and *Bernard, Are You Okay?*

In various forms of psychotherapy (play therapy, art therapy, drama therapy), puppets are used to express feelings and thoughts, which might otherwise remain hidden or repressed (Bender, 1952; Bernier, 1983; Gerity, 1999; Irwin, 1983; Kors, 1963; Oaklander, 1978; Sommers, 1977). This is especially useful in the resolution of trauma from experiences such as divorce, accidents, domestic violence and child abuse.

In drama therapy and play therapy, clients are engaged in their own spontaneous puppet play, usually with puppets provided for them. For example, a child may be encouraged to select from a variety of stock characters for free puppet play. The therapist takes note of the chosen characters, the roles they play, the plot and narrative of the stories, and the themes. Such information aids in psychological assessment revealing aspects of the child's intelligence, personality, and family dynamics (Irwin, 1983, 1993; Irwin & Malloy, 1975). Children are then encouraged through puppet play to work through emotional conflict or to explore confusing thoughts or experiences (Irwin, Rubin & Shapiro, 1975; Irwin & Shapiro, 1975).

Group puppetry is used as a way to produce original puppet plays around a common theme, such as separation or divorce, in order to provide an enjoyable and therapeutic outlet for children to reveal deep and powerful reactions to events in their lives (Gendler, 1986). Group puppetry also aids in the development of social skills and capitalizes on the individual strengths of the various group members. In some cases, groups of children are engaged in puppet making and the creation of unstructured spontaneous puppet shows (Kors, 1964). In addition to the puppet shows serving as a source of behaviors and expressions to be noted clinically, the ultimate goal is to foster creativity in each child.

In art therapy, the clients are engaged in their own puppet making and the puppets are then used in puppet play activities designed to meet specific therapeutic goals (Bernier, 1983; Gerity, 1999; Steinhardt, 1994). Essential to this approach is the idea that puppets can be made as an extension or representation of the self, parts of self, or aspects of others or of the environment. Combining principles and techniques from art therapy, play therapy, drama therapy, and psychodrama, this approach is sometimes referred to as psychopuppetry (Bernier, 1990; Horovitz, 2002, 2003; Kunsden, 1984). Two effective techniques that can be included in this approach are client directed puppet play and Puppet Playback Theatre (Bernier, 2003).

Client directed puppet play is based on the client-centered approach to play therapy (Axline, 1947/1969; Dorfman, 1951). It involves the client making or selecting puppets for spontaneous puppet play. The client takes on the roles of scriptwriter, actor/puppeteer, and director. The therapist is engaged by the client to assist in the puppet play by taking on roles according to the client's direction.

Axline instructed: "The therapist does not attempt to direct the child's actions or conversation in any manner. The child leads; the therapist follows (1969, p. 73)." The therapist does not creatively offer dialogue or the personality of the character from within, but instead waits to be directed by the client as to what to say or how to act.

This process can be counterintuitive for some therapists, especially those who might naturally participate freely in creative play, contributing towards a balance of input from all participants in the improvisation. However, in this approach of therapeutic puppetry, it is important to give the client control, to allow for more authentic puppet play and storytelling. This allows the client to direct and work through real and/or symbolic scenarios in order to master emotional conflicts.

Puppet Playback Theatre is an adaptation of Playback Theatre (Fox, 1986; Salas, 1993/1996) which is a form of psychodramatic improvisational theatre, created in 1975 by Jonathan Fox and the original Playback Theatre Company. In Playback Theatre, audience members are invited to tell stories from their lives and to watch them enacted on the spot by playback performers using sound, music, movement, and improvisational drama. Playback Theatre can be entertaining, educational, and therapeutic. It affirms the importance of personal and universal experiences and provides opportunities for viewing life from new perspectives.

Sometimes, Playback Theatre companies use puppets or found objects as puppets in their work instead of the actors acting out the story. According to Salas (1993/1996),

> In this imaginative, ritual context, we can readily endow household objects with human characteristics, just as small children do in their play. In a Playback performance, a scene done with "puppets" instead of visible actors can provide theatrical variety. It is an opportunity for a different kind of expression and response. Anything can serve as a puppet. Instead of coming prepared with objects, you can involve the audience in finding objects around the room – a plant, a shoe, a ruler. (p. 41)

This technique, most commonly called object puppetry or object theatre, has many rich therapeutic possibilities.

In my own work as an art therapist, especially with victims of domestic violence and/or child abuse, I have experimented with using puppets instead of actors in Playback Theatre, incorporating the evocative symbolic expression of puppets and animated objects as well as techniques unique to puppetry. Usually, the therapy group members take turns as storytellers, audience, and puppeteers/actors using ready-made puppets, their own puppets made in art therapy, original puppets "orphaned" by previous group members, masks, or found objects. An alternate method is for the therapist to solo perform or "playback" the story with puppets or objects. In either case, the therapist serves as the conductor, facilitating the storytelling, the performance, and group discussion processes.

In clinical settings, Puppet Playback Theatre can be added as a technique in creative arts therapies (art, music, drama, dance/movement, and poetry therapies) practice. In addition to attending to the general goals of therapy, Puppet Playback Theatre can be utilized to foster spontaneous and authentic expression as well as to facilitate communication between participants and the therapist.

In non-clinical settings such as classrooms, Puppet Playback Theatre can foster class cohesiveness, cultural and diversity awareness, and socialization. The improvisational nature of Playback Theatre encourages development of language/communication skills, memory, problem solving, cognitive processing, and creativity.

Puppetry is also used in speech therapy, to assist in language development and speech modification; occupational therapy, to assist in improvement of activities of daily living; physical therapy, to challenge and coax the patient to cooperate with exercises; and pain management, to provide diversional activity and stress relief. Puppetry has also been used therapeutically in specialized settings such as therapeutic or alternative schools, nursing homes and prisons (Aronoff, 1996, 1997).

In educational settings, teachers may find that puppetry activities have therapeutic value even when the intent of the activity is educational. As expected, in the classroom, puppetry can be found to foster creativity, language development, socialization, and problem solving. It can also serve as an outlet for emotions and impulses, which might otherwise find their way into non-productive or disruptive behaviors.

Without attempting to be therapists, teachers can effectively engage students in puppetry that has educational and therapeutic value. Additionally, teachers may find that particular themes or characteristics of the puppets or puppet play (i.e., violence, suicide, homicide, substance abuse, self-degradation, etc.) indicate a need for a referral to a qualified mental health provider for assessment or intervention.

In the following chapter, the terms therapy and therapeutic, are used broadly. The range of therapeutic applications of puppetry is still being expanded and the field is in a constant state of being defined. The qualifications and credentialing required for people to practice some form of therapeutic puppetry is variable depending on the setting, although most practitioners in hospitals or formal clinical settings have advanced degrees, certifications or licenses in clinical specialties such as art therapy, drama therapy, professional counseling, social work, child life, etc.

# References

Aronoff, M. (1994). Introducing puppets in preparation. *Cascade,* 10-11.

Aronoff, M. (1996). Puppetry as a therapeutic medium: An introduction. *British Journal of Therapeutic Rehabilitation, 3,* 210-214.

Aronoff, M. (Winter, 1997). Therapy. *The Puppetry Journal, 25.*

Axline, V. (1947/1969). *Play therapy.* New York: Ballentine.

Bender, L. (1952). *Child psychiatric techniques.* Springfield, IL: Charles C Thomas.

Bender, L. & Woltmann, A. (1936). The use of puppet shows as a therapeutic method for behavior problems in children. *American Journal of Orthopsychiatry, 6,* 341-354.

Bernier, M. (1983). *Puppetry as an art therapy technique with emotionally disturbed children.* Unpublished master's thesis, Hahnemann University, Philadelphia, PA.

Bernier, M. (1990). *Psychopuppetry.* Unpublished manuscript, Eastern Virginia Medical School, Norfolk, VA.

Bernier, M. (2003). *Puppet Playback Theatre.* Unpublished manuscript, Eastern Virginia Medical School, Norfolk, VA.

Cassell, S. (1965). Effect of brief puppet therapy upon the emotional responses of children undergoing cardiac catheterization. *Journal of Consulting Psychology, 29,* 1-8.

Chiles, D. (2001). The therapeutic use of puppetry in a health care setting. *National Festival Workshop Manual: 2001 A Puppet Odyssey.* Puppeteers of America.

Chiles, D. (2005). http://www.hospitalpuppet.com

Cole, N. A. (1993). *Lend them a hand: Therapeutic puppetry.* R.R. #2, Milford, Ontario, Canada, KOK 2PO: Arthur Cole.

Dorfman, E. (1951). Play therapy. In C. R. Rodgers (1965). *Client-centered therapy.* Boston: Houghton Mifflin.

Fox, J. (1986). *Acts of service: Spontaneity, commitment, tradition in the nonscripted theatre.* New Paltz, NY: Tusitala.

Gendler, M. (1986). Group puppetry with school-age children: Rational, procedure and therapeutic implications. *The Arts in Psychotherapy, 13,* 45-52.

Gerity, L. (1999). *Creativity and the dissociative patient: Puppets, narrative, and art in the treatment of survivors of childhood trauma.* London: Jessica Kingsley.

Horovitz, E.G. (2002). *Art therapy and speech/language therapy: An interdisciplinary approach* [video]. (Available from Julia Productions Inc., Rochester, NY, www. arttxfilms.com.)

Horovitz, E.G. (2003). *Paddle to the sea: A psychopuppetry film* [video]. (Available from Julia Productions Inc., Rochester, NY, www.arttxfilms.com.)

Irwin, E. (1983). The diagnostic and therapeutic use of pretend play. In C. Schaefer & K. O'Connor (Eds.). *Handbook of play therapy* (pp.148-173). New York: John Wiley & Sons.

Irwin, E. (1993). Using puppets for assessment. In C. Schaefer & D. Cangelosi (Eds.). *Play therapy techniques* (pp. 69-81). New Jersey: Jason Aronson.

Irwin, E. & Malloy, E. (1975). Family puppet interview. *Family Process, 14,* 179-191.

Irwin, E. & Shapiro, M. (1975). Puppetry as a diagnostic and therapeutic technique. In I. Jakab (Ed.). *Psychiatry and Art, 4.* New York: Karger.

Irwin, E., Rubin, J., & Shapiro, M. (1975). Art and drama: Partners in therapy. *American Journal of Psychotherapy, 29,* 107-116.

Kors, P. (1963). The use of puppetry in psychotherapy. *American Journal of Psychotherapy, 17,* 54-63.

Kors, P. (1964). Unstructured puppet shows as group procedure in therapy with children. *Psychiatric Quarterly Supplement, 38*(1), 56-75.

Kunsden, W. W. (1984). Psychopuppetry, non-directive group play therapy using puppets as the intermediary object: A comparison with traditional non-directive group counseling or no counseling in the treatment of emotionally handicapped elementary school children. *Dissertation Abstracts International, 48.* (DA 8425281)

Linn, S. (1977). Puppets and hospitalized children: Talking about feelings. *Journal of the Association for the Care of Children in Hospitals, 5*(4), 5-11.

Linn, S. (1978). Puppet therapy in hospitals: Helping children cope. *Journal of the American Medical Women's Association, 33*(2), 61-65.

Oaklander, V. (1978). *Windows to our children* (pp.104-108). Moab, UT: Real People Press.

Oatman, K. (1981). *Breaking through the barrier.* Willowdale, Ontario, CA: Ontario Puppetry Association Publishing Co.

Petrillo, M. & Sanger, S. (1980). *Emotional care of hospitalized children: An environmental approach.* Philadelphia: Lippincott.

Renfro, N. (1984). *Puppetry, language, and the special child: Discovering alternate languages.* Austin, Texas: Nancy Renfro Studios.

Salas, J. (1993/1996). *Improvising real life: Personal story in Playback Theatre.* Dubuque, IA: Kendall/Hunt.

Schneider, F. (1976). Puppetry as preparation for surgery. *Puppetry Journal, March/April,* 3-8.

Sommers, S. (1977). Marionette making and self-awareness. *American Journal of Art Therapy, 16*(2), 51-53.

Steinhardt, L. (1994). Creating the autonomous image through puppet theatre and art therapy. *The Arts in Psychotherapy, 21*(3), 205-218.

Sullivan, D. (1982). *Pocketful of puppets: Activities for the special child with mental, physical, and multiple handicaps.* Austin, Texas: Nancy Renfro.

# CHAPTER 20

## PUPPETRY AS A THERAPEUTIC MEDIUM: AN INTRODUCTION
## Mickey Aronoff

### Abstract

This article introduces puppetry's history and role in the therapeutic milieu, primarily with children, but also with adults; how, why, and in what situations it is effective, including current examples of practice drawn mainly from the author's own practice, begun in hospitals in the U.S. in the early 1970s.

### Introduction

As more and more people in the therapeutic arena turn to the creative, expressive arts as tools for empowerment and transformation, therapists wishing to incorporate puppetry into their fields of practice need professional education in puppet theatre arts in order to know how to use and transfer puppetry skills to best effect.

Therapeutic puppetry, in its simplest - and most obvious - definition, is the use of puppet theatre arts in therapy. To examine puppetry's usefulness in therapy, we must first look at its history and form.

Prehistoric evidence shows that ritualistic puppet practice precedes theatrical use (Robertson, 1992). Worldwide, shamans still use puppets as spiritual guides, as storytellers, as mediators between the gods and people, to reflect on universal or personal conditions, or in the healing process. Examples are given on the Native American tradition by Geertz and Lomatuway'ma (1987); on Balinese practice by Chaplin (1994); and on practice in Africa, as shown by Dagan (1990).

## What is performance puppetry?

A puppet is an inanimate object. Many types of puppets - rod, glove, finger, marionette, shadow, body, giant, object - stem from many traditions. Subtypes, combinations and differences exist; puppets must always be designed for specific use - for ease of handling and for symbolizing meaning.

In performance, the puppet's expression is derived more from movement than from text. Without a puppeteer to provide the human energy behind the object - dramatically animating it for the purpose of communicating with an audience, without the audience to see that movement, the puppet lacks meaning.

Training for the professional puppeteer of excellence can take upwards of 10 years and becomes a lifetime's work. A multi-talented puppeteer may devise all aspects of the performance and work "solo;" specialists may collaborate with up to 50 others.

Presently marginalized within theatre arts (while growing in popularity), puppet theatre is not a "technique" but exists as a creative, expressive art form in its own right. Depending on the degree of complexity, a performance can embrace and incorporate not only puppetry and mime, but art, sculpture, music, drama, dance, scenography, lighting, etc. Good practice and bad practice exist not just in terms of performance technique but also in terms of social and individual responsibility regarding content, as well as images presented and used.

## How Puppetry Works as a Therapeutic Tool

Puppets empower by offering the motivation and the means to make feelings known (Aronoff, 1991). Puppets are visual symbols that, through their body language as well as through text, can offer opportunities for "reading" expression. Puppetry's complexity provides endless tools to the client and to the therapist, synthesizing artistic skills in everyone, whatever their level of development, expertise or aesthetic taste. Clients thus have more at their disposal to aid with self-projection and the trying on of new identities than they would with a single art form. Manipulating a puppet may not be to everyone's taste or disposition, but there luckily remains the business of script writing, prop building, etc. In short, there is something for everyone. Access is universal, holistic.

Puppets protect: what is expressed can be denied and blamed on the puppet, so that inner emotional worlds are revealed in non-threatening ways. Renfro (1984) speaks of puppets as "socially acceptable outlets." Psychotherapists refer to Winnicott's theories of play (1971) and speak of the puppet's ability to act as a transitional object. As projective media, puppets free the capacity for self-expression, allowing people to rehearse feelings before "owning" them. In the case of selective mutism, puppets may even act as advocates for children (Cole, 1993).

As Wilson et al. (1992) have shown there are many different approaches to child psychotherapy. Within these different approaches, puppets provide standard play therapy material. Irwin (1983) outlines the roots of pretend play in the course of child development and its diagnostic and therapeutic use in the treatment of children. McMahon (1992) shows the development of play across many areas: sensory/creative, physical, exploratory, social and symbolic. Because puppet theatre arts offer a never-ending range of materials, themes and ways to work, it can deftly fit across all these categories.

With all these tools at hand, many stories arise through play. Play may be based on reality or fantasy; a sensitive therapeutic process will help determine this. Content may not reflect what is happening in a child's life but may reveal a child's preoccupations. Oster et al. (1988) report, "A story based on personal experience may hold greater significance for understanding the individual, but even stories based on popular culture may reveal important interests and attitudes."

Witnessing someone's immediate and obvious delight and pride in putting feeling and life into a previously lifeless object, one can observe how readily empowering animating a puppet can be. Self-esteem can be seen to be raised as soon as a puppet speaks or moves; further action and development are likely to occur. It is a self-encouraging process.

The client-puppeteer, whether in individual therapy or group work, can be seen to be director, actor and audience simultaneously. Here, puppetry's

advantage over other methods is its safe indirectness: one can "rehearse" for "real" life by first focusing on the puppet and what that puppet can do. When puppets help release and tell stories, they act as vehicles for change in personal and social situations.

Aronoff (1992) speaks of puppet making and performance in group work, where critical sensitivity develops with learning and reinforcement. Through informed choice and experimentation, project work creates the habit of decision-making, stretching intelligence. Experimentation with new ideas is empowering, offering metaphors that clients can build on. New identities are tried on, and self-expression gives the opportunity for discussions and for sharing feelings within a group.

When puppetry is not linked to work or retraining, it can be perceived as unique - not as a consolidation of past experience. It therefore provides a less stressful medium "than retraining" through which people can practice old skills and test their current competencies. Physically, puppetry can improve voice and fine motor skills, concentration and memory. Mostly, puppetry is enjoyable, creating a non-threatening atmosphere within which trusting relationships can be formed and social isolation is diminished.

## Who uses puppets for self-expression?

As opportunities for using puppetry increase, more adults are taking advantage of the medium and do so in individual or group therapeutic situations. Children, however, are the most likely to want to use (and to be offered!) puppets, although not all children elect to use them. However, when a therapist is skilled and uses puppetry engagingly, clients (children or adult) are more likely to want to participate. Physical disabilities should not be a factor preventing puppet play when puppets are designed to accommodate. However, one must respect a person's wish not to enter into play because of pain, tiredness, lack of self-esteem, or any other reason.

Emotional and physical development are taken into consideration when using puppets. In child psychotherapy, as Irwin (1983) shows, some children's inability to play may reflect complex problems. Indeed, there may be contraindications for using play therapy at all, as shown by West (1992). For example, some children may have psychoses and the inability to distinguish fantasy from reality.

## Who practices therapeutic puppetry?

As training opportunities and exposure to puppetry increase, more therapists can incorporate puppetry into their practice. Therapeutic puppetry practice differs, depending, of course, on the practitioner's culture, time, context, training, etc. Acceptance by the community-at-large, however, remains a problem as knowledge of this fairly new field remains scant.

Full-time Western therapeutic puppetry practitioners are rare; the field is fairly new, and to be well grounded in therapy and puppet theatre arts is a lengthy process. Many part-time users of the puppet are found in the fields of psychotherapy, play therapy, social work, speech therapy, occupational therapy, health education, drama therapy, and puppetry in special needs work. The little therapeutic puppetry training that exists normally trains for the use of the puppet as an effective medium for those already working in therapeutic settings. Given receptive situations, one can, however, "grandmother" oneself into the work and pioneer new ground, as in the author's case, for whom early therapeutic training involved casework in protective services to children and therapeutic puppetry in pediatric teaching hospitals. Resources world-wide available to those wanting training in the use of the puppet include more than 50 centers dedicated to puppetry and as many training schools, puppet theatre productions, workshops, conferences, 150 puppetry festivals yearly, and 9,000 books on the subject across many languages.

## Examples of Practice

Because it can be used as a tool for counseling, education, physical strengthening and/or recreation, areas of practice are infinite. As Woltmann (1960) and Irwin (1993) have shown, puppetry is used in areas of psychotherapeutic assessment and treatment of children. Projective, symbolic play is important, as children cannot always be direct.

Debbie Jans, a Scottish speech therapist, in 1992, described to me her work with children too young to use a mirror for learning, demonstrating how they could instead mimic mouth movements made by a wide-mouthed puppet with pronounced tongue, teeth, tonsils and uvula. Learning of prepositions can be reinforced by animating them with puppet movements. At a 1992 conference in Krasnodar (Aronoff, 1994), I heard Russian speech therapists speak of their collaboration with state puppet theatres, finding that when some youngsters manipulated puppets, stuttering disappeared.

My own clinical experience spans diverse client groups and service settings through employment as a play therapist, a puppet therapist, and currently as a special needs puppetry consultant. The following examples come from my own casework.

- Children on a psychiatric assessment unit push through fears and insecurities and strong individual needs to participate in group puppetry projects. Learning, making, manipulating, and performing all give opportunities for self-expression. As these are practiced, self-esteem is raised; children who initially refuse to participate or enter into puppetry activity go on in subsequent sessions to perform. Staff members are provided another assessment mode for social and communication skills in the client group, while learning and developing specialized play skills.

- In working on areas of grief with children facing life-threatening illness, puppets help release the voice that tells the stories children need to tell in order to share the pain of their loss (Aronoff, Dec. 1994 - Jan. 1995).

- Puppets help prepare children for medical procedures and surgery, and they help release feelings associated with this. Hospitals are strange and stressful places and may disempower children. Fear freezes language, and children may imagine a causal relationship between what they think and what happens to them. Linn (1978) states children feel unsafe expressing anger to medical personnel, thinking this may provoke an injection.

  Used interactively, puppets help release emotions having to do with fears relative to treatment. Once fear is minimized, children can be educated, and coping skills can be taught. Self-esteem and confidence are raised as children role-play what they undergo in reality. One eleven-year-old girl with whom I worked was embarrassed to cry during lumbar punctures. Through practice with puppets she reached her own goal - to relax enough so that she could stay calm during procedures.

- In the hospital, recreational puppetry, involving and incorporating puppet making and/or performance, provides distraction from the more serious medical/surgical side of hospitalization. Plays can have themes that avoid or playfully incorporate hospital-related issues; either provides release. Thus, the fun relief that craft and the giving of shows offer is therapeutic as well.

- In a high security prison, prisoners in a pre-release program have the opportunity to learn how to resolve personal issues assertively rather than aggressively, using puppets in a fun and relaxed atmosphere.

- In a center for adults who are wheelchair users, clients wrote poems related to issues of disability, fleshing them out using shadow puppetry. Testing of new skills, working symbolically, and performing for the community raised self-esteem enormously.

- In a special school for children with profound and complex learning and physical disabilities, a topic about insects motivated a child to exercise his arms while buzzing his bee puppet between flower and hive.

- Young adults with epilepsy bonded in weekend-long puppetry projects and devised humorous sketches based on issues important to them.

## Key Points

- Puppetry is an art form in its own right that has historical and transcultural roots.
- Puppetry can provide an effective expressive medium for use in therapy.
- The therapeutic puppetry practitioner needs to be effective with both therapy and puppetry.

- Western cultures are more familiar with the "passive entertainment" aspect of puppetry, whilst an "active participant" role offers several therapeutic opportunities.
- Therapeutic puppetry facilitates communication in many ways.

## Issues Arising

- The need to establish training.
- There remains the challenge of pursuing therapeutic puppetry work in clinical institutions where the management and organizational structure can work against the practice of creative therapy.
- There is a need for adequate supervision of therapeutic and puppetry practice to ensure sustained quality of service.
- There is a need for more research.

## Conclusion

Puppets can do things and change in ways people can't. This transformational quality is also what puppets offer to people: they can help people do things they can't do unaided in self-exploration, self-expression, and individual or social change. Puppets enable access - access to one's inner life, thought processes, creativity and social contact; language is extended. Renfro (1984) reports that the puppet's power is to be found in its visual form that "exists on an animated plane;" it is through the integration of the visual and verbal aspects of this medium that language takes on a new dimension.

The puppet is a powerful tool. Since the puppet can be blamed for what is expressed (thereby absolving the puppeteer from all responsibility), the deepest of feelings can surface; clients may not even realize how much they may have disclosed or uncovered for themselves. This process can be an aid in therapy if the therapist is sufficiently sensitive and skilled.

A lot can be learned from puppets used just as a "talking tool," but they are much more than mere mouthpieces. When the scope of puppetry activity widens to encompass puppet making and performance, clients have an increased chance for expression and therapists a greater chance to understand and guide clients. The greatest gifts a therapist can offer a client are a map with many roads and vehicles for traveling. That, coupled with clients being offered choices (and control within their choices), is necessary to ensure that the creative process can become a healing one. Sharing fundamentals of communication and transformation, puppets and therapy are well matched. When the powers of speech and gesture are stripped away, puppets can help return them, along with dignity and self-worth.

## References

Aronoff, A. (1991). Puppets for change. *Animations, 56,* Feb./Mar.

Aronoff, A. (1992). A soul in the palm of a hand. *Therapy Weekly, 19*(10), 8.

Aronoff, A. (Dec. 1994 – Jan. 1995). Unmasking our grief. *Scottish Child, 11.*

Aronoff, A. (Sept.1994). Introducing puppets in preparation. *Cascade, 13,* 10-11.

Aronoff, M. (Nov.1994). Reflections on Russian therapeutic puppetry (Part I). *British UNIMA Bulletin, 87,* 26-30.

Aronoff, A. (Autumn 1994). Scottish Mask & Puppet Centre. *Disability News,* 45-46.

Chaplin, E. (1994). *Sociology and visual representation (*pp. 207-212). London: Routledge.

Cole, N. (1993). *Lend them a hand: Therapeutic puppetry (*p. 32*).* Box 45, Milford, Ontario, KOK 2PO, Canada.

Dagan, E.A. (1990). *Emotions in motion: Theatrical puppets and masks from black Africa.* Montreal: Galerie Amrad African Arts.

Geertz, A. & Lomatuway'ma, M. (1987). *Children of Cottonwood: Piety and ceremonialism in Hopi Indian puppetry.* Lincoln & London: University of Nebraska Press.

Irwin, E. (1983). The diagnostic and therapeutic use of pretend play. In C. Schaefer & K. O'Connor (Eds.), *Handbook of play therapy* (pp.148-173). New York: John Wiley & Sons.

Irwin, E. (1993). Using puppets for assessment. In C. Schaefer & D. Cangelosi (Eds.), *Play therapy techniques* (pp. 69-81). New Jersey: Jason Aronson.

Linn, S. (1978). Puppet therapy in hospitals: Helping children cope. *Journal of the American Medical Women's Association, Feb.,* 62.

McMahon, L. (1992). *The handbook of play therapy.* London: Routledge.

Oster, G., Caro, J., Eagen, D. & Lillo, M. (1988). *Assessing adolescents.* New York: Pergamon Press.

Renfro, N. (1984). *Puppetry, language, and the special child: Discovering alternate languages.* Austin, TX: Nancy Renfro Studios.

Robertson, A. (1992). *Museum of automata.* York: Tower Street.

West, J. (1992). *Child-centred play therapy.* London: Edward Arnold.

Wilson, K., Kendrick, P. & Ryan, V. (1992). *Play therapy: A non-directive approach for children and adolescents.* London: Ballière-Tindall.

Winnicott, D.W. (1971). *Playing and reality.* London: Tavistock.

Woltmann, A. (1960). Spontaneous puppetry by children as a projective method. In A. Rabin & M. Howarth (Eds.). *Projective techniques with children* (pp. 305-312). New York: Grune & Stratton.

# CHAPTER 21

## PSYCHOPUPPETRY:
## ANIMATED SYMBOLS IN THERAPY

### Matthew Bernier

When therapeutic puppetry is provided in the context of psychotherapy, it is sometimes referred to as psychopuppetry (Bernier, 1990; Horovitz, 2002, 2003; Kunsden, 1984). Typically, versions of this approach are offered by mental health professionals such as creative arts therapists (art, dance/movement, music, poetry, drama), psychodramatists, play therapists, psychologists or social workers. Puppetry is an integration of art forms and usually, psychopuppetry combines principles and techniques from art therapy, play therapy, drama therapy, psychodrama, and of course the puppetry arts.

As an art therapist, my work has naturally included the art process and products of puppetry; making the puppets and exploring the symbolic meaning of the puppets. However, since my background before art therapy, in addition to psychology, was also in theatre arts and puppetry, it was natural for me to begin to see the possibilities of integrating the modalities of play, creative dramatics, movement, and mask work into my practice of art therapy and psychopuppetry.

In art therapy, the clients are engaged in their own puppet making and the puppets are then used in structured or spontaneous puppet play activities designed to meet specific therapeutic goals (Bernier, 1983; Gerity, 1999; Sommers, 1977; Steinhardt, 1994). Essential to this approach is the idea that puppets can be made as an extension or representation of the self, parts of self, or aspects of others or of the environment.

Puppets are sometimes made as conscious self-representations or representations of others, but more often, puppet characters emerge that embody unconscious dynamics or parts of self that are not as easily or openly expressed. For instance, a shy person can create an extroverted character. A contained person can create an angry character.

Psychopuppetry can be practiced according to a variety of psychotherapy approaches such as psychodynamic, Jungian, imaginal, gestalt (Oaklander, 1978) and cognitive behavioral. Due to the integrative nature of puppetry, most clinicians are likely to use an integrative approach. Psychopuppetry techniques can be used with individuals, groups, couples, or families.

In all of the various versions and applications of therapeutic puppetry or psychopuppetry, puppets serve as animated symbols. It is important for clinicians to understand the theories about symbolism as they attempt to understand the symbolic language of their clients as expressed through their puppets, puppet play, behaviors, and verbal associations.

Symbolism has been studied extensively (i.e., Deri, 1984; Fromm, 1951; Jung, 1964) and its role in psychotherapy and the fostering of "good mental health" (Deri, 1984) is an important one. Symbols help us make sense of the world, connecting our inner and outer realities. Anything in our outside world can become symbolic. Symbols carry meaning and have feelings attached to them. Some symbols have universal meaning such as mother, birth, loss, and death. Other symbols have very personal meaning. Personal experiences or parts of those experiences may be stored mentally as symbols and may be triggered or retrieved by external symbols. When symbols are animated, as in puppetry, they take on even more of a life of their own with multi-leveled meanings, which can become integral parts of the therapeutic process. Everything that occurs in psychopuppetry can be understood symbolically.

While working as an art therapist at a shelter for victims of domestic violence, I used psychopuppetry as a means for the children to express and explore the unspeakable stories of their lives. Working with children, as young as two years old, and others who simply either didn't have the language to describe their experiences or feelings, or were too afraid to tell, puppetry and dramatic activity proved to be very effective.

Sometimes the puppetry work would emerge out of other artwork such as drawings about violence or abuse or family life in general. Whenever there was a story to be told and characters who needed to express themselves, puppets served the purpose. Other times, the children would specifically ask to create puppets or to engage in puppet play with the puppets they had already made.

Typically, I prefer to encourage the use of simple and familiar materials to begin puppet making. Paper bag, sock, box and bottle head puppets are constructed easily within an art therapy session and can be ready quickly for dramatic action. In cases where I could work more long-term, and when the child had the necessary developmental abilities, we would construct puppets from papier mache and fabric.

Almost every child I worked with at the shelter made a puppet, and many made more than one. Sometimes puppets transformed into new puppet characters and the children were free to modify their puppets accordingly. Empowerment and self-control were always fostered in the process. Sometimes, when children "finished" their work with their puppets or when they left the shelter without taking their puppets with them, these orphaned puppets were adopted by new children to use in their work. Symbolically, the children were constantly making "order out of chaos" and beauty out of "damages goods."

One day, Jimmy, an 8-year-old Caucasian boy appeared at the art room door holding a pair of worn out socks. He asked if he could make a sock puppet, having seen puppets the other children had made. He was surprised to learn that not only could he make his own puppet, but that I had a ready supply of socks and other materials for him to use. He did not have to use what was perhaps his only pair of socks brought with him to the shelter.

Jimmy was invited to attend an art therapy group with several other children. During the session, Jimmy made a simple sock puppet with a face crudely drawn on with markers. He attached long strips of cloth for arms and two found hands from a "parts box" that I kept on hand. Along the length of the arms, Jimmy drew several red dots.

His peers began to become interested in what he had done and one spoke up saying, "Your puppet has the chicken pox!" "No," said another boy, "it's the measles." "You're both wrong," declared Jimmy. "They're bullet holes!" Jimmy proceeded to use his puppet to tell the story of how he, his mother and younger bother and sister came to the shelter. His father had a gun and put it to Jimmy's head, telling his wife, "Don't even think about leaving me or I will use this gun to kill one of you." Apparently, prior to that, Jimmy's father had flashed his gun around the house saying that he had to have the gun to protect himself from the "bad guys." Jimmy was truly confused who the bad guy was after repeatedly seeing his father abuse his mother. Shortly after that incident, Jimmy's mother took her children and found their way to the shelter.

The children were eager to use their puppets in puppet play. They took turns telling their stories, casting them from each others puppets or the existing puppets in the room, and playing out their scenes. The unspeakable truths about domestic violence, child abuse, and substance abuse were safely spoken and dramatized through puppetry.

Upon leaving the art room, one of the non-clinical staff members saw the children leaving with their puppets. She exclaimed, "Oh how cute! You made puppets today." She didn't seem to notice that these weren't just any ordinary puppets and she certainly didn't realize the stories that had just been acted out were far from cute. The children didn't seem to mind. They had successfully used their puppets and puppet play symbolically and therapeutically and were able to put closure on that work for now.

Psychopuppetry involves many psychological concepts with implications for therapeutic puppetry. The following are some examples of these concepts and their symbolism implications.

## Psychological Concepts with Implications for Therapeutic Puppetry

**Developmental Levels:** When performing puppet shows for an audience or when engaging people in their own puppet making and puppet play, it is important to remember that individuals of each age group tend to function at different levels of development in various areas of functioning including: physical, cognitive, emotional, sexual, social, artistic, etc. Developmental levels can vary within an age group depending on factors such as intelligence, experience, socialization, physical exercise, and exposure to factors such as: creative expression, cultural activities, violence, etc. Individuals can often be challenged to participate in puppetry that encourages higher levels of functioning. However, they should not be expected to grasp concepts or to perform skills for which they are not yet developmentally ready.

**Control/Self-Control:** Healthy parents help their children to develop self-control (impulse control) by teaching them to conform to the rules of the family and of society. The development of self-control involves the sense of will, responsibility, and competence (as in toilet training) (Erikson, 1978). In child development, children learn that it is exciting and interesting to attain mastery over their body and gain approval by their parents by the display of new abilities such as toilet training and tying their shoes. This self-control eventually is generalized to other behaviors such as the regulation of aggression and the use of manners and appropriate self-expression. An adaptive result is a sense of personal control over the body, its movements, and its products and a sense that one is in accord with the family and society. Maladaptive outcomes include the feelings of shame and self-doubt which are then reflected in associated dysfunctional behaviors and symptoms (Erikson, 1963; Newman & Newman, 2003).

Children initially behave in ways which reflect their efforts to gain parental approval and they place responsibility and blame on external forces for meeting or not meeting their needs. This is sometimes referred to as external locus of control (Rotter, 1966). Eventually, children develop some degree of an internal locus of control as they recognize their ability to shape their own lives, meet their own needs and create or perform for their own self-approval and personal satisfaction (Rotter, 1966).

In puppetry, the puppets are created by the artist out of raw materials. This process requires motivation, imagination, frustration tolerance, and impulse control. The artist selects the type of puppets to be made, the materials, and the construction methods. More successfully constructed puppets are the result of a greater degree of self-control used in the puppet making process.

The completed puppets are lifeless objects until someone controls them. Depending on the type of puppet, the control takes place from below (rod), inside (hand), above (marionette) or from behind (table-top rod, bunraku, shadow). Even the sticks that marionette strings are attached to are called the controller. The process of learning to manipulate puppets effectively presents opportunities to exercise, relax, practice, or modify control, self-control and locus of control.

The puppeteer is symbolically in control of the imaginary characters and their stories as well as the world in which they live. Puppetry provides metaphors for variations of control and opportunities to practice degrees and styles of control which may be associated with various roles (i.e., parent, child, villain, or hero). Even variations in movement of the puppet character are the result of degrees of control used in manipulation of the puppet.

Puppet manipulation can offer opportunities to practice modulation and control of efforts (energy force from within) (Laban, 1960) and shapes (body configurations in space (Lamb, 1965) of movement. Laban described the effort dynamics of movement as:

Space: direct/indirect
Weight *(force)*: strong/light
Time: quick/slow *(sustained)*
Flow: bound/free

Lamb defined shape in terms of three factors:

1. Its flow determined by changes between body parts towards or away from each other
2. Its direction being the paths that movement makes in space
3. Shaping, which is the adaptation or molding of movement *(contained, expansive, etc.)*. (Halprin, 2003, p. 61)

These factors are ways in which inner impulses and energies are manifested in movement; either consciously or unconsciously controlled.

The puppeteer usually consciously controls the puppet. However, when the puppeteer client/patient is regressed, aggressive, sexually provocative, etc., there is the possibility for self-control to be dismissed in favor of acting-out behaviors which can be blamed or projected onto the puppet. The therapist must allow for some degree of loss of control in the creative process, while at the same time providing adequate structure and limit setting to encourage a productive and satisfying outcome as well as self-growth. What the puppet learns to do, the client learns to do as well. When the puppet is in control, the client is in control.

**Metaphor/Symbolic Expression:** In spontaneous puppet play, puppets can take on any role, either real or symbolic as determined by the puppeteer. Also, puppets can play realistic roles that are representations or metaphors for something else. For instance, the police officer puppet can be a metaphor for parental authority, while the lost puppy may be symbolic of the child. Inanimate or non-human objects can be symbolically personified as they represent real life.

In puppetry, any object that can be manipulated with movement can be used symbolically to represent something. Symbols stand for something else not present, but they also have feelings associated to them and they carry meaning (Deri, 1984; Jung, 1964). Puppetry, as do other forms of theatre, asks the viewer to suspend reality and to enter into an imaginary and symbolic world. Even though the viewer knows consciously that the puppet is only cloth or wood, the puppet and the puppet show can be evocative (evokes feelings) or provocative (stimulates thoughts or actions) because the symbolic connections are so strong.

**Intermediary Object:** In therapeutic puppetry sessions, puppets can be used to gain the attention of the clients, especially when they are avoidant, anxious or withdrawn. Puppets can serve as a valuable means of communication between the therapist and the client when the client is unwilling or unable to focus attention on the situation. Clients often respond to questions from the puppet that they do not respond to when asked directly by the therapist (Rojas-Bermudez, 1969).

Resistance can be attributed to the fear of being invaded or penetrated by the therapist asking questions. The puppet becomes useful in therapy because it is innocuous and does not have all of the human characteristics which might cause fear. Puppets can be objects that intermediate between people (Rojas-Bermudez, 1969).

The puppets as "intermediary objects," are able to enter the personal territory without releasing alarm reactions. Puppets can be a means for the patient to respond indirectly to the therapist. They also are useful as a stimulus for the expression of certain unconscious aspects of conflicting behavior. The puppets can take on these roles instead (Rojas-Bermudez, 1969).

**Defense Mechanisms:** Unconscious psychic maneuvers are used to protect against painful feelings such as shame, guilt or anxiety, or fears such as the loss of love, rejection or abandonment (Moore & Fine, 1990). Defenses may delete or distort reality. Examples of defense mechanisms are repression, projection, regression, denial, and avoidance. Defenses are evidenced by various behaviors, verbalizations or symptoms. It is interesting to see manifestations of defenses and/or their sources in spontaneous puppet play.

**Adaptive Regression in the Service of the Ego:** Regression refers to a return to a more developmentally immature level of mental functioning. It is regarded as one of the mechanisms of defense which a person uses when a specific situation is anxiety provoking or uncomfortable (Moore & Fine, 1990). Puppet play often stirs up a tendency for participants to act silly and to lessen ordinary verbal and behavioral inhibitions. It often presents itself as an opportunity to "get away with" doing things that might otherwise not be done in real life because they may cause consequences such as guilt, shame, or restrictions or punishments.

In other words, "it's not me who is acting so strange or inappropriate. It's the puppet doing it." In an effort to effectively express and explore anxiety provoking conflicts or to relax inhibitions in order to unleash creativity, some degree of regression may actually be healthy and necessary. In this case, the regression may be considered adaptive if it serves the goal of building ego strength (Kris, 1952). However, it is only adaptive if the individual is still able to respond to rules of safety and reality and is successfully able to regain self-control and an adequate level of functioning when the puppet play is finished.

In psychopuppetry, the therapist must monitor the degree to which the clients can make use of adaptive regression and must be prepared to provide structure or limit setting when necessary.

**Projection:** Projection is one of the defense mechanisms whereby a personally unacceptable impulse or idea is attributed to the external world (Moore & Fine, 1990). In puppetry, these impulses or ideas can be projected onto the puppet and/or the role it is playing, or they can be projected onto someone or something else by way of the puppet. The puppet serves as a vehicle for projection and thereby as a method of providing self relief or a sense of safety.

In therapeutic puppetry, this is often seen when puppets are used to carry out terrible or terrifying acts that might be impossible or inappropriate for the puppeteer to do in real life. As described by Hammer (1958) and many others, projection also refers to the mental process of imposing personal associations onto an ambiguous stimulus or form. In puppetry, a certain puppet may be chosen to play a certain role based on who or what that puppet reminds the person of or how it makes the person feel.

**Return of the Repressed:** Repression is one of the defense mechanisms by which an idea or memory is excluded from consciousness in order to protect against the associated painful feelings (Freud, 1926). "If the repressive forces give way, the *return of the repressed* (content) may cause neurotic symptoms, parapraxes (linguistic slips), and related dream content" (Moore & Fine, 1990, p. 167).

The repressed content can also be manifested in artwork, even in the form of unconsciously added characteristics to a puppet. Repressed material frequently shows up in spontaneous puppet play and becomes the content for therapeutic intervention. Repressed content can be stirred up or triggered by external stimuli such as sounds, smells, and visual imagery as in artwork, movies, plays and puppet shows. Adults who had previously been abused as children may experience the return of the repressed after hearing a related story or watching a show. Therapy sessions themselves can stir up repressed content both in the nature of the art and play materials (fabrics, colors, puppets, etc.) and techniques used in therapy and in the dynamics of the therapeutic relationship.

**Repetition Compulsion/Repetition for Mastery:** Some people may be seen to repeat distressing or even painful situations in the course of their lives. Repetition compulsion can also be seen in children's play where the repetitions serve to master the experience of loss or they may relate to the "repetition of various passively experienced traumatic events (Moore & Fine, 1990, p. 165).

In therapeutic puppet play, it is common to see children, for instance, using the puppets to repeatedly act out situations of abuse or accidents as if in an effort to "get it out of their system." Developmentally, repetition for mastery also occurs as part of the learning process as the acquisition of new skills provides a sense of pleasure and competence (Greenacre, 1959; Mishne, 1983).

**Closure:** Closure involves psychologically "putting a lid" on what gets dealt with or "opened up" in the therapeutic session. In order for puppetry activities to be therapeutic, they should provide closure of specific emotional conflicts or particularly disturbing or distressing thoughts. The puppetry activity itself should have a distinct beginning, middle and end. Effective closure includes ending stories and puppet play and the appropriate putting away of puppets, supplies, props, etc. Puppets can have special resting places where they can safely remain until the next time they are needed. Closure can also include specific rituals or routines such as hand washing, closing the curtains of a puppet stage and turning off the lights when leaving the room.

# References

Bernier, M. (1983). *Puppetry as an art therapy technique with emotionally disturbed children.* Unpublished master's thesis, Hahnemann University, Philadelphia, PA.

Bernier, M. (1990). *Psychopuppetry.* Unpublished manuscript, Eastern Virginia Medical School, Norfolk, VA.

Deri, S. (1984). *Symbolization and creativity.* New York: International Universities Press.

Erikson, E. H. (1963). *Childhood and society (2ⁿᵈ ed.).* New York: Norton.

Erikson, E. H. (1978). Reflections on Dr. Borg's life cycle. In E.H. Erikson (Ed.), *Adulthood* (pp. 1-31). New York: Horton.

Freud, S. (1926). Inhibitions, symptoms and anxiety. *Standard edition of the complete works of Sigmund Freud.* London: MacMillan.

Fromm, E. (1951). *The forgotten language.* New York: Grove Press.

Greenacre, P. (1959). Play in relation to creative imagination. *The Psychoanalytic Study of the Child, 14,* 61-81.

Halprin, D. (2003). *The expressive body in life, art and therapy: Working with movement, metaphor and meaning.* London: Jessica Kingsley.

Hammer, E. (1958). *The clinical application of projective drawings.* Springfield, IL: Charles C Thomas.

Horovitz, E.G. (2002). *Art therapy and speech/language therapy: An interdisciplinary Approach* [video]. (Available from Julia Productions Inc., Rochester, NY, www.arttxfilms.com.)

Horovitz, E.G. (2003). *Paddle to the sea: A psychopuppetry film* [video]. (Available from Julia Productions Inc., Rochester, NY, www.arttxfilms.com.)

Jung, C. G. (Ed.) (1964). *Man and his symbols.* New York: Doubleday.

Kris, E. (1952). *Psychoanalytic explorations in art.* New York: International Universities Press.

Kunsden, W. W. (1984). Psychopuppetry, non-directive group play therapy using puppets as the intermediary object: A comparison with traditional non-directive group counseling or no counseling in the treatment of emotionally handicapped elementary school children. *Dissertation Abstracts International, 48.* (DA 8425281).

Laban, R. (1960). *The mastery of movement.* London: MacDonald & Evans.

Lamb, W. (1965). *Posture and gesture: An introduction to the study of physical behavior.* London: Gerald Duckworth.

Mishne, J. (1983). *Clinical work with children.* New York: The Free Press.

Moore, B. & Fine, B. (Eds.) (1990). *Psychoanalytic terms and concepts.* New Haven: American Psychological Association & Yale University Press.

Newman, B. & Newman, P. (2003). *Development through life: A psychosocial approach (8ᵗʰ ed.).* Belmont, CA: Wadsworth/Thompson Learning.

Oaklander, V. (1978). *Windows to our children* (pp.104-108). Moab, UT: Real People Press.

Rojas-Bermudez, J. (1969). The intermediary object. *Group Psychotherapy,22,* 149-154.

Rotter, J. B. (1966). Generalized expectancies for internal versus external control of reinforcement. *Psychological Monographs, 80(1),* (Whole No. 609).

Sommers, S. (1977). Marionette making and self-awareness. *American Journal of Art Therapy, 16*(2), 51-53.

Steinhardt, L. (1994). Creating the autonomous image through puppet theatre and art therapy. *The Arts in Psychotherapy, 21*(3), 205-218.

# CHAPTER 22

## THE PUPPET AS THERAPIST

## Joan Brown

A child is taught not to talk to strangers. Then his mother takes him to a doctor who sticks him with a needle and a dentist whose instruments, even before treatment, are strange and scary. Is it any wonder that a child clams up when his mother brings him to a counselor/stranger?

I'm a mostly retired psychotherapist who has counseled children and their families in private practice and a community mental health center. A new client - whether man, woman, or child - is fearful. What will the therapist ask? What will happen? How long must I come to her office?

During an initial counseling session, just to test my assessment of people, I penned on the corner of my note pad a guess as to what the real problem would be. Many adults need two to three visits before they trot out the reason for seeking guidance.

So imagine a child's worries! Mother wants Tommy to sit on the couch in a room with a stranger and answer every question she asks. He is not to cry and not to lie; except Mother has given Tommy a second message. He is not to tell the therapist about the fights Mommy and Daddy have, or that broken glass was all over the kitchen floor. He is not to say that Daddy paddled his little sister much too hard on Saturday, then slammed the door and wasn't seen for two days. "Just tell the lady about school, how your teacher doesn't help you, and that the principal said you should get some counseling." Poor Tommy!

One of the counselors in my community solves the fear problem by taking children in his car for ice cream—not exactly what I'd call a smart idea! Other counselors have an office full of toys and even a sand box where pretend family members—four inches high and made of plastic—walk around an imaginary town. I thought there had to be a less complicated idea for reaching children, plus I'm not much for sand.

I grew up at the end of the Great Depression and the beginning of World War II. My parents had little to give me in the way of toys, but in those days even rich children had few toys. A Shirley Temple doll was my prized possession. She was so beautiful! Perfect curls; always smiling; dotted Swiss dress; white buttoned shoes. She and I had long talks under an old desk where I did my homework.

One day my mother gave me an empty shoe box and some cloth. "Shirley could use a bed," she said. Shirley liked the bed! But she also needed a chair, a trunk, and a dresser with a "pocketbook" mirror. Soon she had visitors: a brown bear and a bedraggled baby doll. They suggested their friend have a kitchen and a living room. Oh, what marvelous conversations they had! They talked about school and the playground and a black and white cat that disappeared. I dramatized their lives at night in bed; I changed my voice as I spoke for them in the back of my daddy's Chevy; they went with me to Grandmother's house. They were true-blue friends.

Shirley and her buddies were probably lurking in my memories when I began to draw stick figures with a child client. "Look here, Tommy," I would say to a youngster, "this is you at your house. Can you draw your mother? Is she inside or out by the car?" Before long, we had Daddy in the picture, and sister, best friend, and dog.

Still, they were stick figures, the same renderings that Tommy drew at school. Sticks do not talk, do not walk, do not even look like real people. And, while Tommy may be six years old, he is not stupid.

Enter hand puppets! First, a non-specific sex puppet; then a boy puppet, a girl puppet, a mother-type puppet. "Look, Tommy. This is my friend. He lives over there in that bookcase, runs around the building at night when I'm not here. Would you want to try to get him to stop that, convince him to stay in that bookcase when I'm at home asleep?"

Tommy doesn't call the counselor an idiot, because he can see on her face that she's playing some kind of silly game. Besides, he's never held a puppet, so why not go along with the therapist's dopey behavior? "Let me try," he insists, determination mixed with a grin. Before long, Tommy is the puppet, the therapist is inside a second puppet, and they are on page two of the therapy book of change.

Of note is that a child does not feel at fault when a puppet squeals on a family's lifestyle. A puppet (his friend), not the child, tells about the dirty pictures uncle hid behind a dresser and what happened in the shower. There is time later to walk Tommy through ownership, help him to value his role.

In 1998, this counselor locked her door and came home to semi-retirement. Soon I found myself writing children's stories and buying cloth at Wal-Mart. The sewing machine was out every day, next to the buttons, yarn, and sketches. I went around the house being puppet voices, expressing their joy, their concerns. In my head I was creating their houses and furniture. I went to flea markets to find them bicycles and foot lockers. People saw me in my Chrysler van, conversing with no one.

In 2000, "The Puppet People" became a show designed for children ages 3 to 12. The puppets go to schools, Ys, country clubs, libraries, and private homes. Eleven short shows (children have a brief attention span) are available, usually six selected for a specific age or site. Each story offers a moral that a good therapist would offer a child: don't enter the house of a stranger; share what you have with the needy; tell the truth. If a customer wishes, I offer an adjunct course for parents or teachers on how to make simple hand puppets, or a question time when children and puppet/therapist can "analyze" the meaning of the stories:" Why shouldn't we punch someone? Is it okay to reject a classmate because he's a different color? Does Mother know more than I do?"

My quiet goal is to encourage parents to create puppets with their children for pleasure. But a puppet is also an emotional release, a trusted pal and secret-keeper, and an introduction to the essentials of theatre: story, actors, costumes, music, set, and stage.

So the psychotherapist is back in business, except now, advice emerges from 25 surrogate "therapists" who look like people, a snake, three bears, a horse, a mouse, and a very clever talking tree.

# CHAPTER 23

## TRAUMA, PUPPET MAKING, AND NARRATIVE: CREATING MOMENTS OF REPRIEVE

### Lani Gerity

I worked as an art therapist in New York City with a group of patients who were traumatized as children. Because of their experiences of physical, sexual, and psychological trauma when they were very young, a developmental rupture in their sense of self and body image lead to symptoms, defensive strategies, and over time, a variety of diagnoses. As I worked with these patients in an art room, I repeatedly observed this rupture and defensive stance within the artistic expressions of self; artwork depicting separation, dissociation, and aggression towards the self.

What I also noticed was that over time, particularly in the puppet making group, the creative process was being used to repair disturbed body images, to bring together dissociated parts of the self, and to provide the artists with a sense of history, causality, and meaning. Over time, I observed a diminishment of feelings of alienation and estrangement and the encouragement and growth of a stable community; this by a population better known for instability and dissociated sense of history.

In *Women Who Run with the Wolves* (Estés, 1992), Clarissa Pinkola Estés tells a fantastic story of a bone collector, an old woman who gathers bones in a barren landscape, until she has a complete skeleton. As she sings over these bones, the flesh, skin and hair begin to grow back, and life is restored. As fantastic as this story may sound, it tells my experience with this group of artists and the amazing transformations of lumps of papier mache and cloth into magical, animated, little creatures, a room in a dreary inner-city day treatment facility into a land filled with possibility, and the most difficult of patients into warm, generous human beings.

In trying to understand the changes I saw in the artwork and in the stories these patients were beginning to tell, I began to ask myself Murray, Epston, and White's (1992) questions about narrative, which I paraphrased to fit this situation.

- What were these artists' original life experiences?
- What meaning did the artists give these experiences?
- What kinds of narratives did they originally tell about these experiences?
- How did these narratives affect their lives and relationships?
- How did they come to see their experiences in a new way?
- How did they express these new views?
- How did the expression of their new views affect their lives and relationships?

Arthur Frank's (1995) ideas about story telling are also extremely helpful, especially with the question, "What kinds of narratives did they tell?" Frank describes a process of "colonization," in which a patient hands over his or her body and life narrative to someone else; in his book it is usually a "biomedical expert." The individuals I was working with in New York had, as children, been forced into a similar form of colonization by their abusers. As they became adults, they repeated this colonization in their various relationships, in peer and family relations and in their relationships with the psychiatric community. In the process of making puppets with their attached stories, however, the dissociative patient was able to reclaim the authority to tell his or her own story, and to construct a new life narrative from the "wreckage" of their early childhood trauma.

Frank (1995) categorizes life narratives into three types, which we can clearly see in these patients' stories and artwork. He describes one type of story telling as "chaos narrative" in which life events just happen and there is no meaning to be made. Much of the adult survivor's life history was experienced as chaotic, pain filled, events and violations, which were then reflected in the artwork. "Restitution narratives" have a clearer meaning threaded through them. These stories describe attempts to return to a previous state of health or imagined happiness. Patients, who move from chaos narratives in their search for meaning, focus on early abusers or even on the current "colonizer" in their lives. They begin to tell restitution narratives, which can be boiled down to: "If I could only get out of this relationship than everything would be OK."

Frank also describes what he calls a quest narrative, in which illness or life challenges are seen as part of a spiritual journey. This kind of narrative was beyond the experience of most of the dissociative patients until they began to work in the art room, until they began to develop a sense of agency in their own lives. The patients seemed to be able to distance themselves from their problems as they worked on their puppets. They would find artistic challenges, solve these, and see their resolutions in terms of their strengths and abilities. They could then anchor these strengths into the puppets they were working on. It seemed that as improvement could be found in their work and lives, the artists created little markers that could not be denied, and that in fact were often sought out like touch stones of comfort and moments of reprieve.

In the puppet making group, there would be ongoing stories that developed organically, weaving together a tribal history. These hand puppets (very animated, three-dimensional, miniature beings) seemed to easily pull empathy from the hardest hearts. Changes would be documented and remembered in the oral history of the group. Often the original trauma and misfortune could be retold in a more distanced way through the life and struggle of the puppet. This distancing gave them the opportunity to use a part of the mind, which created hope and dreams and new possibilities, a part of the mind that could conceive of life as a spiritual journey. These hopes would then be anchored into the form of the puppet; some new clothing, new hair or a new expression would mark the change.

Although each artist has his or her own amazing story of transformation, I'll tell you Jack's story and the story of his puppet Bogdan. I had often heard Jack say, "Anything could happen in Puppetland," an optimistic statement about the world of imagination, the world of possibilities. He had not always been able to hold such an optimistic view. Jack was an adult survivor of childhood trauma. He told stories of rage and victimization for many, many years. He described his early life as being filled with seductive, unpredictable, often enraged adults: his mother and a series of shadowy, sometimes violent boyfriends.

He had first come to our center in late adolescence. He trusted no one, had little sense of object constancy, and struggled with his sexual identity, alcoholism, and agoraphobia. During the ten years that followed, he developed a reputation as the worst, most hateful, frightening borderline patient one could work with. Psychiatrists dreaded their appointments with him. Jack had been asked to leave every verbal group he'd ever been a part of and every staff member lived in fear that he would be assigned to them. As a kind of therapeutic last ditch effort, it was suggested that Jack try art therapy.

Although the prospect of Jack coming to art groups was intimidating, I showed him where the materials were kept and told him whatever he did in the art room would be all right as long as it was on the paper. He seemed to appreciate having this place where self expression was really allowed, even encouraged. He gradually became a regular in many of the art groups during the week and after many, many pictures of guillotines, bombings, dismembered body parts, and death and destruction, he slowly allowed others within the art room to see a less hostile aspect of himself. At last, he was able to work quietly and expressively, but each piece seemed self contained, each session seemed isolated and removed from the reality of his life, as if the art room were a sanctuary that needed to be kept protected from the danger of the "real world." He would talk about the real world "impinging" on him, and that the art room was his refuge. I hoped to begin to find a way to help him integrate these split off aspects of his life.

When he asked if he could join puppet making, I was delighted, even relieved. I saw from my work with others that this modality provided great potential for integration and a real way to anchor gains and growth. Indeed, it seemed the things Jack and the other group members learned in puppet making could be integrated into their lives. Myths, a sense of history and context were woven around the puppets. Their stories grew or evolved from week to week and the creators would carry the stories beyond the confines of the art room, musing over the meaning while riding the subway or cooking a meal. Jack used images well, expressing much of what had been inexpressible, but now, with the creation of puppets, he could make something else, new stories that could be reflected upon and linked to his "real" life, stories with possibilities.

Through participating in Puppetland adventures, Jack experimented with various parts of himself, with new ways of interacting. He was able to create a narrative to explain his puppet Bogdan's reactions to the world, and from the puppet's story, his own suffering and motivations became clearer to him. He found it easier to talk about the puppet's fears and shame than his own, so he spoke in an empathic way for Bogdan, discovering that within his own imagination lay the magic of possibilities, generosity, and caring. It gradually dawned on him that Bogdan's difficulties were very like his own and that Jack actually felt a great deal better when he found solutions for Bogdan's difficulties.

Bogdan's story begins in the Ukraine, before the days of Stalin. Bogdan had experienced a happy childhood but then came the shadow and cold of the Siberian work camps, which were "unspeakable in their horror." While cutting down trees and suffering from the bitter cold, Bogdan vowed to himself that one day he would be free, that he would be warm and his stomach would be full. Bogdan suffered from memories of a woman in the cell next to his being beaten, tortured, and raped. Part of the horror of the memories was his inability to do anything to help her. Another part of the horror of the story was that this woman was his mother. After telling this aspect of Bogdan's narrative, Jack fell silent for a long time. Bogdan and Jack truly knew the meaning of regret and sorrow.

Jack was fond of saying that Bogdan had a hunter's fire in his heart. He overcame the ice and oppression of Siberia and came to America. Bogdan often "blessed that day," because America was "a land of great opportunity, freedom, goodness, and safety." "You can make a real killing on Wall Street," he was fond of saying with a Ukrainian lilt. The hunter's fire in his heart led him to acquire a sizable import-export business as well as an estate in an area where the boundaries of Long Island and Puppetland overlapped. These triumphs had not taken away the pain and regret from the memories of the work camps, however, so he tried to numb that pain and wall it off with the finest fire-water available, with very little success. Fate, being a capricious thing, had provided him with great suffering as well as the opportunities to learn and thrive, but he would have to be awake to act on these.

In Bogdan's personal story, Jack was able to describe the helplessness and misery of his adolescence. He placed Bogdan in a Siberian work camp where he was forced to suffer physically as well as emotionally, where he was paralyzed in his inability to help his mother. Bogdan's great excitement at finding freedom in America, and on Wall Street, paralleled Jack's gratitude at finding the art room and more specifically the puppet making group. The freedom of expression that he found in that group was, for him, priceless and the ability to tell his own story with enough distance and through this small, animated hand puppet was humanizing.

At last this was a place where Jack felt he could trust others. But in all the most interesting stories I have heard, the hero is put to the test and the story of Puppetland was no different. Jack and Bogdan were about to be tested. This was the day that was later referred to as the day of the Big Hunt. One of the puppeteers, an older woman, had come in to the session looking to create a situation with Jack. We, the group leaders, had been warned and were well prepared. I had brought in a mysterious rod puppet with long black hair and a body of blue fur. Du Rand (Du Rand & Gerity, 1996) decided that her puppet, Ungar, would take Bogdan on a hunt if he was willing, so that Jack would be able to experience his own rage with awareness and containment, and then sublimate it into something that would be useful for the community. The awareness could occur because Jack knew Bogdan was a representation of himself, containment could occur in the enactment of a great hunt, and something positive could be created from the rage because "anything is possible in Puppetland."

Both of the interventions worked very well, the hunt was a great success and Jack seemed genuinely delighted to find this female puppet, which he named Jadwega, immediately picked up, and spoke through. It seemed to provide him with an outlet for a softer voice, a kinder aspect of himself that was something new and unexplored. So, Jadwega, and all she represented, became a reason to stay, a reason to maintain the balance of the group, to avoid a battle "to the death," or the eviction from the group. The hunt provided an outlet for the rage, a socially acceptable one. The tribe was well fed for months to come.

White (1988/9, p. 6) writes about freeing people up to take a lighter, more effective and less stressed approach to "deadly serious" problems. We can see that on the "day of the Big Hunt," Jack externalized his situation, by retelling his story through Bogdan, and this did create a sense of expanded choice and hope.

"Puppetland" was a perfect setting for the unfolding of quest narratives for puppets and puppeteers. These narratives truly belonged to the tellers. They were no longer a meaningless string of events and no longer about being colonized by their abusers or the psychiatric community. They were able to see their lives as their own unique narrative of an unfolding journey. Years after his Puppetland experiences, Jack attributed his feeling better to the reawakening of the ability to dream and hope that had occurred within Puppetland.

Another patient explained the magic that she felt was a part of this puppet making group in this way:

> When I think back to Puppetland I think of bright colors, special music, playfulness, laughter and freedom. And joy...and innocence...and trust. And all those things triumphed, in Puppetland, over the deep anguish, fear and disillusionment that darkened the lives of its human inhabitants. Puppetland lives in my memory as ... a bottomless 'treasure box' filled to the brim with wonderful, mysterious, shiny things that you can explore to your heart's content...lovely little jewels, tiny dolls and figures, interesting pictures, fabulous fabrics. A huge toy store where everything you want is yours already. And Puppetland's celebrations live in my memory as...well...absolute joy.

> ...There have never been any parties to rival Puppetland's celebrations. I know in reality Puppetland consisted of a handful of... emotionally disturbed adults making puppets and dolls with paper, paste, fabric, needle and thread at long wooden tables in a big, somewhat run-down room on the second floor of a day program for mentally ill adults.

But there were two Puppetlands: the external and the internal. And the internal Puppetland transcended everything.

As an art therapist, I see the restorative value of the puppet making and the connected stories as many layered. The first layer lies in the actual puppet making, being on a deep pre-verbal level, a way for people to repair their body image, through art as therapy; through the creation of whole body image representations where they once only created representations of dismemberment and dissociation.

Another art as therapy aspect of this process is the ability and freedom the puppet makers had to mark the learning and wisdom gained, metaphorically, through the changing appearance and embellishments of their puppets. One very clear example of this was an interaction between two finger puppets who each focused on, experiencing the world in one way only. Mr. Mad only saw the world with an angry heart. Wolfie was a very blue dog and only felt sadness. The puppeteers began to wonder about this. Was one right and one wrong? Or what if they had hearts that were of other colors; if Wolfie or Mr. Mad had red hearts they might feel anger, and if they added a yellow heart (since "anything was possible in Puppetland") they might feel joy, while a blue heart would allow for sadness. A blossoming of little felt hearts appeared on many puppets that day.

Often these stories seemed to effect change in a mysterious way. Sometimes the group members would put their puppets down and talk about the subversive qualities of the process, that they could feel things shift and change, but they couldn't figure it out. It seemed also that change could occur as they shared these stories, handing down the group narrative to newcomers as they sat around the metaphorical campfire.

And then there's a sense of community that is created when individuals share a history, stories, and moments of reprieve together; when they listen deeply, with empathy, to these stories. And there's much healing and growth that occurs with this kind of listening. The empathic listening had a way of bringing out warm, generous feelings in the participants and the celebrations were needed to provide a vehicle for people to create gifts for each other.

Puppetland was known for its celebrations. All transitions, leave takings, and special events were marked with music, food, gifts, and laughter. On one of these occasions, a particularly beloved intern was leaving, so the puppeteers brought many gifts of food and artwork. The intern prepared a story of a wise old woman in the forest, who could be visited at any time for wisdom and comfort. The wise old woman had given the intern little beads to give the puppets that would be a kind of guide on their journeys. It seemed the intern had given us a wonderful group myth. Although we were loosing her and her puppet, there was this reparative gift, this archetypal Wise Old Woman that had come to life in story.

Some time went by and it became clear that the group could benefit by the addition of this character, a nurturing, caring, community elder, in puppet form. Once the Wise Old Woman was finished, she was brought to life by the group as a whole. Each member had a chance to hold her or work her, and to listen for something about who she was and what gift she had to give to the individual. We all listened carefully as the puppet was passed around and in this way she developed a kind of group character.

We learned that she had gifts for each of us, that she was 104, and that she lived in an underground hogan or kiva. It was also discovered that she had knowledge of the earth, its herbs, seasons, and life in general. All of the aspects of this puppet were warm and generous. All her gifts were good and simple. From the Wise Old Woman's emergence I learned about the importance of generosity.

At yet another gathering, at the end of another intern's time at our center, the puppeteers were sitting around the art room table. I asked if the puppets could make a list of things they felt they were holding on to and things they felt that they could let go of. A list of the puppets' concerns would be more accessible than individual concerns hidden under layers of resistance and denial. Most of the lists of things being held on to included: fears, emptiness, sadness, reality, and despair. Most of the lists of things that could be let go of were identical. I then asked everyone to turn the paper over and to write down a gift for their puppet, the thing they needed most. Some of the gifts were abstract things like happiness, friendship, and feeling whole. Most were concrete things that would bring the puppet (or puppeteer) happiness: art, maps, dance classes, a ride on the Central Park Carousel, a sapling, a peppermint stick, art supplies, and three wishes for friends.

When the writing was done, Jack asked if he could read the lists and the gifts to the group, without giving the name of the puppet. The group agreed to this suggestion, eager to hear what everyone else had written. When I picked up the pieces of paper after the group was over, I saw that Jack had added additional gifts to all the sheets of paper. He had not read these additions, he was not looking for acknowledgment of what he had done or for the generous feelings he was having towards the group members. They were simply his wishes for the puppet and the puppeteer, and in each case they were strong, wise, and compassionate gifts.

Of all the kinds of groups I ran at this bleak inner-city mental health center, I never found such acts of generosity, such moments of reprieve as I found in this group. I suspected, at the end of this session, that all would be well, that we all had the tools or "guides" we needed to carry on within us.

In looking back over these narratives, and remembering these various puppets and of course the puppeteers, I can see that by looking for the answers to Murray, Epston, and White's questions about narrative have shown us very clearly the ameliorative effects of a group of this kind. The puppeteers began to have new life experiences for themselves through the puppets. The new experiences broadened their view of the world. They expressed this in the unfolding narratives and in the art making aspect of creating and embellishing their puppets. They began to develop empathy for their own puppets and narratives, for their own personal stories and selves, which the puppets represented, and most of all for each other. This was expressed through the celebrations and the giving of gifts in Puppetland.

If I could give you one thing from this experience of Puppetland, it would be that you have an adventurous heart, that if you come upon an opportunity to create puppets and quest narratives for these puppets, you take it and see where the adventure leads you.

## References

Du Rand, L. & Gerity, L. (1996). Puppetry: A collaboration between drama therapy and art therapy. *Dramascope: The National Association for Drama Therapy Newsletter*, *XVI*(2), *Summer/Fall*, 9-10.

Estés, C. P. (1992). *The women who run with the wolves.* New York: Ballantine Books.

Frank, A. (1995). *The wounded storyteller.* Chicago: Univ. of Chicago Press.

Gerity, L. (1999). *Creativity and the dissociative patient: Puppets, narrative, and art in the treatment of survivors of childhood trauma.* London: Jessica Kingsley.

Murray, K., Epston, D. & White, M. (1992). A proposal for re-authoring therapy. In S. McNamee & K.J. Gergen (Eds.) *Therapy as social construction.* London: Sage.

White, M. (1988/9). The externalizing of the problem and the re-authoring of lives and relationships. In M. White (Ed.), *Selected Papers* (pp. 5-28). Adelaide, Australia: Dulwich Centre Publications.

# CHAPTER 24

## FREDDIE AND FRIENDS:
## PUPPETRY AND PLAY IN THE HOSPITAL

### Helene Hugel

For children, the hospital can be an unfamiliar and frightening environment. The beds are unusual and machines are strange; tubing, plastic pouches, nozzles, equipment that sticks to you, sticks into you, and is sticky, and nearly everyone is wearing plastic gloves. The effects of hospitalization on children have been recorded to include fear, anxiety, stress, and harm to a child's future development. According to Save the Children Fund (1989), amongst the elements likely to cause stress are painful procedures, separation from family and friends, and finally, an aspect which I would like to focus on, the alien environment or "Not Knowing their Space" (p. 9).

Both play in the hospital and the arts in healthcare are utilized individually to alleviate the potential effects of the unusual hospital environment for children. Play helps to normalize the environment, "offering an experience of the everyday and familiar in an unfamiliar world" as described by Richard Lansdown in his book, *Children in Hospital* (Lansdown, 1996, p. 65). Art helps by "improving the quality of the health environment by linking art, architecture, and interior design at every opportunity" (Senior & Croall, 1993, p. 4).

How can an artist collaborate and compliment the role of hospital play in providing for the holistic well-being of children in the hospital? All children's hospitals and most pediatric wards in Ireland have created roles for Hospital Play Specialists. The Hospital Play Specialist provides developmental, emotional, and social support for the hospitalized child and their families. Among their many responsibilities, they strive to create a safe and suitable child friendly environment in which the child can learn to "Know their Space." This implies that although the roles of the arts in healthcare and play in the hospital are very different, they are both powerful tools with some common objectives. Hospital Play Specialists are known to utilize both the creative arts and the performing arts in their work and the artist may be striving to enhance and make the hospital environment more child-friendly as well as developing the child creatively and imaginatively.

It has been suggested by a Senior Hospital Play Specialist from the UK that play is a child's language. Through play, children explore and discover the world around them, learning to understand objects, relationships, the environment and themselves, as well as being able to express their feelings and create opinions.

If play is accepted as the child's language, then artists, as Play Specialists, can learn to understand the importance of play, the role of the Hospital Play Specialist and can learn to speak their language. Liisa Piironen, a Professor Emerita of Art Education at the University of Art and Design in Helsinki, has this to say about Play and Art:

> In play and in the arts there are several mutual parameters such as creativity, imagination, transformation, and associative thinking. Play is a motivating element for all ages and it makes possible to move around safely without straining self-esteem in an area where skills and knowledge are not adequate. For this reason, play can be a connecting and integrating element in the making of art. (2003)

## Project

I decided to utilize the language of imaginary play combined with the art of puppetry and explore their potential in the context of a children's hospital. Both imaginary play and puppetry are very powerful tools. Imaginary play, sometimes also known as fantasy play, pretend play, make-believe play, symbolic play, is the natural result of brain development in which the child begins to become capable of representing one thing (symbol) for another, through objects, motions, and eventually language. It is that which enables a child to see an object as something other than what it is.

Puppetry combines both the benefits of the creative and dramatic arts and in particular, has a unique quality to transform perceptions of everyday objects. This is sometimes called object theatre. The transformative power of imaginary play and puppetry became the focus of this residency.

## Presenting Stella

Stella may look a bit familiar. She is a stethoscope. But Stella isn't just a stethoscope. She walks and talks, dances and sings, with help of course.

## Aim

Stella, myself, and our other medical friends like Freddie Cannula and Beeeep aspired to empower the children to transform their clinical hospital environment through puppetry and play. We animated hospital objects, explored the bed as a play space, and also made and played with puppets created from hospital materials.

**Objective**

Our objective was to make hospital equipment more familiar and fun; something of which the children gain mastery and have ownership.

**Setting**

The residency lasted a total of 19 sessions, run once a week, mainly in the playroom on one of the wards which catered to a variety of acute and chronic illnesses, such as cystic fibrosis and renal conditions. The sessions lasted for an hour at a time, scheduled between school and dinner. I was assisted by a hospital play specialist from a neighboring ward who brought over some of her children and also by a 4th year student on placement from Trinity College's Drama Degree Program.

Due to the nature of hospitalization, attendance, age range, and needs were unpredictable and varied. Therefore, the sessions needed to be self-contained, flexible, and adaptable to a broad range of participants. Group sizes varied from four to ten children, including siblings, plus parents and occasional ward staff. Four years and older was the requested age range, with the eldest participant recorded at fourteen years old.

The result was a series of what I would term "play sessions," which attempt to utilize the language of play to develop creative and imaginative skills. That is, they encourage curiosity, spontaneity, exploration, discovery, and mastery. Overall, they are designed to empower the child to transform the clinical nature of their environment. These play sessions all endeavor to draw on my performance, puppet making, and storytelling skills as a puppeteer in which the puppets, like Stella and Freddie, assist in facilitation. Most sessions are structured on an imaginative and flexible story framework which introduces the activity and also encourages and makes time and space for spontaneous and free-play to occur. The story frame-work is flexible and allows for the group's imaginative ideas to directly affect the activity in the workshop. This, in turn, encourages a playful and imaginative environment which is motivating, non-achievement based, and, I believe, contributes to the healing process.

A total of seven sessions were created, tested, and further developed, each one being tried at least twice. Some took place on a one to one basis, at the bedside of the patient, but most occurred in the playroom with a group of children. These seven workshops included:

1. The Magic Toy Box: animating hospital equipment
2. The Bandage Buddies: making sock puppets from hospital materials (using a bandage instead of a sock)
3. Bed-Bugs: using simple mix and match puppets to transform the bed into an imaginative play space
4. Who is Freddie?: making puppets from T-connectors (those little things which attach to the canulla) and giving them character
   (Optional: making a home for Freddie)
5. The X-ray Men: making shadow puppets from old X-rays; also using a lighting box to examine the X-rays

149

6. The Little Spittals: making and playing with finger puppets made from hospital equipment (including syringes)
7. "Beeeeeep": building machines into "walk about" puppet characters I would like to describe in more detail three of the seven play sessions.

## The Magic Toy Box: Animating Hospital Equipment

After the group discovers the Magic Toy Box which makes anything which falls inside come alive, Stella Stethoscope appears from within. She plays with the children and introduces the idea of animating equipment. The children are then encouraged to discover what or who else has fallen into the Magic Toy Box. The equipment is physically transformed using a kit of small and large eyes and hair which the children can attach to their selected piece of equipment wherever they choose. We then play imaginatively, giving our equipment a voice, name, character and personality. The session ends with each piece of equipment starring on Stella's Talk Show.

Some of these characters can be seen in the puppets. An oxygenating mask before the play session is now called Masky, as christened by one patient who in fact had previously received treatment using one of these masks. A nebuliser became a crocodile. A buretrol was transformed into a dragon who lived in Scotland in a river of chocolate. Interestingly, I discovered that each child chose a piece of equipment with which they had had previous medical experience.

## Who is Freddie?: Making Puppets from T-Connectors and Giving them Character

The name "Freddie" is used as a child-friendly term for the cannula and attaching T-connector, which is often inserted into a vein in order to provide easy and less painful access for medication, bloods, or IV drips. The name was coined by a pediatric consultant and has now spread across Ireland and is used by most hospital staff working with children. Receiving a cannula can be a frightening experience for some children and Hospital Play Specialists work through play to prepare and educate children about this procedure. I saw the opportunity to build on both the existing pet-name of Freddie and the familiarizing work of the Hospital Play Specialists.

During this Play Session, children meet a very shy and timid Freddie puppet who is hiding in my pocket. They coax him to come out, only to discover that he is lost and can't remember who he is or where he lives. The children assist Freddie in finding his memory and then make their own Freddie puppets from T-connectors, with the option of making a Freddie home. In general, the children responded very positively to this workshop and again, related to their own experiences of receiving a cannula.

## Beeeeeep

We built a blood pressure monitor machine into a 'walk about' puppet character. Beeeeeep is a hospital machine onto which I have attached a moving mouth. This mouth is designed to be unnoticeable until Beeeeeep finds his voice at the beginning of the play session. As the children entered the play room, they were curious as to why the machine was there. Later, they were surprised when it began to speak. As a group, the children transformed the machine, adding eyes, hair, a nose, and a personality. Then we played games with Beeeeeep, like Simon Says and Copy Cat. These encouraged the children to master a large piece of hospital equipment in a playful manner; controlling a machine which was normally inaccessible.

## Conclusion

So, what was the overall outcome? In general, situations were observed in which children demonstrated an increased sense of association, ownership and mastery over their environment. There were also circumstances in which was recorded a shift in perception of the hospital environment in which the children could be seen and heard to become more familiar with and to Know their Space. To illustrate, I would like to present a few example stories.

## The Story of a Shift in Perception (Drawing of Beeeeeps)

At the end of the first Beeeeeep workshop, the Hospital Play Specialist accompanied her children back to the neighboring ward. As they walked out of one ward, down the long hall and back into the other ward, the children occupied themselves with a game of "eye-spy the blood pressure monitor machine." Look there's a Beeeeeep! Look there's another Beeeeeep. And there, there's Beeeeeep again! Even without his raggy hair and red nose, the image of Beeeeeep, the walking talking hospital machine, was vivid in the children's imaginations.

## The Story of Association and Ownership

During the very beginning of the Who's Freddie play session, while the children passed the Freddie puppet around the circle, one five year old boy began to talk to the canulla attached to his hand and make it talk back. "Look, I have a Freddie too!" he said proudly. "Hello Freddie!" he said. Later, we discovered that his Freddie was the sister of my Freddie Puppet. During the second Who's Freddie play session, another child exclaimed, "Look, I have a Freddie, but with no hair."

## The Story of Empowerment

A buretrol is the piece of equipment which regulates a drip. Initially, I had doubts about putting this piece of equipment into the Magic Toy Box. I thought it appeared less interesting and perhaps too strange or out of context when detached from its tubing. However, I put it in anyway. It was chosen many times by the children. As seen earlier, it became a Dragon for one child. Another girl, aged nine, transformed it into a Tortoise. I interviewed her, and asked her thoughts about this piece of equipment. These were her replies:

I chose it because I knew what it was and it was easy to do stuff with. I knew there wasn't anything dangerous about it and I remembered it from when the nurse (used) it for my antibiotic.

She described the first time she saw one.

> It was scary because the nurse came with a big needle injection thing. The nurse filled it with fluid. I didn't like it because when I first saw it there was a sharp thing. It was scary.

She described how it felt to play with the buretrol.

> I felt kinda shy at the beginning...but as soon as I got the eyes and hair and everything on the tube, I felt better. Not shy anymore.

She commented:

> It looks better (with the eyes and hair) cuz it wasn't scary anymore.

When asked whether she would remember the Tortoise she said,

> Yes, probably, because they use this (the buretrol) to take the pain away after my operation and remembering the Tortoise will take my mind off of it.

## And finally...

After, a Magic Toy Box session, I heard a young boy aged about eight years leave the playroom to tell his mother what he had made. "Anything can be a puppet you know," he said to her.

Among these results, other benefits were observed. These included:

- Increased self-esteem and confidence, for those few children who participated over more than two weeks
- Self-expression and communication
- Socializing
- The puppets provided an opportunity for the children to interact playfully with staff and adults in general.

## Recommendations

This artist's residency not only seemed to benefit the participants and staff involved, but was hugely rewarding, enriching, and inspiring for myself as an artist. I am eager to continue to develop this type of transformative work as well as investigate further opportunities for collaboration between play and the arts within healthcare.

In looking ahead to the future and in considering the aim of some arts in healthcare providers, which is to consider a policy based approach to the Arts and Health in Ireland, I would propose a recommendation. This recommendation is based on my experience of my residency and my parallel training in Hospital Play.

**Training**. Firstly, training should be made available for artists wishing to work with children in hospital. I feel this is hugely important based on my experience of my own parallel training in Hospital Play. It gave me enormous insight into the effects of hospitalization on children, importance of play, and the role of the Hospital Play Specialist. It taught me how to make observations, and to monitor and evaluate my work. I became aware of the workings of a hospital and the development of children. This all greatly informed my work, assisted my relations with hospital staff, made me aware of health and safety, and most of all put me in tune with the hospitalized child.

In particular, it sharpened my understanding of the power of a child's imagination, how to focus its potential, and how to avoid harm by confusing fact and fiction. This is a very important point in relation to transforming hospital equipment.

Secondly, training for Hospital Play Specialists could also include the importance of art and health. Here, students could reflect on the role of Art and Health in children's hospitals. Also, they could consider how art, artists, and art and health organizations can be utilized as a resource to assist the Hospital Play Specialist's role in alleviating the effects of hospitalization, and in creating a more child-friendly environment. This is an opportune time to encourage this topic within Hospital Play Specialist training. The first course of its kind in the Republic of Ireland is to be potentially launched in September 2005.

Through education and awareness, the Artist and the Hospital Play Specialist, can learn how best to complement each other. This, in turn, will create opportunities for collaboration and emerging projects which enrich the fields of both Hospital Play and the Arts in Health and maximize their impact and benefits for the child; both speaking the same language, the child's language, the language of play.

(Editor's Note: In the United States, Hospital Play Specialists are called Child Life Specialists. More information about Arts in Health can be found on the internet by searching for Arts in Healthcare and the Society for the Arts in Healthcare.)

## References

Lansdown, R. (1996). *Children in hospital.* Oxford: Oxford University Press.

Piironen, L. (2003). The power of play in art education. *Centre for Creative* Communities Newsletter, Dec.

Save the Children (1991). *Hospital - a deprived environment for children?: The case for hospital play schemes.* Belfast: Save the Children UK.

Senior, P. & Croall, J. (1993). *Helping to heal: The arts in health care.* London: Calouste Gulbenkian Foundation.

## Acknowledgments
The Children, their Parents and Families
All the Staff on the Ward
The Play Specialist and The Hospital Play Department
The Clinical Engineering Department
The Seamstress
Stores
Nursing Administration
Sarah-Jayne, the 4th year Drama Student
Veronica McGuire

# CHAPTER 25

## STEPPING INTO A PUPPET'S WORLD:
## AN ACCOUNT OF EXPLORING PUPPETRY'S ROLE AS A HEALING ART FORM FOR YOUNG CHILDREN IN A RESIDENTIAL HOME BY A PUPPETEER IN RESIDENCE*

### Helene Hugel

*(Residency Duration: 1 hour a week over 11 weeks, supplemented by staff training. This account will focus on the final stage of the residency.)

Mr. Fox lives in a big house on a hill, surrounded by a deep dark forest, full of traps. Living in the middle of the forest are Mr. Farmer, Mrs. Farmer, and their last chicken, Miss Hen. Up high, above the forest flies Mrs. Swan, who keeps a watchful eye on everyone down below. The small library of the residential home has been transformed into the world of cunning Mr. Fox. His three-level house, made from cardboard boxes, sits at one end of the room surrounded by various textures of green cloth, representing his forest. Hidden under and in and around the cloth are traps: a large onion net, a cage made from a cereal box, ghoul-y large hands, and rope. At a distance from Mr. Fox's house is Mr. Farmer's residence: another box which, after sometime, acquired a high protective cardboard wall and surrounding blue fabric "water." Inside the wall sits Miss Hen on her nest of colorful eggs, which hide a little chick. Mrs. Swan sits near-by on a table, ready to participate. Also around the room, lie puppets made by the children involved with the first half of the residency. The child enters the room for his second session with Mr. Fox. He sees Mr. Fox's house, his forest, and his neighbors and becomes transported through imaginative play into the puppet's world. Both the care-workers and I, the puppeteer, are delighted and amazed at his response.

This scene was co-created by two child-care workers and a puppeteer for use in a series of therapeutic puppetry and play sessions with a young child in out-of-home care. The puppets, their characters, and their story were designed in collaboration with the staff. The puppets, props, and their homes were made by the puppeteer, all to be kept by the home. The key character, Mr. Fox, and his background originated from a brainstorming meeting between the two child-care workers and the puppeteer. At the start of this meeting, it was agreed that the key issues to be addressed were: truth / telling lies, responsibility / consequences, expressing emotions, and self-esteem. The story, Pinocchio, was used as our starting point. It was then decided that the most appealing character to encourage imaginative play around these issues was a fox who was given the following characteristics: trickster/sly/ cunning, thief, quiet, tells "wild" tales, plays pranks, entertainer/charming, and master of disguise.

Based on these ideas, the puppeteer created a story with the above characters and then presented the story, the characters, and the scene to the child using dramatic storytelling, and "audience" interaction and participation during the first play session. The child's reaction was very positive. He was delighted, curious, and captivated by the story and the characters and engaged in spontaneous imaginative play to which the puppeteer and child-care workers responded by playing with him.

Originally the fox and his story were created by the puppeteer and staff to direct the imaginative play to confront the targeted issues. When the child was introduced to Mr. Fox, to the other characters, and to their environments, he seemed transported into an imaginary world where he began to take the lead and facilitate the play. The child felt free to use whichever puppet suited his expression. The puppeteer and child care-workers began to play along side, providing reactions, consequences, and observations to the child's activity or else they were directed by the child himself.

After observing the reaction of the child, both staff and puppeteer agreed that the child benefited greatly from free-play (non-directive) with the puppets. However, because the story was created to present key issues, these issues arose naturally within the free-play. The key story presented in the beginning became a catalyst for the child's self-expression and a means for himself to confront these issues in his own time. From time to time, the puppeteer would expand on the story to incite further free-play and was prepared for each session to do so if necessary (i.e., adding a story of a little chick who liked to climb to high places). Or the puppeteer might provide a making session in the art room to allow the child to creatively affect the main story himself, i.e., before the second to last play session, a making session in the art room was facilitated to "personalize" Mr. Fox's house. The child felt it important to add a chimney, a TV, and a ladder up the side of the house for the fox to climb. These attributes were in turn used to incite further play in the final two sessions. In fact, the child was independently inspired to bring a perforated cardboard box to one of the play sessions and used it as one of Mr. Fox's traps. Or the puppeteer might prepare the play environment as usual, but leave one significant thing different, i.e., after a previous session in which the little chick's story was told, the puppeteer placed the little chick, sitting high on the farmer's roof. This was responded to immediately when the child walked into the room.

As a conclusion to the residency, a presentation of the puppets and set was planned for the rest of the children and staff in the house. The aim being to integrate the puppets, props, story, etc. into the home's regular play agenda. One of the care-workers facilitated the presentation of Mr. Fox and his props by using the puppet to tell his story to the children and some of the staff. She also encouraged the children's puppet play, which was initiated upon hearing the story. The children were keen to try all the puppets and curious about the farmer's and fox's house. One child was very keen to make a horse puppet to live on the farm. Another was eager to make a house similar to Mr. Fox's house. This excitement was well received by the staff who undertook to investigate programming further puppetry and play activity for the other children in the home.

As puppeteer in residence, I found this experience was extremely informative and inspiring. I found the combination of using puppets, play, interactive storytelling, props, and large set pieces very useful in facilitating self-expression and inciting communication with a young child in out-of-home care. The combination of these factors created a particular environment, which was useful to facilitating the healing process. This environment is tangible. The child can step into it. The puppets used were hand puppets and could be worn; the fox's house was large enough to crawl into the bottom floor. The farmer's protective cardboard wall around his house was large enough for the child to sit in, surrounded by it, which the child did at the end of the residency. Inside the wall he took his favorite puppets, instructed that the wall gates were to be locked, announced that it was nighttime, and proceeded to pretend to peacefully fall asleep. Using large sets and props with the puppets seems to imaginatively transform the room and immediately incite reactions and encourage spontaneous play and free-expression. Mickey Aronoff (1997), a special needs puppetry consultant, and Lenore Steinhardt (1994), an art therapist, support this view:

> Puppetry is a theatrical form. While a child can make a puppet be expressive without a context for that puppet's character, the presence of an environment heightens and lends authority to the puppet's expression. Indeed props or scenic elements can offer the reason or motivation for expression...Making puppets, props and scenery and devising stories tells you more about children's inner worlds. (Aronoff, 1997, p. 14)

> ...the important and decisive factor, which tremendously deepened the experience and heightened the intensity of cathartic revelation...is felt by the author to be the building of an individual/theatre environment for each person's puppets...Art therapy context infers that spontaneous artwork (i.e. the puppet) done in therapy is an autonomous image with a life and story of its own. McNiff (1991) suggests that our images want to speak to us and that we undergo a process of dialoguing with them, asking them how they feel and what they need from us...Theatre

provided the integrative function of connecting the making of the puppets and their stories in a spontaneous performance... (Steinhardt, 1994, pp. 205-06)

Utilizing props and scenery in combination with puppetry could also encourage a shift from expression through an object (the puppet) to independent self-expression without the object. Later in the sessions, the child began to act out Mr. Fox himself, without the use of the puppet.

After my experience of this residency, I am keen to develop this type of interactive, imaginary play session using puppetry. I am aware that the creation of the initial key character Mr. Fox and his appealing story was crucial to our success. I am also very aware of the potential benefits of creating (or facilitating the creation of) a physical creative environment for the puppet play to occur. In the future, with the opportunity of a longer residency, I would like to explore the benefits of allowing participants to create the puppetry environments themselves. Finally, an underpinning factor of importance to be mentioned was the collaboration between the child-care staff and me. This collaboration enriched both our experiences and the child's. It also facilitated a well-rounded work process and a beneficial exchange of skill.

Mr. Fox

## References

Aronoff, M. (1997). Puppetry projects with children in psychiatric assessment units of pediatric hospitals. *La Marionnette et Les Ages de la Vie, Comte Rendu VIIIéme Colloque International, Organisé par Association "Marionnette et Thérapie"*, 14-18.

Steinhardt, L. (1994). Creating the autonomous image through puppet theatre and art therapy. *The Arts in Psychotherapy, 21(3)*, 205-218.

**Acknowledgment from the puppeteer:** My exploration of puppetry and play was inspired by my collaboration with my colleague Niamh Lawlor while working together in Puca Puppets. Niamh introduced me to the area of puppetry and play after having attended discussions with Richard Lewis from the Touchstone Centre, NYC in IMMA (The Irish Museum of Modern Art). Niamh Lawlor, puppeteer, can be contacted at Puca Puppets:
Phone: 00 353 1 210 0320

This residency was funded by the South Side Partnership.

For further information on puppetry in Ireland contact UNIMA Ireland (The National Branch of the International Association for Puppeteers) at unimaireland@eircom.net. c/o 18 Irishtown Rd.; Irishtown; Dublin 4; Ireland.

# CHAPTER 26

## PUPPETS ENRICH CHILDREN WITH AUTISM

### Marlene Joyce

In November 2001, a friend and I participated in a Teach-In at a St. Petersburg, Florida elementary school. We performed the story "Shingebiss" about a courageous duck and how his fortitude overcame "Big Chief North Wind." We used a fleece marionette duck for Shingebiss and a long sheer white silk on a stick for the wind. The Wind tried to starve the duck, to freeze him and to make the duck afraid, but his courage triumphed. We entertained several second grade classes and we were also asked to take our puppets to the two classes of children diagnosed with autism in the school. They had never before been able to participate in this day of special events when community adults showcase talents and interests for the children.

For the children with exceptional needs, we chose a different story, "The Little House." In this tale, several fleece animals are invited to live together in a basket, until it becomes too crowded and the house comes apart, then they all return to their homes. It was interesting to see the delight of the children and their interest in playing with the animals. I sat on the floor with the children in a semi-circle around the cloth that was partially on my lap. I told the story a second time while the children moved the animals. As I was putting everything away, it became apparent that some children did not wish to relinquish their animal. I realized that this group of children might enjoy and learn from more contact with puppets.

At the beginning of the September 2002 school year, I called the teacher of the kindergarten/first grade class, ages 5-7 years, to offer my puppetry. We met to discuss this possibility and decided to pursue this together. She requested that I come for one hour every Tuesday afternoon, at the same time weekly, to fit the rigid schedule these children need. She explained that her general goals were to help the children to attend to the story and participate appropriately. In addition, she had different goals for each of the seven boys in the class: focusing for 3-5 minutes on the activity, participating, not interrupting, remaining seated in a chair, etc.

Drawing on my experience as a Waldorf teacher, I felt I could begin to meet her goals most effectively by presenting simple stories with a variety of puppets. Since these children are self-absorbed and have social, communication, and behavioral inadequacies, I planned to begin with soft, airy materials that attract younger children and gradually move to heavier, more solid material like the felt cloth table puppets and then to Shingebiss, a wooden duck.

At our first time together, I handed out a silk scarf the color of the wind in our story to each child. I began to sing a song about the wind as I moved the silk through the air. "I'm the wind, I breeze and blow, mmm mmm, hear me whisper, hear me whisper. In a tree, listen to me, mmm mmm, hear me whisper, hear me whisper." All the children began to move the silks. Some wrapped them around themselves, others danced with them, and all except one child was engaged. Two children hummed the song as the teachers and I sang it several times.

The seven children and an assistant then settled into a semi-circle of chairs to watch "The Land With No Story" with cloth marionettes and a piece of silk wind. I told the story and moved the puppets with the help of the teacher and her assistant. After the story, each child again moved the silks as we sang the song. I left several silks for the children to use during the week.

The teacher and I took a few moments to evaluate this session, and we were both pleased with the response of the children. We planned the next month, when her focus would be on Halloween, harvest, and a visit to a Pumpkin Patch. I was delighted when the teacher suggested that she present a related craft to follow each puppet story.

I wanted to fit my story and artistic presentation to the teacher's autumn curriculum, so I decided to use fleece table puppets to illustrate a story about Farmer Brown, his wife and two children planting a pumpkin patch. We began the presentation by placing a long piece of blue sky-colored silk fabric over the scene and billowed it as we took it off and lay it in front of the table on the floor as if it were a "curtain" going up. The story told of the children planting seeds, which grew into pumpkins in their own pumpkin patch. Then, the children carved them into jack-o'-lanterns. I adapted a poem into a song and the words explained how to carve a pumpkin. At the end of the performance, we planned to replace the sky-blue silk over the scene, as if it were a curtain coming down. This day, when we looked beneath the table where we laid the silk, it was gone. One of the boys had quietly wrapped himself in it and was sitting happily enveloped in it. The craft chosen by the teacher was to make a jack-o'-lantern. Each child tore black paper and pasted it onto an orange pumpkin to make a face.

The following week, we repeated the same story with the Brown family planting the seeds, which grew into pumpkins in the field and carving them into jack-o'-lanterns. The appearance of Hedgy the Hedgehog and Squirrel Nutkin was added to the story. They had been hidden in the silk landscape.

To our surprise, at the end of the story, several of the children rushed to the table and began to touch and move the puppets. I began to sing and encouraged this play with care; however, it became a scramble. It took some minutes to regain decorum, but the children were becoming engaged!

For the craft following the story, each child was given a paper lunch bag to which they attached cut outs: seeds, stem, leaves, flower, and finally, a pumpkin to make a jack- o'-lantern. This activity required sequencing, eye-hand coordination, and the use of glue.

The following week, since one child had shown great interest in moving the fleece puppets with care, I invited him to help me with the story. The Pumpkin Patch Story began with Hedgy the Hedgehog and ended with Squirrel Nutkin. The helpful child stood in front of the table and blocked the view of the other children, and immediately their attention was lost.  Our silk "curtain" again was used by a child to wrap himself, so we used another. The craft was to cut pumpkin cookies off of a log roll. They were baked and the children had them for their snack.

The final week of October, I wanted to transition to the next story; so I did an abbreviated Pumpkin Patch story with the addition of Mother Earth calling Hedgy the Hedgehog and Squirrel Nutkin to sleep for the winter. The set-up was elaborate with an under and above ground setting. I sang the Wind song and a new "Mother Earth" song about a beetle and a butterfly sleeping on a log underground. The children were more settled this day, and the child who helped me the previous week noticed that Farmer Brown's two children were not included in this story and asked where they were. There was no time for a craft after this performance.

In November, Mother Earth became the focus of our story. She called the butterflies, beetles, Hedgy the Hedgehog, Squirrel Nutkin and the flower children to sleep underground in their beds. Then she knit a blanket of fall colors to keep them warm through the winter. When the story was finished, I invited all the children to take a puppet from the story to move. There was a rather controlled swarm upon the scene and the children were very rough with these fleece puppets. I realized that we needed to use much more sturdy puppets for the children to work with them.

In December, as the class curriculum introduced winter, I brought the Shingebiss story. The children were now getting used to my appearance and welcomed me with interest. I began to set up the materials in-the-round on the floor with the children sitting on chairs in a semi-circle. There was a lot of curiosity as I was setting the scene. Children would come over and sit in a chair to wait for the start. Some children picked up the pieces of the scene and then replaced them imitating the way I had placed them.

Shingebiss was a wooden pull toy with leather flapping feet. The children wanted to handle the duck, move the logs for his home and his little fleece fire as well as play in the silk "snow" which surrounded the fleece snow. I gave them each what interested them, and after they had spent some time with it, we replaced it and began the story. After the story, once again, they all handled the silk snow.

We did the Shingebiss story again, and this time rather than setting up the scene with the silk, I gave each child a portion to feel and move before placing it. Other parts of the scene were moved and handled. When everyone was ready, I set the scene as they watched, sitting in their chairs, and told the story as the children listening quietly. At the end of the story, each child moved Shingebiss and played with the silk as I was taking it up. After the story, the teacher held up cards and asked each child to say a word relating to winter. They all were able to do this.

In our last session, I set up Shingebiss and we told the story in the round with the children choosing an animal and a making a house of logs for it. Then, in turn each animal moved by a child, caught some fish and gave it to the duck saying, "I don't eat fish, but you do, so please take mine for your dinner." Each child was able to do this with some prompting. The children became puppeteers, moving all the animals to meet in a circle around a fire to have a celebration of friendship.

I felt that we accomplished our goal of gradually helping the children become interested and engaged in the story to the point of participating with the characters. This held their attention while it was their turn and, since our group was not large, they watched their classmates as well.

Gradually bringing more "earthy" durable puppets allowed the children to play with them and move them as part of the story. The nature stories were easy for the children to relate to, while reinforcing and enhancing the curriculum with artistic elements of color, textured and flowing fabrics, song, and movement.

In her evaluation, the teacher remarked that the students were achieving the goals she had for them individually and she wrote, "Overall the students are taking a lot away from these therapy sessions."

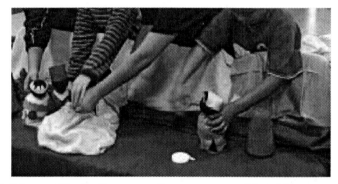

Children with Autism enacting a scene with table puppets.

## References

Aulie, J. & Meyerkort, M. (1978/1999). Shingebiss: A Chippewa Indian tale. In *Winter: A collection of poems, songs and stories for young children* (p. 86). Stourbridge, England: Wynstones Press.

Down, S. (2000). The land with no stories (Adapted from an African Tale). In *Multicultural stories: A resource book for teachers and parents*. Boulder, CO: Storyarts Publications.

Foster, N. (Ed.) (1998). I'm the wind from late autumn circle. In *Let us form a ring: An acorn hill anthology* (p. 9). Silver Spring, MD: Acorn Hill Children's Center.

Foster, N. (Ibid), Mother earth circle play (p. 25).

von Olfers, S. (1990). *The story of the root-children*. Edinburgh, England: Floris Books.

# CHAPTER 27

## ACCESSING THE POWER OF PUPPETS IN THERAPEUTIC AND EDUCATIONAL SETTINGS

### Wendy Passmore-Godfrey

Wendy Passmore-Godfrey and frog development puppets.

The scene is repeated throughout history and over many cultures: a rapt audience watches a small (or large) wooden (or cloth, leather, paper...) human-like object (or animal or some other thing) speak (or sing or be silent or just breathe...).

They are caught up in the object's thoughts and feelings. They are entering the object's world and cheering for its success (or its downfall...).

And what of the man (or woman or child) behind the object as it moves to music, interacts with its world, converses...? What thoughts or feelings is the person expressing through this object - questions, explorations, anger, love, outreach, exploration, teaching...? Reaching back into the process, when the object was created (or found), what soul was sculpted (sewn, carved, stapled, molded or imagined...) into its shape?

A puppet's power is its inherent nature to "become" anything it is designed to be. Puppets synthesize ideas. They are the essence of a thought, concept or character. As such, they can represent qualities such as tolerance, peace, etc., quickly and without needing qualifiers or explanation. They can teach without needing qualifications, model without ego. They can express without consequences. They can speak for us as a proxy. This is what makes puppetry such an effective medium in so many therapeutic and educational settings and what has fascinated audiences since a shaman-caveman created the first puppet from a bone and a flickering fire's shadow.

The power of puppets, as Michael Malkin writes in the Atlanta Center for Puppetry Arts Museum Catalogue, is that they "...*can transcend personal and even cultural selfhood. They are our undeveloped spirits and unrealized thoughts that need to escape... to do things we cannot or dare not do...*" (1995).

## What are the strengths of puppetry in a therapeutic setting?

I had been teaching at a school with deaf and hard of hearing students. One class had produced beautiful black light puppet/masks that sat on their heads, allowing their hands to still sign. One student, a child who was not given to fantasy, excelled in his monster conversations. Fingers flying, he talked about his character's favorite food, rotten fish eyeballs, his imagination released by the puppet's power as proxy!

Irwin (1983), in her discussion of the diagnostic and therapeutic use of pretend play in play therapy, states, "For many, communicating through puppets is physically safe and fun. Used as a tool in assessment, puppet play provides symbolic, non-verbal, and interactional data" (p. 159).

Repeatedly, therapists and teachers see that puppetry "works." Matthew Bernier, an art therapist, in his seminar, breaks down *why* this unique art form "works":

- Allows projection of conflicts onto an intermediary or distancing object.
- Externalizes anxiety allowing for observation and fostering of insight.
- Can express exhibitionistic strivings which may not otherwise be expressed.
- Satisfies creative urgings and provides sense of accomplishment in making a simple or complex puppet.
- Allows control and mastery over elements in life. One can add/delete parts of a story, change endings, etc.

- Puppets can play a variety of roles, human and non-human; symbolic characters can represent conscious or unconscious elements and even inanimate objects.
- Symbolic characters may allow for free expression of aggressive and sexual themes without causing shame, fear or guilt.
- The hands of the client become the energy of the puppet. The client "controls" the puppet.
- Provides an opportunity to re-enact real life stories; remembering, repeating, working through.
- Provides an opportunity for self-confrontation of the drama of existence.
- Group puppetry encourages socialization and teamwork; a chance to practice and master interpersonal skills and roles.
- Psychopuppetry: puppets can act and speak for the client to the group and allow for role reversal. (Bernier, 2000)

## How to Use Puppetry in a Therapeutic and Educational Setting

In the therapeutic and educational setting, puppetry can be used in numerous ways including:
- client puppet *making* (either for themselves or to pass along to another, i.e., adults creating puppets for children).
- client puppet *using* (in spontaneous puppet play, dialogues, scripted puppet play, soliloquy).
- client *interacting* (client talks *to* a puppet used by the facilitator).
- client assessment.

As puppet theatre arts have the potential to span and encompass all the creative expressive arts forms - music, art, drama, play, writing, and more, projects and activities can be multifaceted. Puppetry works on many different levels – from simple to sophisticated, philosophical to fun, and can therefore be used when working with people of all ages as well as groups, individuals, families or couples. The following project descriptions provide ideas on how to use puppetry in a couple of different settings and can be adapted, extended, simplified, etc.

## Shadow Puppetry

Shadow puppets may have been the first puppets in history, perhaps taken up by a caveman shaman to make his message to the hunters more effective! In times since, their mysterious shimmering imagery have been used to represent "another world" – the "dream," the "will of the gods," the "voices of the dead," etc. in the performing cultures of China, India, Persia, Greece, Indonesia, and Egypt.

Beyond the basic human fascination in light and shadow, the strengths of this puppet genre include:
- Anonymity of puppeteer is increased - get to hide behind a screen.
- Makes connections between abstract/representation silhouette and object itself, between 2-D and 3-D concepts.

- Refers to ethnic traditions of shadow puppetry.
- Wheel chair accessible.
- Shadows can simply be made in the sunlight – no technical requirement.
- Puppets can be simply made or even be "found objects," eliminating concerns of "artistic ability."
- Works well in partners – with one person holding a flashlight or a solo puppeteer can use a headlamp.
- Can do "hand over" easily.
- Extends to a more complex project when utilizing other light projection sources, i.e., overhead, slide, film or video projector or even the traditional oil lamp (with great caution).
- Projects can also utilize cinemagraphic concepts of fades, close-ups, stop action.

**A Shadow Puppet Project**

The following activity explores color, shape, animals, movement, music, and emotions. It is suggested for ages 6-9 years. Shadows can be shown against a wall in a sunbeam or behind a screen using an overhead projector, lamp, flashlights or the sun.

A basic shadow puppet screen can be made by stretching material over a frame and hanging it from the ceiling or doorway. Material can be a white sheet, a piece of white paper, frosted Mylar, etc. Unless the budget extends to a professional rear projection screen, the recommended material is a white or beige shower curtain. A frame can be made from a cardboard box, copper piping, a hula hoop, an old picture frame - recommended is a set of canvas stretch bars found in an art supply store. Make sure the screen is big enough for the puppeteer to move the puppet freely around and bigger if multiple puppets will be shown.

**Materials:**
black tag/light weight card paper
colored cellophane
straws or bamboo sticks
masking tape
glue sticks
scissors
brass fasteners/split pins
CD player
various music i.e.: classical, jazz, new age
simple pictures of animals *as a resource*

**Method:**

a) Read "My Many Colored Days" by Dr. Seuss (1996). This delightful book, published after his death, is about colors and how they describe our moods and includes lines like; "Then comes a yellow day and wheeeeee, I'm a busy buzzzy bee." (A web search gives many other lesson activities related to this book.)

Discussion can be opened on a number of topics:

- clarifying the names of feelings.
- occasions for different feelings, the differences and commonalities of how people express them.
- the concept that color represents different things – starting with red for danger.
- the complexity of color symbolism – red also is used for love
- movement and/or music that (subjectively) goes with feelings

b) Ask participants to fill in this equation:

**emotion = color + animal + movement + music.**

For example: Glee = yellow + bee + flying in circles + Prokofiev's "Flight of the Bumblebee" (or a song from Raffi – amend to appropriate age!)

c) Generate a puppet using the decisions made for the equation:

- draw the silhouette of an animal on the black paper, cut it out.
- cut out stripes, spots, stars, or any shape
- fill in holes with the selected color of cellophane
- tape on a stick or straw

Other things can be added to create an interesting silhouette
( i.e.: paper doily, feathers, lace, etc.). Be careful not to weigh down the cardboard with too many additions.

Another interesting addition is a moving part – a leg that dangles or a head that turns using a brass fastener/split pin.

A moving part

171

d) Show the puppet by holding it up behind the screen – make sure the puppet is clear and not overshadowed by a part of the puppeteer. Move the puppet to the music.

Further tips for manipulation include:
- Practice entering and exiting.
- Experiment with fading the puppet in and out.
- Keep movements consistent with the chosen emotion.
- Try speaking a typical phrase that goes with the emotion (i.e.: tired: "I'm bagged" or a line from the Dr. Seuss book).
- Partner up with someone with a puppet of different mood and have a conversation.

**Extensions**

If an overhead projector is being used, backgrounds can be created by drawing on an overhead transparency, or make a color photo transparency (perhaps a photo of a time or place that matches the emotion)

For older students, the concept of shape and its relation to emotion can be discussed. References can be made to art (i.e.: the excited whirls of Van Gogh, the cold, intellectual lines of Mondrian, the peaceful, horizontal lines of a landscape, the languid curves of various reclining nudes!).

A mad cat                            A calm fish

**A Sensory Object Puppetry Project**

The genre of Object Puppetry is very interesting in the therapeutic and educational setting as it incorporates more directly than other types of puppetry, the concepts of symbolism, stereotyping, metaphor, etc. It also asks participants to think about their observations and understanding of people and situations. As there is no construction involved in the project it allows the drama and presenting to happen immediately. Furthermore if participants doubt their "artistic ability" they don't need to worry as their puppet is already made! The following lesson plan is suggested for ages 10-15 years or older.

**Materials:**
Gather objects/things from all categories (i.e.: workshop tools or supplies, kitchen implements, office supplies, nature, consider the sensory elements – texture, smell, sound, color, etc.).
Avoid toys and items already representing something else (i.e.: figurines, as well as objects that are too multifaceted, i.e.: tape player, mix master).

**Method**
a) Review basic puppet manipulation techniques:
  • If the puppeteer is visible try to always give focus to the puppet, keep you eyes on the puppet, speak and think through the puppet.
  • Imagine how a human would move or express the action and copy it (within the puppet's limitations).
  • Make sure the puppet makes eye contact with its audience or the object it is working with.
  • Make a different voice for the puppet – it's not you, so it doesn't talk in your voice! Remember you can also "talk" in sounds.
  • Practice basic moves like, yes, no, breathing, walking, thinking, sneezing and figure out the puppet's 'body vocabulary' for its different feelings (i.e.: How does it move when it's worried?)
b) Have Participants select an object and think about the qualities of the object, relating them to the general qualities of a person.
  • Is it soft, prickly or flexible?
  • Is it natural or manmade?
  • Is it part of a group or an independent item?
  • Is it brightly colored or more subdued tones?
  • Does its smell have pleasant memories?
  • Does it make loud obnoxious noise or a little single sound or a complex sound, etc.?
c) Construct and attach eyes to match the nature of the puppet – they can be cut from paper or be more elaborate.
d) Play some drama games with the puppets; try to keep the puppets acting 'in character'.

Everybody gets a turn as this goes around the circle. It is really only a means of getting the puppets/puppeteers to talk. "A is for ….", "B is for…"

This is a call and response game that puts no pressure on what is actually said:
*Person A*: "Did you know …?" (Make up something to finish the sentence, i.e.: that my grandmother likes oysters.)

*Group*: "You don't say!"
*Person A*: "I just did say!
*Group:* "So you did."

Before you play this one everyone needs to take a pledge of secrecy. The puppets whisper their secret in the puppeteer's ear and the puppeteers tell the group. This is an exercise to get the participants to think of the puppet as a separate entity with its own "life," although it may bring out some interesting items to talk about later.

"My secret is …" (i.e.: that I'm scared to be put in the storage box)

e) Allow time for discussion.

**Extensions**
- Provide a "Story Starters" to get a mini play going: "Your puppet is walking down a path and smells….this smell (mustard, cinnamon, vinegar, cow manure). "Your puppet was reaching up to a shelf and felt …. (a pine cone, fur, glue, a marble). "Your puppet heard a noise in the other room ….it was (a can opener, coins dropping, a zipper, a growl)."
- Provide "Story Enders" which are more difficult but equally fun: "and so he lived to the end of his days in a red bucket," "she took up her quill cyber pen and cartooned the whole adventure," etc.
- Have the object represent an occupation (i.e.: an egg-flip is a cook, a mirror is a makeup artist, a flag is a politician) and ask participants to act out a "day in the life" of someone with that job.

The power of the puppet medium in therapeutic and educational settings relates directly to our human inclination to animate objects around us, whether we put words in our dog's mouth or kick the tire when the car has broken down on the side of the road. When this inclination is combined with a wish or a need to communicate our thoughts, puppets become "ideas in motion." A puppet, static on a shelf doesn't have the power - a person is always required to provide the spark of spirit that moves through the puppet to the viewers. The audience watches, engaged in a communal imagining of "life" brought forth from "non-life."

Expressing and exploring our myriad of human thoughts (personal, universal, challenging, comforting…) to an audience (of one or two or many) united with the performer in listening (exploring, interpreting, disagreeing…) with the thoughts - this is "Puppet Power."

**General Puppet Tips**
In conclusion, here are a few more tips on puppet use:
- Keep it really simple, don't rush the project, be gentle on yourself, and think "outside of the box" (unless your puppet is a box!). Expose yourself to other good puppetry examples.

- When choosing materials for puppets provide both shiny and new and older and used as well as natural or man made. Clients can pick what appeals to them.
- Provide a "dignified" home for the puppet when it is not in use. Throwing them head-first into a box destroys the characterization you've been working in. They can sit in a box that is specially decorated for them, or carefully placed into a box at the very least.
- A multi-step puppet project can be broken into several sessions and gives great satisfaction in accomplishment as well as a sustained attention activity.
- Puppets can be made on the pretext of being made for someone else as a gift.
- A neutral face puppet can feel lots of different emotions, but a puppet with a face in one expression is usually stuck. (Note that rules can always be broken.)
- It is better to custom-make your puppets, but if you need to buy one, pick a comfortable one, not hard or breakable or complicated - probably a hand puppet or hand/mouth puppet; make sure the eyes are visible.
- Children seem to like animals better than humans.
- Make sure your human puppets are diverse in age, culture, etc.
- Don't assume that children will know that a puppet is not a living or magical thing. If necessary show the child how the puppet works, how your hand goes into it. Maybe start with finger puppets as the least threatening of all puppet types.

## References

Bernier, M. (2000). *Psychopuppetry.* Unpublished manuscript, Eastern Virginia Medical School, Norfolk, VA.

Irwin, E. (1983). The diagnostic and therapeutic use of pretend play. In C. E. Schaefer & K.J. O'Connor, *Handbook of play therapy.* New York: John Wiley & Sons.

Malkin, M. (1995). *Puppets: The power of wonder.* Atlanta: Center for Puppetry Arts.

Seuss, D. (1996). *My many colored days.* New York: Knopf Books for Young Readers.

# CHAPTER 28

## PUPPETS IN RECOVERY©

## Paula Shutman*

HEALTHY INNER CHILD: Yes, I want to write an article for this book!

BLUE BOY: No one will read it. No one listens to me. I don't have anything worthwhile to say. I'm stupid.

BLACK HAIRED BOY: Why bother? Don't even try.

BAG LADY: I'm a failure. I don't even have a college degree. I dropped out of college. I'm a failure. I'm not important.

WISE WOMAN: I've been wanting to write about my experience with my puppets. This is a great opportunity!

BAG LADY: I'm afraid I'll fail. I'll put it off, write it later.

CREATIVE INNTER CHILD: No! I spent lots of time making and playing with them. I want to tell people about them too!

STRAIGHT A STUDENT: (raises her hand and waves it high) I can write it! I know I can do this! I'm so excited!

So you have met some of my inner children puppet characters! They each have their individual stories and they are all part of me. I have made and used puppets therapeutically for fifteen years in my ongoing recovery from an eating disorder. I am not a trained psychotherapist nor a professional puppeteer, at least not yet. This article is an expression of my experience making and using puppets as part of my own healing process.

When I was introduced to the "inner child" in my first therapy group, it was suggested that we each buy a doll to represent our "inner child." The inner child is a therapeutic method used in accessing the feelings experienced in childhood. It involves "re-parenting" the young part of us that experienced childhood trauma including incest and abuse. I bought a baby doll, but was unable to relate to her in a nurturing way. Instead, she elicited anger and I couldn't use her. However, later as my therapy progressed, she became a symbol of my spiritual inner child. I became inspired to make an inner child puppet after watching a puppeteer on the Mr. Rogers Neighborhood show on public television. She manipulated two large puppets that looked and acted exactly like real children and thus the idea was born.

My puppets have helped me speak and find my voice. They helped me name, recognize and feel emotions that I have forgotten and repressed since childhood. They also helped me recognize habitual negative thought patterns associated with the feelings. I grew up in a family that did not talk about feelings. The predominant feeling expressed was anger, which frightened and inhibited me. I retreated into a fantasy world and creativity to express my feelings, which may be why puppetry works for me. As a result, I am now more aware of my feelings and can verbalize them better.

The first puppet I made was my healthy inner child. She is extremely verbal, direct and happy. As therapy progressed, I found myself overwhelmed and devastated by a conglomeration of unintelligible intense painful suppressed feelings. In an effort to differentiate one feeling from the next, I gave each new feeling a personality and a full character emerged as an inner child. I have many characters, children as well as adults, some male and some female. They represent different stages of growth from the crying baby through adolescence and on to adulthood.

Because thoughts and emotions come and pass quickly, I constructed the puppets in such a manner that I could change characters quickly to accommodate the pattern of feelings and thoughts that arose. By identifying an emotion as an inner child puppet character, I was able to get some distance from, and able to experience emotions, without having to run away from them. This was how I came to know and experience shame, abandonment, loneliness, terror, fear, rage, sadness, hopelessness, and despair. Thus my puppets helped me to access my unconscious in a non-threatening manner.

I was determined to face these feelings and knew I had to refrain from overeating to feel them. All my life I had been using food as a way to medicate myself so I wouldn't feel. I knew it was these intense feelings buried deep in my unconscious that were driving me to overeat. Painful as it was to not overeat, I was determined and attended Overeaters Anonymous for support.

As time progressed, I learned more about myself through dialoguing with the "inner children." Also, more characters emerged from my subconscious, such as the ballerina. My involvement with psychodrama helped me to look at these feelings in a more unified way and to experience the strengths and beauty of the healthy inner child – the whole child. One of my characters, the wise woman (strong nurturing adult) was made real to me in psychodrama. In addition, I think puppets can be used to help one focus and cultivate positive thoughts and behaviors. Puppets can also be used as a substitute for people in acting out individual psychodramas.

I believe puppets are powerful tools for transformation and can bring new dimensions to adult psychotherapy. Puppet use is experiential and integrative. It involves the visual and tactile senses as well as speech and body movement. It can externalize and bring perspective to a situation. Puppetry brings out playfulness and lightheartedness and connects us with the child within. Puppets are non-threatening and can create a buffer between the event and corresponding emotions. The experience can be similar to watching a play and identifying with the main character, but not having to relive the trauma. Puppets can be useful in cognitive therapy, psychodrama, inner child therapy, role-playing, and behavioral modification. It's less threatening to have your puppet try out a new behavior first, like writing an article to be part of this book.

* Written by Paula's "Straight A Student" inner child.

HEALTHY INNER CHILD: Bye! I'm finished! I did it! Hope you liked it! (Squeals and jumps up and down)

# PART THREE:

# RESEARCH

# CHAPTER 29

## MONITORING AND EVALUATING PUPPETRY PROJECTS: WHY AND HOW?

## David Silver

### Puppetry and Evaluation

Puppetry serves many purposes that cover the whole gamut from entertainment to education. A wide range of approaches and practices has been applied to raise awareness on a vast array of educational, therapeutic, socio-political and health themes, all toward the same goal - engaging individuals and communities in bringing about change. But even though this shared goal is commonly acknowledged, surprisingly little effort has been directed toward knowing what change, if any, has taken place as a result of puppetry performances.

This article will address several key issues facing puppeteers who are concerned with measuring the impact of their performances: the meaning and purposes of evaluating impact, commonly encountered obstacles, and how impact can be measured.

### 1. What is meant by *impact?*

In simplest terms, impact is the result of a project's final goal. In the context of puppet theater evaluation, *impact* may be understood as demonstrable *"significant or sustainable new skills and information necessary for audiences to make their own choices"* (AREPP). A meaningful and lasting impact on their audiences is probably, above all, what most performers desire. But how do you know you've achieved that hope?

## 2. Why assess or evaluate impact? What needs to be assessed?

Evaluation is a daily human activity, an essential step in the process of integrating learning and moving on to new discoveries. Evaluation supports the desire to understand more deeply, see the truth more clearly, and act more effectively (Moriarty, 1997).

As communication programs utilizing entertainment/education approaches such as Puppet Theater grow more sophisticated and strategic, evaluation is not keeping pace with their innovation. Educators, funders, project planners, script writers and performing puppeteers alike are asking for more information on results for the feedback essential to improving future performances.

Purpose of measuring impact. While some may view information collection for monitoring and evaluation as only a reporting or a project requirement, the routine use of information leads to improved quality, greater impact, and a more cost effective effort. Measuring the impact of a puppet theater project can provide a wealth of useful information:

- Target audience response: Monitoring and evaluating examines the responses of the individuals and community to the messages and inputs of the puppetry project. Such feedback helps ensure acceptability and usefulness of future performances.
- Target audience impact: Measuring a puppetry project's impact on individuals or the community paints a clearer picture of the effect of the project on quality of life and living standards, such as empowerment, health, civil liberties, and relationship to environment.
- Assessing progress: As with any project, impact evaluation is necessary to determine if the project objectives are being achieved.
- Identifying strengths and weaknesses: Impact evaluation identifies where a project needs improvement and how it can be done.
- Effectiveness: Measuring impact shows which activities have worked and which need to be further improved. Measuring the impact of a puppetry theatre project should have the same fundamental outcome as working on improving the script and acting techniques: "so you can do the next one (project or performance) better."
- Sharing experiences: The evaluation process highlights both the mistakes to be addressed and the positive approaches that should be continued, expanded, and shared.
- Advocacy and support: Identifying the specific impact and results on influencing individuals or a community provides evidence and marketing facts for attracting future support from communities, local partner organizations, and donors. Impact evaluation demonstrates to donors that the money they are investing in this educational effort is having an impact.
- Achievement: Professional puppeteers, like others involved in communication, need to be constantly aware of what they have actually accomplished. Additionally, for community-based puppeteers, determining both short-term

and long-term impact can provide encouragement and re-enforcement of feelings of control, competency and self-worth.
(Adapted from Barton, 1997; *CARE-Uganda: Guidelines to Monitoring and Evaluation*)

Thus, as in other education projects, puppetry in education projects need logical information systems that serve to maintain and strengthen the project, as well as to meet the needs of all potential information users, including the target population.

## 3. Why hasn't impact been assessed?

Determining the overall impact of puppetry as a tool for education and development has been difficult due to both a lack of documentation and the lack of established methods. Although artists may be well focused on the production, they may not have the long-term perspective nor the time and skills for looking at and documenting the long-term impact of their efforts. While the limited information available, anecdotal reports, and intuition, all indicate some level of impact, the general lack of pooled information coupled with the wide variety of methods, concepts, and organizational capacity of puppetry groups make it difficult to provide more conclusive documentation on impact. Furthermore, the issue of attribution - how to be satisfied that results (effects, impacts) claimed for the project are actually due to project interventions and not to other outside factors - is often very difficult to establish.

Monitoring and evaluating the impact of puppetry projects is also more complex than traditional donor projects. Measuring emotions and attitudes, beliefs, cultural practices and behavior change is much more difficult than determining a percentage of children immunized or attending school, for example. Nor are the results of puppetry performances readily visible, like a new school building or increased agricultural production. Furthermore, as artists who are creative in nature and more oriented to human emotions, puppeteers may value neither spending time nor evaluating their work beyond the stage and the immediate audience. Nevertheless, while the term "project evaluation" might appear bureaucratic, in practice, puppeteers as artists are constantly "evaluating" their performances as they rehearse.

## 4. How can we measure impact?

As discussed in Section 2 above, measuring the impact of a puppet theater project can provide useful information about target audience response, target audience impact, project progress, project strengths and weaknesses, as well as the overall effectiveness of a project. But what specific information do we want to gather in order to substantiate each of these areas, and how do we go about the task of collecting it?

Indicators.  Just as in other jobs in our daily lives, a set of tools has been developed to help accomplish the task of information gathering and analyzing. To start with, it is necessary to first define a set of criteria used to check whether proposed changes have occurred. An *indicator* is a tool designed to provide a standard against which to measure or assess or show the success or progress of a project against stated targets. Indicators can be established to specifically measure each level of a particular project:

- <u>Final goal</u>: To assess actual change in the conditions of the basic problem identified.
- <u>Intermediate goal</u>: To describe target population responses to project outputs, *e.g.,* behavior change, reactions and perceptions;
- <u>Output level</u>: To describe project products, *i.e.,* the direct outcome of project activities and inputs for which the project is responsible, and
- <u>Activities level</u>: To describe what project activities took place.

It is useful to first develop a list of what changes we hoped to see as a result of what we said we were going to do. Some examples for a puppetry education project might include:

- To increase the size of the audience reached
- To promote audience changes in attitudes, perceptions, and feelings toward the performance themes and messages
- To promote audience changes in behavior toward intended message as a result of exposure to the puppet performances
- To increase audience acceptability of the presentation form (*i.e.,* puppetry) of the messages
- To encourage audience participation

This type of "hoped for changes" indicator is called a conceptual indicator.

But how do we then go about measuring each of these conceptual indicators? The first example, *"to increase the size of the audience reached,"* is pretty straightforward. All we need to record is the number of audience members attending our puppetry performance from the project's inception to its completion. This type of numerical information is called *quantitative data.*

The next change listed for what we hoped to see is a bit more challenging, *"to promote audience changes in attitudes, perceptions and feelings toward the performance themes and messages."* To accomplish this hurdle, we must convert our conceptual indicator into an operational indicator that can answer the question: *"What data can we actually measure in the field?"*

One measurable approach is to ask a sample of audience members if they are able to describe a change in their attitude toward the intended performance theme attributable to seeing one of the puppetry project performances. The type of information that can best be described in words such as descriptions of events, observed behaviors and direct quotations is called *qualitative data.* Qualitative data are needed when the attitudes, beliefs, and perceptions of the target population must be known in order to understand its reactions and responses to project services.

**5. But how can we be sure what the audience members' attitudes were before seeing the puppetry performance?**

<u>Baseline research</u>.  Many projects are too hastily developed in response to available funds, omitting a thorough analysis of the community needs and situation. The practice of conducting baseline research serves many functions that are vital to the monitoring and evaluation process. Baseline research is essential:

- to understand existing knowledge, attitude, and practices (KAP) in different thematic areas as civil society, health and education;
- to develop appropriate themes and messages as part of a strategic communication-based intervention program, such as puppet theater, in order to bridge these knowledge gaps and change attitudes; and
- to define a measurable set of appropriate indicators to determine program progress.

Puppet theater groups can use baseline research to determine knowledge gaps and misconceptions in order to more accurately formulate their strategy and performance approach. They then can follow selected audience members over time to observe how effective the performance has been and to help develop new performances. In this way, impact evaluation becomes a process that is integrated into the performance process itself, enhancing its effectiveness.

**6. But what kinds of methods can be used to gather information about each indicator?**

<u>Data collection methods</u>.  Conducting pre and post performance audience interviews and focus groups have been a traditional way of obtaining information on the immediate impact of a performance in behavior change communication programs. Interviews, for example, which inquire into another person's perceptions about one or more topics may be structured (*e.g.,* questionnaire survey with "yes/no" choices and circling stated responses) providing quantitative data, or open-ended (*e.g.,* in-depth interviews) which provide qualitative data.  Although usually easier to collect, compare, and summarize than qualitative information, quantitative data leaves out explanations, the human voices, and the actual nature of what is going on. Accordingly, an integrated monitoring and evaluation system for puppetry theater projects incorporates information systems requiring the collection of both quantitative and qualitative data.

Other creative approaches have been taken to monitor and evaluate popular theater projects. These include video taping audience responses, measuring change in the use of related community services such as patient or counseling visits, tracking a selected number of the audience and observing their behavior for a certain timeframe, interviewing household members of an audience member, and observation and feedback in the community. Regardless of which methods are selected, the main purpose is to create an up-and-running monitoring system that is integrated into the routine project activities so that adjustments can be made on an ongoing basis rather than waiting for a final evaluation.

Finally, the information system plan should include arrangements for analysis and interpretation of all data that is collected. In this way, the project can ensure that raw data is converted into useful information for facilitating decision-making and other applications. Data analysis is an entire subject unto itself. Nevertheless, most, if not all project monitoring and evaluation can be done with descriptive statistics and qualitative summaries - there is little or no need for complex statistics for most projects.

## 7. Keeping track of it all: Now, how can you keep all these different components of your project's information system straight?

In order to provide a working reference to guide the overall project components including monitoring and evaluation, a tool known as a logical framework, or log frame, is used. The format of a completed log frame is usually a four-column grid that shows the linkages between project intentions (goals, objectives), assessments of achievements (indicators), ways of checking progress (means of verification) and expected events or situations outside project control that can influence the project (assumptions).

## Conclusion

Despite the methodological obstacles inherent in measuring the impact of puppetry in education projects, developing a comprehensive yet feasible plan for monitoring and evaluation (M&E) will provide many benefits for the projects. These include the ability to more accurately measure target population response, target population impact, achievement, project progress, strengths and weaknesses, and effectiveness. An ongoing M&E system will also highlight, in a timely fashion, both the mistakes and the positive approaches that should be continued, expanded, and shared. Identifying the specific impact and results on influencing a community will also provide evidence and marketing facts for attracting future support from communities, local partner organizations, and donors.

## Reference

Barton, T. (1997). *CARE-Uganda: Guidelines to monitoring and evaluation.* Uganda: CARE International.

# CONTRIBUTORS

**Tova Ackerman** (Brooklyn, NY) Director of Puppetry in Practice (PIP), has degrees in the fields of Early Childhood Education (B.A.), Special Education, Supervision and Administration and Teaching English as a Second Language (M.A., Ed.D.), and served as a Board of Education teacher for 25 years. As an Adjunct Professor at Brooklyn College for more than 20 years, she was also part of the Active Learning through Drama program at Lesley College where she gave a graduate seminar in the use of puppet drama to facilitate English language learning. She has taught English as a Second Language in Jiao Tong University, Shanghai and is currently studying Mandarin Chinese. Throughout her career, Dr. Ackerman has applied her curiosity, creativity and special interests in linguistics, to building new approaches in working with ESL/bilingual children.

In 1980, Dr. Ackerman founded Puppetry in Practice (PIP) at Brooklyn College, CUNY, a program that brings the excitement of puppet theatre and the folklores of different cultures into the classroom. Since its inception it has served as a resource center for teachers in New York City. PIP recently completed a two-year folklore project, "Folktales: Structuring Meaning in Our Lives," funded by The National Endowment for the Humanities. The project involved using puppet theatre in two K-5 programs in the New York City school system. PIP is currently focusing on a research project that connects the development of literacy skills with puppet theatre.

**Mickey Aronoff** (Albuquerque, NM) has worked for three decades in the USA, Great Britain, and Singapore as a therapeutic and educational practitioner, consultant, and trainer in puppet theatre arts. She is Therapy Consultant for Puppeteers of America, a member of UNIMA-USA, and a board member of Loren Kahn Puppet and Object Theatre. She has authored many articles about her work.

**Matthew Bernier, MCAT, ATR-BC** (Portsmouth, VA) is a registered and board certified art therapist and a puppeteer. His undergraduate education includes psychology and theatre arts, and he has a master's degree in creative arts in therapy. He is an Associate Professor of Psychiatry and Behavioral Sciences at Eastern Virginia Medical School where he teaches in the Graduate Art Therapy Program. He specializes in the treatment of individuals and families who have experienced domestic violence and/or physical or sexual abuse. He has been involved with puppetry since childhood and is nationally known for his long-time charismatic involvement with therapeutic puppetry, combining his knowledge of art psychotherapy, symbolism, and dramatic enactment. He has presented many workshops and presentations on a variety of topics at schools and conferences, locally, nationally, and internationally. He serves as the president of the Southeastern Virginia Puppetry Guild and as a trustee on the Board of Trustees of the Puppeteers of America. He is a member of the Union Internationale de la Marionnette and the American Art Therapy Association. As an artist, in addition to puppetry, his interests include working with found objects through collage, assemblage, and mixed media. He is also an instructor of ballroom dancing.

**Joan Brown** (Mansfield, OH) is a licensed social worker and puppeteer.

**Bruce Chessé** (Portland, OR) is a second-generation puppeteer with more than 40 years experience in Puppetry in Education. He is an internationally recognized puppet designer, manipulator, actor, director, and teacher. Bruce is Artistic Director of the Oregon Puppet Theatre (OPT) and performs annually for audiences at festivals, schools, museums, and community events. His creations include commissioned works, giant parade puppets, puppets and programs for video and TV, and repertory productions. He is the author/publisher of the OPT Video *Making Puppets in the Primary Grades* (1992), and co-author or editor of three best-selling books on puppetry: *Puppets from polyfoam: Spongees* (Chesse & Armstrong, 1976), *Titeres de polyfoam: Esponjaditos* (Chesse & Armstrong, 1976), and *Puppets for dreaming and scheming: A puppet sourcebook* (Sims & Armstrong, 1978). He was the first recipient of the Puppeteers of America's Marjorie Batchelder McPharlin Award for contributions in the field of education.

**Suzanne Down** (Victoria, BC, CA) is long-time founder and Director of Juniper Tree School of Story and Puppetry Arts, now based out of Vancouver Island B.C. The school offers certificate training in educational, artistic, and therapeutic puppetry, which will be offered on both coasts of the U.S. starting summer 2005. Conferences, workshops, and puppetry intensives, and consultations are offered internationally. Suzanne has developed the Puppets for World Change Institute, which encourages the use of puppetry to awaken social change, including projects such as the International Puppets for Peace Day, and the Hope Puppet Project which researches and promotes therapeutic puppetry for underserved children. She is Co-Chair of the North American Association for the Renewal of Puppetry Arts - an international Waldorf School inspired association.

**Hobey Ford** (Weaverville, NC) (Golden Rod Puppets) Winner of puppetry's highest honor, the UNIMA Citation of Excellence, and recipient of three Jim Henson Foundation grants, Hobey Ford is known for excellence in puppetry performance, storytelling, and innovation in puppetry craft. He has created both the "Foamies" and the clever hand puppet known as "Peepers." His intricate shadow puppetry work and creation of the original rod puppets, the "Foamies," have earned him a place in the Kennedy Center's Partnership in Education Program. Through this program, Hobey travels the country teaching puppetry techniques and doing performances for teachers. Hobey's performances incorporate a variety of puppetry styles including Bunraku, rod, marionettes, "Foamies," and shadow puppetry. Hobey adapts folktales from various cultures for many of his performances, always adding a special "Golden Rod" twist. He uses his own voice to create characters and sound effects, tell stories, and sing. Hobey utilizes his artistic study at The State University of New York at Purchase and the University of North Carolina at Asheville to design and construct all of his Golden Rod Puppets and the beautiful sets that surround them. Hobey also draws on his early experiences growing up in coastal Connecticut or living in a Nevada Native American community in writing the scripts for some of his performances such as "Whale Walker" and "Turtle Island Tales." Hobey Ford's Golden Rod Puppets maintain a busy schedule performing and teaching in schools, performing arts centers, museums, libraries and festivals. Hobey presents shadow puppet workshops for students and two Kennedy Center workshops for teachers: "Telling Folktales with Shadow Puppets" and "From Larvae to Butterfly: Metamorphosis through Puppetry." He lives in the North Carolina mountains with his wife and three daughters, all talented artists as well.

**Elizabeth Freeman** (Wakefield, MA) has been a member of the Boston Area Guild of Puppetry and Puppeteers of America since attending the MIT festival in 1989. She has been a regular classroom teacher, Title One teacher, and professional development leader since 1968, from nipa huts in the Philippines to urban classrooms in Pennsylvania and Massachusetts. Liz is currently an elementary special education teacher in Lowell, MA, working with many bilingual students integrating puppetry across the curriculum. She is also the coordinator for the Linden Tree Coffeehouse in Wakefield, MA and assistant director for Puppets: Education Magic Institute, a conference for educators.

**Lani Gerity, PhD, ATR-BC** (Prospect, Nova Scotia, CA) is a puppet maker, book artist, author, and registered and board certified art therapist. She holds a doctorate from NYU in Art Therapy. She continues to write, lead puppet making/narrative workshops, and teaches both in the US and in Canada.

**Ronni Gerstel** (Palm Springs, FL), the creative spirit behind Flamingo Park Puppets and partner in ZingThing puppets, has been a professional puppeteer, puppet builder and instructor for 14 years. She regularly tours elementary schools throughout Palm Beach County, Florida, performing educational programs for the Mental Health Association, the Solid Waste Authority, and the Palm Beach County School District. She has produced and performed in original productions for the Jewish National Fund, the School District's Multicultural Department, the Palm Beach Zoo, and the Puppetry Arts Center of the Palm Beaches. Ronni has created and directed puppetry programs for children in arts camps and after-school programs in underserved communities. The goal of these programs is to encourage cooperation and creativity, and boost self-esteem among young people. Ronni has been awarded grants from the Community Foundation for Palm Beach and Martin Counties, and the Neighborhood Arts Residency Program to create puppet programs with young people, which promote tolerance and understanding. As an artist with the Center for Creative Education, Ronni partners with teachers to teach curriculum through the art of puppetry. She won two "outstanding collaboration" awards for her work with the Center. Another classroom collaboration is featured in the documentary, "Project LEAP: Learning Out Loud." Ronni also teaches seminars on "Puppets in Education" for the school district, local museums, and art centers, and at Puppetry festivals.

**Joy Gwynne Ginther** (Tijeras, NM) and her Pink Elephant Theatre present exciting, colorful, and educational programs featuring magic and puppets. Whether performing on a traditional puppet stage or by operating her zany puppets on top of her guitar, Joy presents stories that are captivating for audiences of all ages. Joy holds a Master's Degree in Art Education.

**Farryl Hadari** (Tel Aviv, Israel) is the chairperson of the Art Studies Division of the Seminar Hakibbutzim College in Tel Aviv, Israel. She teaches puppetry as an educational and therapeutic tool as well as an art form in the Special Education, Elementary Education, and Theatre Departments and in the School for Continuing Education. Ms Hadari founded and was the artistic director for many years of the Meitav Puppet Theatre. She produced issue orientated puppet productions on issues such as: understanding differences, Jewish and Arabic coexistence and violence in the classroom. Ms. Hadari has done short and long-term artistic residencies for Jewish communities in numerous states in the United States and in Canada, Mexico and Istanbul. Farryl Hadari's residencies involve becoming aware of the specific character and needs of the community, and then, developing workshops, curriculum enhancements, and other projects that directly address the educational and social needs of the community.

**Sheila Harris** (Remsen, NY) (Telling Times) is a storyteller and educator.

**Helene Hugel** (Dublin, Ireland), puppeteer, was apprentice to Eugene Lambert in Ireland, studied with the London School of Puppetry, and has a qualification in Hospital Play Specialism. She has been working as a professional puppeteer for the past seven years, primarily as co-founder and partner of the award winning Puca Puppets. She became freelance in 2002 to specialize in the field of Art and Health. Through the combination of being awarded an artist's residency in Our Lady's Hospital for Sick Children, Crumlin, and an artist's bursary, she explored the use of puppetry and play to empower children to transform the hospital environment by making puppets from hospital materials and animating hospital equipment. Parallel to this, was the creation of a series of "medical" puppets such as Stella Stethoscope, a walking, talking, working stethoscope. The result is a series of guided hospital play sessions, which utilize performance, storytelling, and making skills to suggest a more non-directive, yet stimulating, child-centered approach to workshop facilitation, which could be useful to the healing process.

**Marlene Joyce** (Burlington, NC) has been active in the education of children since graduating from Miami University, Oxford, Ohio in 1964. She taught fourth grade for eight years in Ohio and Wisconsin, and completed a Master's Degree in Curriculum and Instruction from the University of Madison, Wisconsin in 1974. During a two-year residence in Basel, Switzerland, Ms. Joyce learned of Waldorf Education and in 1997 she attended Sunbridge College in Spring Valley, NY, to receive certification in Waldorf Early Childhood Education. In May, 2004, she received a Masters Degree in Waldorf Education from Sunbridge College, writing her thesis on *Teaching children with puppets: Toward new social forms.* Currently, Ms. Joyce aids public school teachers in using puppets in their daily curriculum as well as helps new parents respond with respect to their newborns through toddlers following indications from Magda Gerber's parenting books. She is also a registered clown and resides in Burlington, NC.

**Susan Linn, Ed D** (Boston, MA), is a psychologist, puppeteer, award-winning producer, and writer. She is Associate Director of the Media Center of the Judge Baker Children's Center and an Instructor in Psychiatry at Harvard Medical School. She is the author of *Consuming kids: The hostile takeover of childhood* (New Press, 2004), which has been praised in publications as diverse as the *Wall Street Journal* and *Mother Jones.* She is also the founder of the national advocacy coalition *Campaign for a Commercial-Free Childhood.* Her writings about the impact of commercial marketing on children have appeared in, among others, *The Washington Post, The Boston Globe, The Christian Science Monitor,* and *The American Prospect.*

Dr. Linn is internationally known for her innovative work using puppets in child psychotherapy. She pioneered this work at Children's Hospital in Boston, where she used puppets to help children cope with their hospital experiences and is now continuing her work at the Children's AIDS Program, which is affiliated with Boston Medical Center. She has lectured about play and puppetry as a tool for psychotherapy throughout North America and Europe and in Israel, Korea, and Japan.

Combining her skills as a writer and performer with her role as a child therapist, Dr. Linn has written and appeared in a number of video programs designed to help children cope with issues ranging from mental illness to death and loss. She has been the psychological consultant to the Leadership Conference Education Fund's anti-bias public service campaigns since 1992 and co-authored their publication, *Talking to children about racism, prejudice and diversity.* To facilitate the creation of children's television programs to promote multicultural understanding, she taught script writing about conflict resolution at Tblisi State University in The Republic of Georgia.

With Family Communications, Inc., the producers of Mister Rogers' Neighborhood, Dr. Linn created *Different and the Same: Helping Children Identify and Prevent Prejudice,* video based classroom materials designed for first to third graders. *Different and the Same* won the 1996 Media Award from the Association of Multicultural Educators and is currently being used in all fifty states.

Dr. Linn's work has been featured nationally on such television programs as *Mr. Rogers' Neighborhood, Today, Good Morning America,* and a variety of nationally syndicated public service announcements addressing issues of importance to children. *This Secret Should Be Told,* a program for children about sexual abuse that aired on WBZ-TV (Boston), won a coveted ACT award, as well as a New England Emmy. Dr. Linn was named Entertainer of the Year by the *Boston Parents' Paper* in 1988. She also received a Citation of Excellence—the highest award an American Puppeteer can receive from The American Chapter of the Union Internationale de la Marionette.

**Mary Mazzacane** (Hamden, CT), an opera singer and solo puppeteer is a former music teacher in the New Haven School System and has been building and performing with puppets for several years. Mary is a graduate of the Yale University School of Music with courses at the Yale School of Drama and is also a graduate of Southern Connecticut State University. Her main focus has been on puppetry in education, which has resulted in the writing of a published book, *Music education through puppetry* (1984). She was the recipient of several awards at Yale and also received an award from Southern Connecticut State University for "Innovative Teaching of Music." She has taught music and puppetry to emotionally and perceptually handicapped children and the gifted and talented children in project "Learn." In addition to being an adjunct instructor in puppetry at SCSU, Mary has taught music at South Central Community College. Articles dealing with her work in "Music Education through Puppetry" have appeared in many periodicals including: The Connecticut Music Educators' Association Magazine, the Puppetry in Education News Journal, the New Haven Register, the Hamden Chronicle and "Animations" Magazine published by the Puppet Center Trust Battersee Arts Center, London, England. Her work has also been televised on WTNH, New Haven, CT. Mary has presented several lectures, demonstrations, and workshops on puppetry in education in several schools, colleges and universities and at the Northeast/Mid-Atlantic Puppet Festival.

Mary performs puppet shows for various schools, churches, clubs, organizations, birthday parties, libraries and fairs in addition to presenting workshops for children and adults which include construction, manipulation, improvisation and performance. Mary is past president of the Connecticut Guild of Puppetry and is a member of the Puppeteers of America.

**Judith O'Hare** (Reading, MA), creator of You and Me Puppets, is the Education Consultant and Chair of the Puppetry in Education and Therapy Committee for the Puppeteers of America and director of Puppets: Education Magic Institute. She is a solo puppeteer who specializes in participatory performances with children and Toy Theater. She has given teacher training workshops in schools and colleges for over 30 years. She teaches graduate courses for the Northeast Consortium/Salem State College and Lesley University. In February of 2002 and 2004, she represented the US at EduPuppets an International Puppet Festival in Kenya where she gave teacher training workshops and performances. She also gave workshops and performances at two universities in Tanzania. She has given workshops in Hong Kong, and China, and presented her workshops, Participatory Puppet Theater and Toy Theater Performances at Puppeteers of America Festivals across the US and in Ottawa, Canada. She has won awards from the Puppeteers of America Northeast Region for her work in puppetry in education, Puppets: Education Magic, a conference for educators, and from Reading, MA, for her contribution to the artistic life of the community both as an arts administrator and founder of Creative Arts, an arts center for children and adults, and for her work as a puppeteer.

**Marianne Parr** (Enumclaw, WA) is a teacher in Auburn, Washington. She began teaching in the public school system in 1973. She earned her BA degree in education from Western Illinois University. She received formal instruction in puppetry at Central Washington University. She has designed and implemented a puppetry in education curriculum for sixth grade students at Mt. Baker Middle School in Auburn, Washington. This curriculum includes a teacher-designed puppet kit for student construction, teacher-written puppet plays that focus on middle school issues, and teacher-designed puppet patterns for costuming. She has written and produced four puppet shows and has presented at faculty in-service offerings. She specializes in rod puppets but also has her students build simple marionettes. Annually, she assists 200 grade six students of all abilities in the construction and performance of rod puppets. Her shows have been a hit with middle school students and parents since 1996. She has been teaching world languages and theater for over 25 years. She has been a member of Puppeteers of America since 1997.

**Wendy Passmore-Godfrey** (Calgary, Alberta, CA), BFA, is Artistic and Founding Director of W.P. Puppet Theatre established in 1991 as a charitable, not for profit Society based in Calgary, Alberta. Annually, WPTS presents over 250 performances and workshops across Canada and internationally, reaching more than 30,000 children and adults. As principal performer and creator, Wendy has hands-on expertise in all aspects of professional puppet theater. Her training includes study with Petr Metasek of DRAK Puppet Theatre, Czechoslovakia at the University of Washington, attending the International Institute of Puppet Arts in Charlesville-Mezieirs, France and going to numerous Puppeteers of America and UNIMA Festivals. Wendy also served five years as a Trustee on the board of Puppeteers of America. As a workshop leader, for children and adults, she sees and teaches the power of puppetry as a medium for communication in many areas beyond performance. WPTS's Vision, and by inclusion Wendy's vision, is to encourage audiences around the world to enjoy, honor and employ the art of puppetry in their exploration of the complexity and wonder of the universe... and to question the human place within the universe. The WPTS motto "Animating the Spirit" is very apt – we not only bring "life" to bits of foam and fur but also bring creativity and joy to our audiences.

**Sharon M. Peck** (Geneseo, NY) is an educator and puppeteer who is committed to improving the literacy lives of students and teachers. She left the elementary classroom to become a professor of literacy at SUNY Geneseo, in western New York. Sharon enjoys working with teachers to implement puppetry in their classrooms, and supporting teacher learning around literacy instruction. She is currently conducting research on puppetry in education. Sharon also performs authentic historical Punch and Judy puppet shows with her sister Deb Peck Kelleher, as The Punchbowl Sisters.

**Paula Shutman** (Nevada, TX) is currently pursuing a college degree in Music Therapy and plans to incorporate the use of puppetry in her work.

**David Silver, MD** (Boulder, CO) is a medical doctor and international public health consultant. He has worked as a technical advisor for health projects in Vietnam, West Bank/Gaza, Uganda, Kenya, India, Indonesia and Guatemala, conducting monitoring/

evaluation, health needs assessment, program planning, participatory action research and training. Utilizing local folk media (storytelling, songs, drama, and puppetry) to communicate health messages and to promote behavior change is a special interest. David is also a founding member of Free Range Theater, a political street theater in the Denver metro area that utilizes giant puppets to raise public awareness.

**Lesley Smith** (Durham, NH) (For ten years, puppeteer/singer/ventriloquist Lesley Smith's Theatre of Life Puppets and Band have entertained and educated students in Kindergarten through eighth grade throughout the Northeast. Her productions cover conflict resolution, bully prevention, tobacco prevention, and environmental education. Scripts carefully reflect the concepts of Wellesley College's Open Circle, Second Step, and William J. Kreidler's conflict resolution material from ESR. As a ventriloquist, Lesley's sidekick Sam Snail creates an intimate relationship with the audience, modeling skills and behaviors that students can then identify with.

Woodland Heights Elementary Guidance Counselor in Laconia NH reported, "I am amazed at how much our students learned in only one short hour. I am even more amazed that they have retained the concepts and are using them in their classrooms and on the playground. Any school who does not see your performance ("Peaceable Kingdom" conflict resolution.) is truly missing out on one of the finest enrichment programs I have viewed." Peggy McCallister, Past President of the National Association of School Principals reports, "It is without hesitation that I recommend Lesley Smith's programs to any school principal! Through her puppets she is able to entertain and teach critical lessons that make a lasting impression. It is rare to find a person who can be as entertaining and engaging with adults, as well as children." The Boston Globe states, "Her smile and presence is as warm and welcoming as her voice! And the emotion and life her puppets exude is something even adults can relish!" NH Public Television applauds, "Lesley Smith is irresistible to children. She's a pied piper, a modern day minstrel, she's absolutely terrific!" The Lowell National Park Series confirmed, "Lesley Smith's music and puppet theatre was one of the most well received components of our season." (Rick Sherburne, Boarding House Park Series Director).

**Carol Sterling** (New York, NY) has worked as a Pennsylvania and New York City based arts education administrator, and has served as a past president of UNIMA-USA, an educational puppetry consultant for the Puppeteers of America and a member of the advisory board for the Puppetry Journal. She is currently a consultant in arts, education and educational puppetry. Carol has authored articles for the *Puppetry Journal* including: "How to Be a Puppeteer in the Schools," and "The Role of Sesame Street in Educational Puppetry." She wrote an article for School Arts Magazine documenting her work on "Giant Puppets," based on her role as a puppeteer-artist in the public schools and in community settings, for New York City's Yankee Stadium and for the Spoleto Festival in Charleston, South Carolina. While serving as Arts Education Consultant for the New Jersey State Department of Education, she wrote *Puppetry in the Classroom*, and conducted educational puppetry workshops for educators, librarians and beyond. Carol is Program Director for Kidville, NY, a Manhattan, NY, educational/enrichment center for New York City families and children ages, newborn to age 5. In the course of her long career as an art educator, Carol has championed the importance of educational puppetry on local, state, regional, national, and international levels.

**Jo Tomalin** (San Francisco, CA) is an Associate Professor in the Theatre Arts Department of San Francisco State University. Originally from England, Jo has lived in the Bay Area for 16 years working in theatre as an actor, director, dialect coach, puppeteer and teacher. Recently she directed "The Trojan Women" for SFSU and "Letters to Anna" a one-woman story poem about a Pioneer woman performed by the author Ellery Akers, for the Marin Fringe Festival. As a puppeteer, Jo performs in small venues and several of her students have formed puppet troupes, which have performed outreach shows in San Francisco schools, museums and libraries. As a workshop presenter, Jo has given workshops at the Great Lakes regional puppet festival at Madison, Wisconsin, West Coast PuppetFest at Asilomar, Monterey, CA, and at Bridges Festival at the University of Connecticut.  She is also an adviser for the Liberal Studies program at SFSU, which is a foundation degree for pre-teaching credential students. Jo received her teaching credential from London University, completed professional postgraduate theatre studies at Ecole Jacques Lecoq, Paris, and is a PhD Candidate in Education: Instructional Design for Online Learning at Capella University, MN.

# BIBLIOGRAPHY

(There are literally thousands of books published on puppetry and related topics. This bibliography includes classics as well as more current books and articles on puppetry, puppetry in education, and puppetry in therapy, and literature with implications for both. Many of these works are dated and some are out of print, but they represent the evolution of the art of puppetry and the development of puppetry in education and therapy. Many puppetry books can be ordered from the Puppeteers of America Puppetry Store, at puppeteers.org/puppetstore.html (store@puppeteers.org) (602-262-2050). Used copies and out of print books are often available from internet book sources such as amazon.com. Also, many university and public libraries have collections of puppetry books.)

## PUPPETRY AND RELATED ARTS

Ackerman, T. (1990). *Puppets and stages.* Brooklyn, N Y: Brooklyn College. (Victorian stage, styrofoam mouse, talker puppet, and shadow puppet.)

Allport, A. J. (1978). *Model theaters and how to make them.* New York: Charles Scribner's Sons

Arnott, P. D. (1964). *Plays without people: Puppetry and serious drama.* Bloomington, IN: Indiana University Press. (Greek classics with marionettes.)

Bacon, M. (1997). *No strings attached: The inside story of Jim Henson's Creature Shop.* Hampshire, England: Macmillan. (Great for technical ideas; wonderful pictures; introduction by Jim Henson; good for older students.)

Baird, B. (1965). *The art of the puppet.* New York: Macmillan. (A must for the library; covers history and development of puppetry as an art form. Reprinted (1966 & 1967) Boston: Plays and (1973) New York: Bonanza)

Baldwin, P. (1992). *Toy theatres of the world.* London: Zwemmer Ltd. (A wonderful resource on Toy Theater designs.)

Bartelt, J. (1993). *Screen play: Shadow puppets on the overhead projector.* Auburn, WA: Jeanine Bartelt.

Bass, E. (1992). *Breaking boundaries: American puppetry in the 1980s.* Atlanta: Center for Puppetry Arts.

Batchelder, M. (1947). *The puppet theatre handbook.* New York: Harper & Row. (She was in the forefront in writing about puppetry in the US.)

Batchelder, M. & Comer, V. L. (1956). *Puppets and plays.* New York: Harper & Row.

Beaton, M. & Beaton, L. (1949/1989). *Marionettes: A hobby for everyone.* New York: Thomas Crowell. (classic)

Bell, J. (Ed.) (2001). *Puppets. masks, and performing objects.* Cambridge: MIT Press.

Bell, J. (2000). *Strings, hands, shadows: A modern puppet history.* Detroit: Detroit Institute for the Arts.

Blumenthal, E. & Taymor, J. (1995). *Julie Taymor: Playing with fire.* New York: Harry Abrams. (Director of "The Lion King" on Broadway. Her work bridges several art forms; extends concepts of puppetry arts; excellent photos.)

Boylan, E. *How to be a puppeteer.* Boston: McCall Press. (She influenced many Boston puppeteers.)

Burgess, R. (1999). *Theater models in paper and card.* East Sussex, England: Guild of Master Craftsman Publications Ltd. (Toy Theater resource.)

Chessé, B. & Armstrong, B. (1975). *Puppets from polyfoam: Spongees.* Walnut Creek, CA: Early Stages Publications. (An original, one of a kind book; great for educators.)

Coad, L. (1975). *Black theatre.* N. Vancouver, BC: Coad Canada Puppets.

Coad, L. (1975). *Classroom stages and black theatre.* N. Vancouver, BC: Coad Canada Puppets.

Coad, L. (1987). *Producing for the puppet theater.* N. Vancouver, BC: Coad Canada Puppets.

Condon, C. (1987). *Try on my shoe.* Chula Vista, CA: Lynn Jennings. (Multicultural folktales and puppet patterns.)

Creegan, G. (1966). *Sir George's book of hand puppetry.* New York: Follett.

Cummings, R. (2002). *101 hand puppets: A beginner's guide to puppeteering.* New York: Dover.

Currell, D. (1970). *Puppetry for school children.* Newton, MA: Charles T. Bradford.

Dwiggins, W.A. (1939). *Marionette in motion.* Detroit: Puppetry Imprints.

Dagan, E. A. (1990). *Emotions in motion: Theatrical puppets and masks from black Africa.* Montreal: Galerie Amrad African Arts.

Devet, D. & Allison, D. (1983). *The wit and wisdom of polyfoam puppet construction.* Charlotte, NC: Grey Seal Puppets.

Devet, D. & Allison, D. (1997). *The foam book.* Charlotte, NC: Grey Seal Puppets. (How to construct polyfoam puppets.)

Doney, M. (1995). *World crafts: Puppets.* New York: Franklin Watts. (Inexpensive; covers many cultures; good for children; easy to read; good pictures.)

Engler, L. & Fijan, C. (1973/1997). *Making puppets come alive.* New York: Taplinger. (A must for any school or professional puppeteer's library! Hand puppet manipulation.)

Feller, R. & Feller, M. (1987). *Fairy tales.* Seattle: The Arts Factory. (Masks and an approach to story development.)

Feller, R. & Feller, M. (1990). *Paper masks and puppets.* Seattle: The Arts Factory.

Fettig, H. (1997). *Rod puppets and table-top puppets:* A handbook of design & technique. Gillingham, England: DaSilva Puppet Books. (This is an updated and expanded version of *Hand and rod puppets.*)

Fijan, C. & B. (1989). *Directing the puppet theatre.* San Jose, CA: Resource Publications. (A basic theater approach to directing.)

Fisher, J. (Ed.) (1995). *Puppetry Yearbook, Vol. 1, 1995.* P of A Bookstore. (Forum for articles on history and practice of puppetry. Written by scholars and performing artists.)

Fling, H. (1983). *Marionettes: How to make and work them.* New York: Dover Craft Publications.

Flower, C. & Fortney, A. (1983). *Puppets, methods and materials.* Worcester, MA: Davis Publications. (Many pictures and construction methods.)

Furguson, H. (1975). *Bring on the puppets!* New York: Morehouse-Barlow.

Gorsline, D. (1980). *What people wore.* Minneola, NY: Dover. (Excellent for costuming.)

Grafton, C. (Ed.) (1979). *Silhouettes: A pictorial archive of varied illustrations.* Minneola, NY: Dover. (Excellent resource for shadow puppet designs.)

Henson Associates (1980). *The art of the Muppets: A retrospective look at twenty-five years of Muppet magic.* New York: Bantam Books.

Henson, C. & The Muppet Workshop. (1994). *The Muppets make puppets.* New York: Workman. (A fun book.)

Huff, M. J. (1998). *Storytelling with puppets, props, & playful tales.* Palo Alto, CA: Monday Morning Books.

Inches, A. (2001). *Jim Henson's designs and doodles: A Muppet sketchbook.* New York: Harry Abrams. (A fun biographical book about Henson and his work.)

Kennedy, J. (2004). *Puppet mania.* Cincinnati: North Light Books. (Many projects, good to use with children and teachers.)

Kominz, L. & Levinson, M. (Eds.) (1990). *The language of the puppet.* Seattle, WA: Pacific Puppetry Press. (Articles about the art of puppetry by major puppetry artists.)

Lafosse, M & Jackson, P. (1998). *Paper pop-ups.* Gloucester, MA: Rockport. (Easy to make pop-up designs that can be used to make scenery and props for Toy Theater or miniature puppet theater. Easy to follow directions.)

Lanchester, W. S. (1969). *Hand puppets and string puppets.* Leicester, England: Dryad Press.

Lasky, K. (1985). *Puppeteer.* New York: Macmillan. (A book about Boston puppeteer Paul Vincent Davis, an artist in action.)

Latshaw, G. (1978). *Puppetry: The ultimate disguise.* New York: Richard Rosen Press.

Latshaw, G. (2000). *The complete book of puppetry.* Minneola, NY: Dover. (Previously out of print book, formerly known as, *Puppetry the Ultimate Disguise.* GREAT!)

Lee, D. T. (1997). *Puppetry: The Taiwan tradition.* Taipei, Taiwan: Government Information Office.

Leleu-Rouvray, G. & Langevin, G. (1993*). Institut International de la Marionette: International bibliography of puppetry, English books, 1945-1990.* Paris: K. G. Saur.

Long, T. C. (1995). *Make your own performing puppets.* New York: Sterling (Charming book includes interesting and easy to make puppets, stages and props with ideas for how to use puppets and masks. Includes ideas for rainforest stories, sets and puppets about dragons, shadow puppets, Toy Theater, marionettes and more.)

Magon, J. (1989). *Staging the puppet show.* Charlemagne Press: N. Vancouver, BC, Canada. (Wonderful resource.)

Malkin, M. (1995). *Puppets: The power of wonder.* Atlanta: Center for Puppetry Arts.

McKay, K. (1980). *Puppetry in Canada.* Ontario, Canada: Ontario Puppetry Association.

McPharlin, P. (1949, 1969). *The puppet theatre in America: A history 1524 to 1948.* Boston: Plays.

Nobleman, R. (1979). *Mime and masks.* Rowayton, CT: New Plays. (Overlook the date; it's a wonderful book and resource.)

Obraztzov, S. (1961). *The Chinese puppet theatre.* Boston: Plays. (A classic)

Philpot, A. R. (1965). *The puppet book.* London: Michael Joseph Press. (Historical)

Philpott, V. (1976). *The funcraft book of puppets.* New York: Scholastic.

Pollocks Toy Theaters Ltd. (Ed.) (1972). *Cinderella or, The Little Glass Slipper.* London, England: Pollocks Toy Theater Ltd. (Text in five languages. Instructions for assembling theatre and performing play.)

Pomaska, A. (1984). *Cut and assemble a fairy tale toy theater.* Minneola, NY: Dover (Full color characters and scenery for "Little Red Riding Hood," "Hansel and Gretel" and "Jack and the Beanstalk.")

Robson, D. & Bailey, V. (1991). *Rainy day puppets.* New York: Gloucester Press.

Reusch, R. (Ed.) (2001). *Shadow theatre.* Germant: Einhorn-Verlag. (Collection of essays and photos by world renown shadow puppeteers. Excellent for advanced students.)

Richmond, A. & Bufano, R. (1950). *Remo Bufano's book of puppetry.* New York: Macmillan. (He was one of the first major US puppet artists who wrote about the art form.)

Richmond, M. H. (Ed.) (1997). *Look what you can make with tubes.* Honesdale, PA: Boyds Mills Press. (A few fun ideas for simple puppets from recycled tubes.)

Roth, C. D. (1975). *The art of making puppets and marionettes.* Radnor, PA: Chilton Book Company.

Rottman, F. (1978). *Easy to make puppets and how to use them.* Glendale, CA: Regal Books.

Rump, N. (1996). *Puppets and masks: Stagecraft and storytelling.* Worcester, MA: Davis. (Many good ideas and approaches to puppet construction and drama.)

Schneebeli-Morrell, D. (1994). *Puppet making.* Seacaucus, NJ: Chartwell Books. (Easy to follow.)

Scholastic. (Ed.) (1993). *The world of theater.* New York: Scholastic. (First printed in France. This is a well illustrated short history of the theater including puppetry and masks. It has interactive parts, and puppets and screen to do a shadow puppet show. Excellent.)

Scott, A. S. (1973). *The puppet theater of Japan.* Rutland, VT. &Tokyo: Charles E. Tuttle.

Simmen, R. (1975). *The world of puppets.* New York: Thomas Crowell. (A very good history of puppetry.)

Sinclair, A. (1995). *The puppetry handbook.* Castlemaine VIC, Australia: Richard Lee Publishing. (An excellent resource on how to construct many types of puppets, theaters and lighting.)

Spinney, C. & Milligan, J. (2003). *The wisdom of Big Bird (and the dark genius of Oscar the Grouch): Lessons from a life in feathers.* New York: Villard Books/ Random House. (A charming personal history by the puppeteer who created Big Bird and Oscar the Grouch for Sesame Street.)

Tichenor, T. (1959). *Folk plays for puppets you can make.* New York: Abington Press. (Tichenor created the puppets for Carnival; his work is part of puppetry history.)

Tilroe, N. (1988). *Movement in puppetry performance.* Wollaston, MA: Touching Hands Publications. (Exercises in hand puppet manipulation.).

Union Internationale de la Marionette (Ed.) (1967). *Puppet theater of the modern world.* (E. Asers & Strick, E. trans.) Boston: Plays. (Collection of essays which discuss puppetry including a philosophy of puppetry in today's world. An interesting point: "puppetry is a reversal of life in that puppets are inanimate objects which come to life as opposed to real life in which the living lose their life in death; a reversal of the life role." Half of the book has beautiful prints. There are several updated editions.)

Van Schuyver, J. (1993). *Storytelling made easy with puppets*. Phoenix: Oryx Press.

Von Seggen, D. (1999). *Puppetry stages*. Englewood, CO: One Way Street.

Wallace, M. (1994). *I can make puppets*. New York: Firefly Books.

Way, B. (1981). *Audience participation: Theatre for young people*. Boston: Bakers Plays.

Wolfe, G. (1995). *3-D Wizardry: Design in paper-mache, plaster and foam*. Worcester, MA: Davis.

Wright, J. (1986). *Rod, shadow and glove: Puppets from the Little Angel Theatre*. London: Robert Hale Press.

Wright, L. (1991). *Masks*. London: Franklin Watt.

Yoder, C. P. (Ed.) (1989). Important puppets. *FACES: A magazine about people*. Peterborough, NH: Cobblestone Publishing, 5(5). (Reprints available by calling FACES.)

## PUPPETRY IN EDUCATION

Astell-Burt, C. (2002). *I am the story: The art of puppetry in education*. London: Souvenir Press. (Teachers like this book.)

Champlin, C. & Renfro, N. (illus.) (1980). *Puppetry and creative dramatics in storytelling*. Austin, TX: Nancy Renfro Studios. (Nancy Renfro has been a writer and collaborator on many wonderful puppetry books for educators. She has left a legacy for puppetry in education.)

Coad, L. (1975). *Using puppets in schools*. N. Vancouver, BC: Coad Canada Puppets.

Crepeau, I. M. & Richards, M. A. (2003). *A show of hands: Using puppets with young children*. St. Paul, MN: Redleaf Press. (Excellent resource.)

Crothers, J. F. (1983). The puppet as an educator. *The puppeteer's library guide: The bibliographic index to the literature of the World Puppet Theatre*, Vol. II. Metuchen, NJ: The Scarecrow Press.

Ewart, F. G. (1998). *Let the shadows speak: Developing children's language through shadow puppetry*. England: Trentham Books.

Frazier, N. & Renfro, N. (illus.) (1987). *Imagination: At play with puppets and dramatics.* Austin, TX: Nancy Renfro Studios.

Fredricks, M. & Segal, J. (1979). *Creative puppetry in the classroom.* New Haven, CT: New Plays.

Hunt, T. & Renfro, N. (1982). *Puppetry in early childhood education.* Austin, TX: Renfro Studios (A must for the early childhood library; grounded in child development; good bibliography.)

Majaron, E. & Kroflin, L. (Eds.) (2002). *The puppet: What a miracle!* Croatia: UNIMA in Education Commission. (A collection of articles by members of UNIMA in Croatia and Slovenia about puppetry in education. A fine resource.)

Mazzacane, M. (1984). *Music education through puppetry.* Hamden, CT: Keynote.

Pearson, M. R. (1992). *Perky puppets with a purpose: A complete guide to puppetry & ventriloquism in Christian ministry.* Springfield, Missouri: Gospel Publishing House. (Covers a broad spectrum of educational puppetry.)

Renfro, N. (1979). *Puppetry and the art of story creation.* Austin, TX. Nancy Renfro Studios.

Renfro, N. (1984). *Puppet shows made easy.* Austin, TX: Nancy Renfro Studios.

Renfro, N. (1984). *Puppetry, language and the special child: Discovering alternative languages.* Austin, TX: Nancy Renfro Studios.

Renfro, N. & Armstrong, B. (1982). *Make amazing puppets.* Santa Barbara, CA: The Learning Works.

Renfro, N. & Hunt, T. (1982). *Pocketful of puppets: Mother Goose.* Austin, TX: Nancy Renfro Studios.

Renfro, N. & Winer, Y. (1983). *Pocketful of puppets: Three plump fish.* Austin, TX: Nancy Renfro Studios.

Roundtree, B., Shuptrine, M., Gordon, J. & Taylor, N. (1989). *Creative teaching with puppets.* Tuscaloosa, AL: The Learning Line.

Santano, T., Pasternack, D. & Vega, A. (1997). *The art of reading.* Brooklyn, NY: Puppetry in Practice.

Schram, T. (1993). *Puppet plays from workshop to performance.* Englewood, Colorado: Teachers Ideas Press.

Schroeder, J. (1995). *Fun puppet skits for schools and libraries.* Westport, CT: Libraries Unlimited.

Shultz, T. L. & Sorenson, L. (1989). *Organic puppet theater.* Santa Cruz, CA: Network Publications. (Using puppetry to teach about the human body.)

Sims, J. (1978). *Puppets for dreaming and scheming*: A puppet sourcebook. Walnut Creek, CA: Early Stages Press. (A great idea book for using puppets with children.)

Speaight, G. (1986). *Theater games for the classroom: A teacher's handbook.* Evanston, IL: Northwestern Univ. Press.

Sylvester, R. (1976). *Teaching bible stories more effectively with puppets.* St. Louis: Concordia Publishing House.

Tierney, J. L. (1995). *Puppetry in early childhood education.* Ann Arbor, MI: Dissertation Services.

Vandergun, A. (1974). *Puppets for the classroom.* Vancouver, BC: Allison Vandergun. (Excellent)

Wade, J. E. (1947). *Puppetry in the curriculum: Board of Education, City of New York, Curriculum Bulletin No.1.* New York: NYC Board of Education.

Wisniewski, D. & Wisniewski, D. (1997). *Worlds of shadows: Teaching with shadow puppets.* Englewood, CO: Teacher Ideas Press. (An excellent resource for shadow puppets!)

Zetlaw, J. & Frank, C. S. *(1985). Alphabet puppets: An interdisciplinary approach to the alphabet.* Carthage, IL: Good Apple.

## PUPPETRY IN THERAPY

Alexander, S. (1988). Puppets as a teaching tool. *Nursing RSA*, 3(9), 24-26.

Aronoff, M. (1996). Puppetry as a therapeutic medium: An introduction. *British Journal of Therapeutic Rehabilitation*, 3, 210-214.

Aronoff, M. (Winter, 1997). Therapy. *The Puppetry Journal*, 25.

Aronoff, A. (1991). Puppets for change. *Animations:* 56, Feb/Mar.

Aronoff, A. (1992). A soul in the palm of a hand. *Therapy Weekly,* 19(10), 8.

Aronoff, A. (Dec 1994-Jan 1995). Unmasking our grief. *Scottish Child, 11.*

Aronoff, A. (Sept 1994). Introducing puppets in preparation. *Cascade, 13,* 10-11.

Aronoff, M. (Nov 1994). Reflections on Russian therapeutic puppetry (Part I). *British UNIMA Bulletin,* No. 87, 26-30.

Aronoff, A. (Autumn 1994). Scottish Mask & Puppet Centre. *Disability News,* 45-46.

Aronoff, M. (1996). Puppetry and ritual: Trance & Beroek. *British UNIMA Bulletin,* Feb, 91.

Aronoff, M. (1997). Puppetry projects with children in psychiatric assessment units of pediatric hospitals. *La Marionnette et Les Ages de la Vie, Comte Rendu Villéme Colloque International, Organisé par Association "Marionnette et Thérapie",* 14-18.

Astell-Burt, C. (1981). *Puppetry for mentally handicapped people.* London: Souvenir Press.

Bender, L. (1952). *Child psychiatric techniques.* Springfield, IL: Charles C Thomas.

Bender, L. & Woltmann, A. (1936). The use of puppet shows as a therapeutic method for behavior problems in children. *American Journal of Orthopsychiatry,* 6, 341-354.

Bernier, M. (1983). *Puppetry as an art therapy technique with emotionally disturbed children.* Unpublished master's thesis, Hahnemann University, Philadelphia, PA.

Cassell, S. (1965). Effect of brief puppet therapy upon the emotional responses of children undergoing cardiac catheterization. *Journal of Consulting Psychology, 29,* 1-8.

Chiles, D. (2001). The therapeutic use of puppetry in a health care setting. *National Festival Workshop Manual: 2001 A Puppet Odyssey.* Puppeteers of America.

Cole, N. A. (1993). *Lend them a hand: Therapeutic puppetry.* Box 45, Milford, Ontario, Canada, KOK 2PO: Arthur Cole.

Du Rand, L. & Gerity, L. (1996). Puppetry: A collaboration between drama therapy and art therapy. *Dramascope: The National Association for Drama Therapy Newsletter,* Vol. XVI, 2, Summer/Fall 1996, 9-10.

Gendler, M. (1986). Group puppetry with school-age children: Rationale, procedure and therapeutic implications. *The Arts in Psychotherapy, 13,* 45-52.

Gerity, L. (1999). *Creativity and the dissociative patient: Puppets, narrative, and art in the treatment of survivors of childhood trauma.* London: Jessica Kingsley.

Gordon, G. (1986). *Puppets for better health: A manual for community workers and teachers*. London: The Macmillan Press.

Irwin, E. (1983). The diagnostic and therapeutic use of pretend play. In C. Schaefer & K. O'Connor (Eds.), *Handbook of play therapy* (pp. 148-173). New York: John Wiley & Sons.

Irwin, E. (1993). Using puppets for assessment. In C. Schaefer & D. Cangelosi (Eds.), *Play therapy techniques* (pp. 69-81). Northvale, New Jersey: Jason Aronson.

Irwin, E., Rubin, J., & Shapiro, M. (1975). Art and drama: Partners in therapy. *American Journal of Psychotherapy, 29,* 107-116.

Irwin, E. & Shapiro, M. (1975). Puppetry as a diagnostic and therapeutic technique. In I. Jakab (Ed.). *Psychiatry and art* (4). New York: S. Karger.

Jenkins, R. & Beckh, E. (1942). Finger puppets and mask making as media for work with children. *American Journal of Orthopsychiatry, 12*(2), 294-300.

Kors, P. (1963). The use of puppetry in psychotherapy. *American Journal of Psychotherapy, 17,* 54-63.

Kors, P. (1964). Unstructured puppet shows as group procedure in therapy with children. *Psychiatric Quarterly Supplement, 38*(1), 56-75.

Lansdown, R. (1996). *Children in Hospital*. Oxford: Oxford University Press.

Linn, S. (1977). Puppets and hospitalized children: Talking about feelings. *Journal of the Association for the Care of Children in Hospitals*, 5(4), 5-11.

Linn, S. (1978). Puppet therapy in hospitals: Helping children cope. *Journal of the American Medical Women's Association*, 33(2), 61-65.

McMahon, L. (1992). *The handbook of play therapy.* London: Routledge.

Oaklander, V. (1978). *Windows to our children (pp. 85-108)*. Moab, UT: Real People Press.

Oatman, K. (1981). *Breaking through the barrier*. Willowdale, Ontario, CA: Ontario Puppetry Association Publishing Co.

Philpott, A. R. (Ed.) (1977). *Puppets and therapy.* Boston: Plays.

Rojas-Bermudez, J. (1969). The intermediary object. *Group Psychotherapy, 22,* 149-154.

Schneider, F. (1976). Puppetry as preparation for surgery. *Puppetry Journal*, (March/April), 3-8.

Sommers, S. (1977). Marionette making and self-awareness. *American Journal of Art Therapy, 16*(2), 51-53.

Steinhardt, L. (1994). Creating the autonomous image through puppet theatre and art therapy. *The Arts in Psychotherapy*, 21, 3, 205-218.

Sullivan, D. (1982). *Pocketful of puppets: Activities for the special child with mental, physical, and multiple handicaps.* Austin, TX: Nancy Renfro Studios.

West, J. (1992). *Child-centred play therapy.* London: Edward Arnold.

Wilson, K., Kendrick, P. & Ryan, V. (1992). *Play therapy: A non-directive approach for children and adolescents.* London: Ballière-Tindall.

Woltmann, A. (1960). Spontaneous puppetry by children as a projective method. In A. Rabin & M. Howarth (Eds.). *Projective techniques with children* (pp. 305-312). New York: Grune & Stratton.

## LITERATURE WITH IMPLICATIONS FOR PUPPETRY IN EDUCATION AND/ OR THERAPY

Arnheim, R. (1954,1974). *Art and visual perception.* Berkeley & Los Angeles: University of California Press.

Bernardi, P. (1992). *Improvisation starters: A collection of 900 improvisation situations for the theater.* Cincinnati: Betterway Books.

Bettlleheim, B. (1977). *The uses of enchantment.* New York: Vintage Press. (A classic resource on the importance of fairy tales for the growth and development of children. Excellent resource.)

Bidwell, S.M. (1990). Using drama to increase motivation, comprehension, and fluency. *Journal of Reading*, 34, 38-41.

Bottomley, J. (1983). *Paper projects for creative kids of all ages.* Boston: Little Brown (Excellent paper sculpting techniques.)

Chaplin, E. (1994). *Sociology and visual representation (pp. 207-212).* London: Routledge.

Clark, R. (1999). *Building expertise: Cognitive methods for training and performance improvement.* Washington, D.C.: International Society for Performance Improvement.

Condon C. & McGinnis, J. (1988). *Helping kids care*: *Harmony building activities for home, church, and school.*, Oak Park, IL: Meyer Stone Books.

Fiske, E. (Ed.) (2000). *Champions for change: The impact of the arts on learning.* Washington, D. C.: The Arts Education Partnership/ The President's Committee on the Arts and the Humanities.

Fowler, C. (1994). Strong arts, strong schools. *Educational Leadership*, 52(3), 4-9.

Frank, A. (1995). *The wounded storyteller.* Chicago: Univ. of Chicago Press.

Gardner, H. (1983/1993). *Frames of mind: The theory of multiple intelligences.* New York: Basic Books.

Hanna, J. (1992). Connections: Arts, academics and productive citizens. *Phi Delta Kappan.* April, 601-607.

Hurwitz, A. (1995). *Children and their art.* Fort Worth, TX: Harcourt Brace.

Lowenfeld, V. & Brittain, W. L. (1987). *Creative and mental growth, 8th ed.* New York: Macmillan. (Originally published in 1947 by Lowenfeld. An excellent approach to art and creativity. Offers a philosophy for creative arts in the public schools. The 3rd ed. includes a chapter on therapeutic aspects of art education. This chapter was removed from later editions.)

Murray, K., Epston, D., & White, M. (1992). A proposal for re-authoring therapy. In S. McNamee & K.J. Gergen (Eds.). *Therapy as social construction.* London: Sage.

Oddleifson, E. (1997). *The balanced mind: An educational and societal imperative.* Hingham, MA: The Center for Arts in the Basic Curriculum (CABC).Reimer, B. (1980). *Arts and the schools.* New York: McGraw-Hill. Sautter, C. (1994). An arts education: School reform strategy. *Phi Delta Kappan.* February, 432-438.

Senior, P. & Croall, J. (1993). *Helping to heal: The arts in health care.* London: Calouste Gulbenkian Foundation.

Spolin, V. (1963). *Improvisation in the theatre.* Chicago: Northeastern Univ. Press. (Perhaps the best book on improvisation acting; great exercises which can easily by adapted to puppetry.)

Spolin, V. (1986). Theater *games for the classroom: A teacher's handbook.* Evanston, IL: Northwestern Univ. Press. (Adaptation of above book.)Sternberg, P. (1998). *Theater for conflict resolution: In the classroom and beyond.* Portsmouth, NH: Heinemann.

Way, B. (1967). *Development through drama.* Atlantic Highlands, NJ: Humanities Press. (Child drama helps to develop the whole child; an excellent text and resource.)

White, M. (1988/9). The externalizing of the problem and the re-authoring of lives and relationships. In M. White (Ed.), *Selected papers* (pp. 5-28). Adelaide, Australia: Dulwich Centre Publications.

Winner, E. (1982). *Invented worlds.* Cambridge, MA: Harvard University Press.

Winnicott, D.W. (1971). *Playing and reality.* London: Tavistock.

# ABOUT THE AUTHORS

**Matthew Bernier, MCAT, ATR-BC** (co-editor), a registered and board certified art therapist and a puppeteer, has education in psychology, theatre arts, and creative arts in therapy. He is an Associate Professor at Eastern Virginia Medical School in the Graduate Art Therapy Program. He is nationally known for his long-time charismatic involvement with therapeutic puppetry, combining his knowledge of art psychotherapy, puppetry, and theatre arts. He serves on the Board of Trustees of the Puppeteers of America and is president of the Southeastern Virginia Puppetry Guild. He has presented therapeutic puppetry workshops across the US and in Canada and Italy.

**Judith O'Hare** (co-editor), creator of You and Me Puppets, is the Education Consultant and Chair of the Puppetry in Education and Therapy Committee for the Puppeteers of America and the director of Puppets: Education Magic Institute. She is a solo puppeteer specializing in participatory performances with children and Toy Theater. She teaches graduate courses for the Northeast Consortium/Salem State College and Lesley University. She has presented her performances, workshops, and teacher trainings on Participatory Puppet Theater and Toy Theater at festivals and in schools and colleges for over 30 years across the US and in Canada, Kenya, Tanzania, Hong Kong, and China. She has won awards from the Puppeteers of America Northeast Region for her work in puppetry in education, and from Reading, MA, for her contribution to the artistic life of the community as an arts administrator and founder of Creative Arts, an arts center for children and adults, and for her work as a puppeteer.

**Twenty-six authors** contributed to this book. They have diverse credentials, experience, and disciplines including: puppeteers, educators (early childhood; elementary; Waldorf; college; graduate school; special, art and music education; and teacher training), child and art therapists, child life specialist, social worker, storyteller, psychologist, and physician. They all have a common denominator of using puppetry in their work.

Printed in the United States
78471LV00002B/79

9 781420 884609